Cashing Out

Cashing Out

The Entrepreneur's Guide to Going Public

James B. Arkebauer

with
Ron Schultz

HarperBusiness
A Division of HarperCollinsPublishers

Library of Congress Cataloging-in-Publication Data

Arkebauer, James B., 1939–
    Cashing Out : the entrepreneur's guide to going public / James B.
Arkebauer, Ronald M. Schultz
        p.   cm.
    ISBN 0–88730–415–X
    1. Going public (Securities)—United States.   2. Going public
(Securities)—Law and legislation—United States.   I. Schultz,
Ronald M., 1951– . II. Title.
HG4963.A75   1991
658.15'224—dc20   91-9869
                                                                        CIP

Printed in the United States of America

91 92 93 94 CC/HC 7 6 5 4 3 2 1

This book is dedicated to
B. H. Arkebauer
and
Sam Schultz

Contents

Preface

I've dealt with the process of taking companies public for 20 years. I've worked with entrepreneurs and their support professionals to assist them in going public. After a while, I began to see the frustration of the people involved. It is, after all, difficult to comprehend all the various aspects and complexities of the process. This is especially true for those who are pressed for time and often don't know the correct questions to ask.

I have been frustrated, in the past, with many business book authors who have had little practical, firsthand experience. Some authors have taken their own company public, or practiced in one of the professional positions, or came from academia. But they often have a narrow point of view and a very specialized perspective. I, on the other hand, have an intimate knowledge of the OTC market as a player, broker, trader, corporate finance officer, and syndicator. Additionally, I've been a public company founder, officer, president, director, and have invested in hundreds of companies, both public and private. I took my first company public in 1970, and have been involved in over 50 IPOs in one capacity or another. Since then, with over two decades of hands-on experience, I have gained a thorough knowledge of business cycles, government actions, and reactions. This includes an understanding of the internal politics, and how all the various players that are central to the process interrelate.

Being involved in a public business is an entrepreneur's ultimate dream. Taking a company public is the major reward. It brings glamour, prestige and is one of the acknowledgments of success in business, but taking a company public is a complex process. It involves many different business disciplines and can be mysterious and confusing, even for those who have been through it several times. It's not surprising that the entrepreneur and their management teams are intimidated. Consequently, they seek helpful information from attorneys, accountants, public relations executives, and other support professionals.

Many of these professionals will acknowledge, however, that they don't have a complete understanding of the complimentary disciplines, or in many cases, a full grasp of the total process.

Some may have only a cursory knowledge of many of the subjects, others may have an in-depth knowledge of some of the subjects. What they share is a common need to gain a greater understanding of the overall process or to gain additional insight in specific areas.

Accountants may be knowledgeable about the financial aspects of the process, but recognize they may be weak in the legal areas. A stockbroker may want more information on the Securities Exchange aspects, a company president may wish to better understand the financial investor relations area, a venture capitalist may want more information on the role of the financial printer, a banker may wish to gain knowledge on how to structure a deal.

The major need of the prospective chief executive officer (CEO) of a public company, and those on the initial public offering (IPO) team, is a fuller understanding of a complicated subject. This book is a complete guide for taking a company public. It explores all of the aspects of this process. Examined also is what a successful offering requires, what roles they play, and more.

I've tried to capture the experience of taking a company public and pass it on to you as knowledge. My entrepreneurial wish for you is that *Cashing Out* will help you gain the experience and capture the dream.

James B. Arkebauer

Acknowledgments

The dedication is to our fathers who were not entrepreneurs, but who set an example of the kind of dedication necessary to foster the entrepreneurial spirit. From the family unit, one builds the framework for future successes and failures. I appreciate many unnamed individuals who fed me the experience of business, sometimes with eyedroppers, other times by the dumptruck load.

Taking a company public is a team effort, not unlike writing a book. The public company entrepreneur needs an effective team as much as an author. My entrepreneurial team goes back 25 years or more.

I'm indebted to the thousands of people whose business plans and entrepreneurial dreams I have shared. I'm also indebted to the hundreds of public company executives I've worked with, and the hundreds of support professionals they have engaged. From them I have learned a lot.

In addition, I am thankful to Harper Business publisher, Mark Greenberg, my editor, Martha Jewett, the production staff, and the marketing department. Special thanks go to my agent, Jeff Herman, and to A. David Silver, who introduced me to Jeff. Without their support, I'm sure that this book would still be in the "red-herring" stage.

My co-author Ron Schultz played a major role in bringing 450 pages of manuscript and 20 hours of tape interviews into final acceptable form. He was a pleasure to work with.

As is true with most long endeavors, someone helps you to dream. Dr. Cheryl Chatfield provided original inspiration and ongoing encouragement. Maita Lester, hours of proofing and unselfish support. To both of them—outstanding entrepreneurs themselves—my simple "Thanks." They understand.

PART I

OVERVIEW OF THE PROCESS

1

Reaching for Success

The Advantages and Disadvantages of Going Public

Going public—two simple words on which hang the dreams, aspirations, and inspiration of many practicing and visionary entrepreneurs. These words represent respect in the business community, and equally important, they can mean great financial reward. These two words, which like the fabled "Open sesame" of Ali Baba, can swing open the door and expand an entrepreneur's company using other people's money. Going public then allows that company owner to revel in the precious benefits gained for owners and investors alike. Ah, the dreams, the fantasies of the entrepreneur contemplating an initial public offering . . . can they ever be more than airy fairy tales? Can they be reality? The answer is unequivocally yes.

As our society continues its evolution from an industrial/manufacturing foundation to a service/information base, we will find that the decade of the nineties will produce an increasing number of entrepreneurial stars. These enterprising company owners are going to become richer faster and take more people with them than ever before. Why? Because as our society has become more global and consequently more complex, we have also become more aware of the problems raised by this increasing diversity. The challenges we will be facing are great. Once again, the doors of opportunity will open to those industrious individuals ready to jump in with an appropriate and timely solution. The spark, however, that will bring these primed issues to flame is capital, and going public is the flint upon which these capital reserves are struck.

3

Basically, going public is the process in which a business owned by one or several individuals is converted into a business owned by many. It involves the offering of part ownership of the company to the general public through the sale of equity or debt securities. The purpose of this book, then, is to examine in detail how successful entrepreneurs build the various teams necessary to accomplish this profitable objective. The following chapters will lay bare the regulatory constraints applied by federal and state governments and expound on the gathering and coordination of the management teams, accountants, lawyers, underwriters, printers, and public relations experts necessary to breathe life into an initial public offering (IPO) and bring the entrepreneur's dream to reality.

The road to public riches is not without pratfalls and pitfalls. The task can be arduous. But we hope this book will help the potential publicteer proceed along this treasured path with eyes open so that he or she may actually reap the capital fruits that lie ahead.

For the Sake of the Company

Why set out upon a road beset with danger? In 1985, Dr. John E. Young of the University of Colorado conducted a study of 562 companies that went public between September 1980 and March 1984. He found that the majority of CEOs cited two fundamental reasons for going public. The first was to raise initial capital as a source for ongoing financing.

Capital is the "wealth used in trade." It is the money invested in a company that allows it to:

- fund start-up operations
- purchase equipment necessary for production
- increase inventories of both raw and finished goods
- support growing receivables
- expand ongoing operations
- support the company's administration
- further research
- develop the next generation of product
- retire prior debt
- increase market share

For a regional company that may be going national, the additional capital that can be raised through an IPO is often a way to attract an acquisition or for purposes of a merger.

Contained within each and every one of these capital purposes is the primary objective for raising capital, to support and sustain the growth of the company.

By way of an IPO, the entrepreneur converts a portion of the ownership of the company into shares of stock and allows investors to purchase that percentage, thereby sharing the business with the general public. The investors hope their added investment will enhance the company's possibility for successful growth and thereby increase the value of their share of the company. This is the second fundamental advantage Young noted for taking a company public: stock value appreciation. The potential monetary reward that an original investor, whether family member, friend, venture capitalist, or of course, corporate founder, can realize from the leveraged selling of a company's stock would makes Ali Baba's hidden treasure seem like pocket change. There are few legal investments that can beat the reward to be gained by an original investor from a successful IPO.

For most people recapitalization and stock value appreciation would seem reason enough to fight the dragons on the road to going public, but there are other advantages a company can gain. A public company has a broader equity base, thus increasing its opportunities for obtaining financing for future efforts. Increasing the bottom-line net worth of a company as well as its debt to equity ratio enables it to borrow at lower interest rates from traditional institutions. If the company's stock performs well after the IPO, it may also obtain further equity capital without having to give as great a percentage of the company away as it did in the initial offering.

Another advantage of going public is the improvement in corporate image. A public company receives more media attention in the financial community than a private firm, and publicity can strengthen competitive position in the marketplace. Favorable trade press attention can attract both new business and new interest in the company. Dun & Bradstreet, Moody's, and Standard & Poor's will often issue special notices on new public companies and follow their progress. The more public exposure a company receives, the greater its chances are for success.

The media, however, are not the only carriers of good news. It is not uncommon for customers, suppliers, and business associates to purchase stock shares in an IPO. This increased involvement in the company and its products or services often results in preferential treatment, ranging from better terms on contracts to increased reliability of delivery schedules.

Since the financial activities of a public company are required to be regularly reported, management has an opportunity to obtain a higher degree of public confidence. Its books are open to the world. This often allows for a greater borrowing flexibility in both straight and convertible debt. Companies can structure deals to fit the dynamics of the current financial marketplace. The added credibility of this open book policy broadens financial avenues such as bonds, debentures, and preferred stock.

Public companies often enjoy an added prestige in the political arena. Shareholders from different areas of the country can influence legislation that might affect the company. This is true on all levels of the political scene, whether in local city councils, state legislatures, or on Capitol Hill.

To the Founders' Advantage

Beyond the gain to the company coffers, the single greatest financial advantage of going public falls to the founders of the company. Now Ali Baba takes his due. The spoils do not all go to the CEOs, but are distributed to passive founding investors and officers and members of the management team who have remained active in the company's daily activities. Their nonmarketable stock investments in their once privately held firm are converted into a marketable stock in a public company. Shares once valued at 1/10th of a cent may, with an IPO rise to 10 cents or more per share. Simple math will reveal that a founder's original $1000 investment is now worth upward of $100,000. One need only think of the initial investment of Apple Computer's Steven Jobs or Microsoft's William Gates and their worth today to illustrate the potential: The percentage of return on a founding investment versus the net worth value of the company can be phenomenal. Typically, a stock sells at 10 to 12 times its earnings. This is known as the price to earnings or P/E ratio. In a small IPO, this ratio may be as high as 30 to 40 times the company's annual earnings.

An IPO also provides founding insiders with the opportunity to diversify their personal investment portfolios. It is common practice for the officers of a private company with a significant track record to have a good part of their personal wealth tied up in their company. An IPO allows these officers to liquify some of their investment. In many cases, officers have made loans to the company, advanced money, or even postponed payment of their salaries. With the proceeds from an IPO, these debts can be cleared up, as well as bank loans to the company secured by officers' signatures or property.

One advantage of going public that a founding officer would probably like to delay as long as possible is minimizing estate tax problems: The payment of taxes on the estate of a company principal would not have to come from company funds, as might be necessary in a privately held firm. The establishment of stock value in a public market simplifies appraisals for inheritance taxes.

As should be increasingly evident, going public offers a wealth of enticements for the founding officers. And to better deal with this new wealth, the liquidity of public stock allows control over the timing of capital gains. As a final bonus, should a founding stockholder wish to secure a personal loan from a financial institution—say to buy that small 20-room cottage on 5 wooded acres—marketable stocks offer a more acceptable form of collateral.

Benefits for the Entire Community of the Company

Founding officers are not the only beneficiaries when a company goes public. There are also added benefits for management and employees working for a public company. Few medium-size or small companies can hope to compete with large companies in salary offers. In a public company, stock options can be an attractive employment inducement. This form of payment is a plus for both the company and the management executive. Cash salaries come directly from the company's earnings, while stock options are paid for by the increased value of the stock itself. A stock option can also be a blessing for the executive dealing with the Internal Revenue Service. In many cases higher salaries result in higher tax brackets, but a stock option permits a portion of compensation to be taxed as longer-term capital gains.

Working for a small public company, management can directly contribute to the profit margins and stock market value of the company. Not only does this provide a certain ego satisfaction, it can prove profitable for the manager as the stock rises in value.

Stock option plans and employee stock option plans are both excellent incentives for quality performance even beyond recruiting good employees. Employee-shareholders can follow their investment in their company in newspapers and financial publications. And if, prior to an initial public offering, employees have had an opportunity to acquire stock, they will also be able to experience Ali Baba's dream come true. The immediate price appreciation of their stock not only creates a pride of accomplishment and long-term loyalty, it makes for wealthier and happier employees.

The Securities Exchanges

The places these dreams become reality are the stock exchanges, for a company can return its profits to its shareholders not only, through periodic dividends, but also through stock value appreciation: The owner of the stock can sell it for a profit if someone believes that the stock is worth more than the selling price, that its price to earnings ratio is undervalued, or that it will rise further.

The primary marketplaces for these stock transactions are the New York Stock Exchange (NYSE), the American Stock Exchange (AMEX), and the over-the-counter market (OTC). The NYSE, which originated under a buttonwood tree at 68 Wall Street in 1792, began its operations on the street with two dozen brokers. Today 1300 members in more than 500 firms with 150 specialists trade 3500 different securities. The AMEX began operations in 1861 on the curb outside the stock exchange and was known as the New York Curb Market until formal adoption of the name American Stock Exchange in 1953. The AMEX now lists about 1000 securities.

The over-the-counter market is the world's oldest and largest market-place for stock transactions. Brought over by European merchants, this negotiated trade market has traditionally been the home for newer and smaller public companies. The name *over the counter* came about when banks, as a supplement to their other services, literally sold securities over their counters; these were purely negotiated sales, as opposed to the auction house sales of the NYSE and AMEX. Over the years, the bankers have been replaced by broker/dealers, who coalesced into a network for buying, selling, and providing quotations on stock prices. This informal network has evolved into today's more formalized OTC market.

In 1971, the National Association of Securities Dealers (NASD) introduced the National Association of Securities Dealers Automated Quotation System (NASDAQ). This system collects and displays up-to-the-minute quotations on over 5500 OTC qualifying firms. (We will discuss the listing requirements for NASDAQ and other markets in greater detail later on.) An even greater number of OTC stocks are traded through the OTC "Pink Sheets." Five times a week, the National Quotations Bureau publishes ask and bid prices on over 11,000 stocks on 5-by-14-inch sheets of pink paper. These sheets also list the market makers for each stock—about 40,000 altogether—so that a broker anywhere in the world can initiate a trade with a single phone call.

All U.S. markets, whether the 11,000-stock strong Pink Sheets or the smaller NYSE, are regulated by both the federal Securities and Exchange Commission (SEC) and state laws. Founded by the Securities Exchange Act of 1934, the SEC enforces the Truth in Securities Act (better known as the Securities Act of 1933), passed by Congress to protect investors in public offerings from unscrupulous dealing. The act requires disclosure statements by public companies and provides criminal and civil penalties for inadequate or inaccurate disclosure of material facts. We will discuss these acts and their regulations in greater detail in chapter 17.

It was the enactment of the '33 and '34 acts that made the IPO process as cumbersome and costly as it has become. Each state additionally regulates the sale of securities. These regulations called *blue-sky laws* were created for much the same reasons as the federal securities acts, to protect gullible investors from promoters offering them the sky, the stars, and the firmament above. As we will see, these laws and regulations require a great deal of time, money, attention, and accountability. And though in the long run the advantages of taking a company public outweigh the disadvantages presented by the process, they should nonetheless be looked at as well.

The Disadvantages of the Public Marketplace

The entrepreneur can easily get carried away by the looming potential of huge benefits that can be gained from going public. That's just part of the story. So, lest you, the reader imagine going public as simply sitting back and waiting for the money to flow in, it behooves us to make a fuller disclosure here. Knowing both the positive and negative sides of the process will better prepare the individual or group contemplating such an important move.

If caution is not observed, the negatives could very well outweigh the positives.

It would be folly for the entrepreneur to think a positive attitude will suffice to win the battle. Rather, one must be prepared for the negatives and pitfalls that keep cropping up at every turn. More often than not, one will meet with the misgivings of family and friends over the intention of sharing a company with the public, as well as the mountains of paperwork and the seemingly endless outlay of money. Patience, persistence, and perseverance are very necessary for the entrepreneur seeking to go public! For there are a multitude of rules to contend with, and mind-boggling regulations and constraints that the entrepreneur must observe before he can finally grab the golden ring.

The primary disadvantages of going public can be grouped under three categories:

1. Disclosure/accountability

2. Control or loss of control

3. Expenses

Most companies would prefer to keep their business and financial activities to themselves and on principle consider it a disadvantage if they must expose the details of their operations. But the SEC requires that all operations of a public company to be public. Inevitably, management suffers some loss of control. Simply filing the forms and paying the fees required of a company going public is costly. In the beginning, there's a lot of money going out and not much coming back. There is also no guarantee the company will ever actually become public.

Disclosure

From an operational standpoint, the company must disclose its marketing methods and indicate the areas to which they apply. This includes mail order, direct sales, representatives, retail outlets, and distributors. In most cases, a company must supply data on how its market areas are defined, the numbers of salespersons, sales by areas, and sales of specific product lines.

While it may seem like a tremendous loss of confidentiality, most competitors, employees, unions, and suppliers, as well as customers have little interest in expending the time or effort required to seek out this information.

Many entrepreneurs consider this type of operational information sacrosanct. But rarely have these financial and statistical disclosures had any detrimental effect on a company's operations. Usually, the price a company charges for its product or service, the cost of materials, and employee compensation are governed by market forces and not compromised by financial disclosure.

For all intents and purposes, the main reason for these disclosures is to assure that management complies with its fiduciary responsibilities to the company shareholders. In a private company, the money at risk belongs to the owners, but in a public company, the money invested and at risk is accountable to its public shareholders. This is also why annual and quarterly reports are required. There's no way around it. A company going public must disclose hard financial facts such as sales, profit margins, competitive positions, and remuneration of officers and directors.

Accountability

Accountability is a form of confession by the company going public. There can be no secrets from the government or the general public for a company going public. It must account for its modus operandi and reveal its inside transactions. These are usually transactions of monetary value between the company and its officers or directors. They include such things as the common ownership of a supplier or a common facilities relationship. For example, if an officer or director is also an owner or shareholder in a firm which supplies to or purchases from the company, those transactions must be reported. It is not unusual or unlawful for the company to lease or sublease office or facility space from an officer or director, but the cost to the company should be no higher (and preferably will be lower) than prevailing market rates. These transactions are termed *non-arm's-length* arrangements and require no formal outside appraisal. Similar principles apply to items like patents, which are often owned by an officer and licensed to the company, and in such cases it is not unusual to have royalty or fee payments revert back to the officer.

This accountability disclosure will continue every quarter for the life of the company. Consequently, management needs to carefully review all insider dealings on a continuing basis. A telling example was contained in the prospectus for one IPO. It disclosed that the president of the company had purchased a swimming pool from the company prior to the public offering. The pool had previously been listed as an asset under the heading of "employee recreational facility." More likely than not, the fact that the pool was located in the president's backyard was a determining factor in the decision to purchase it.

Insider reporting requirements, covered more fully in chapters 17 and 32, concern inside trading. Companies must divulge the names of all officers, directors, and other persons who may be privy to inside information about their company's operations. The company must account for changes in management, any surge in profits, a proposed sale of the company, or any other factor that could affect the price of the company's stock. The term "insider" applies irrespective of an individual's status as a significant shareholder. Those insiders are required to file regular and special reports with the SEC on their stock positions and trading activity in the company's stock. Principals of a company, in particular, must disclose their purchase or sale of company stock. If they fail to do so they can be subject to stiff penalties for what the SEC considers a misuse of their position and authority.

Even the most innocent sale of stock by a principal could be misconstrued by analysts if the reason for it is not reported. For instance, the president of a company may need to sell stock in the company to pay for surgery for a family member. It must be reported, or it could appear to the casual observer that the president is doing something underhanded. This could eventually cause a whole series of unintended disadvantages for the company, including mistrust.

Accountability disclosure can also affect daily decisions by management. Companies have a tendency to shy away from instituting long- or short-term goals that may be of overall benefit to the company but adversely affect the price of the stock. The CEO is constantly being pressured, both internally and externally, to maintain high growth rates. Since financial results must be reported quarterly, the displeasure of brokers and stockholders quickly becomes obvious should sales or earnings fail to meet expectations or projections.

Most companies have no trouble with their accountability reports to the

SEC. Difficulties arise where the CEO must deal on a daily basis with shareholders, brokers, or others with a vested interest. Their money is riding on the company's progress and they want to know what the company is doing for them. Naturally, investors and market makers want information to be promising, or these shareholders and brokers who influence investments in the company could become disenchanted with the company's performance and sell their shares. Unfortunately for management, this is not a group that can be ignored.

Another disadvantage arising from accountability is the process involved in obtaining shareholder approval. There are many standards and procedures that must be followed. For instance, there are regulations on the time length for notification of a shareholders' meeting. There's even a regulation on the size of type in which the proxy is printed. A more serious disadvantage in owning stock in a public company, especially large stock positions, is the invasion of privacy for estate valuation. In a private company, the value is rarely a matter of public record. In a public company, the published daily stock price provides a definite benchmark for the IRS. Of course, it's very possible that the company may be worth more than the stock price indicates.

Control or Loss of Control

As with disclosure/accountability, disadvantages arising from losing some control of a company are bound to affect management's operating style.

After an IPO the primary shareholders will own less percentage of the stock than before. There are a few exceptions, one being the issuance of nonvoting stock or debentures, but in general management must accept the fact that some voting stock control will be lost in going public. As a rule, a public company can anticipate a loss of absolute (51 percent plus) voting control. Even if more than 51 percent is retained by management after the initial public offering, subsequent offerings and acquisitions further dilute control.

A significant loss of control involves timing. Timing often controls the destiny of a company. Invariably, CEOs lose some control over the time spent on day-to-day activities as well as the timing of company decisions and moves for the benefit of the company, the financial community, and the stockholders.

Dealing with the financial community whenever the company's stock prices fall is not an easy task, but management can't control changes in the company's stock prices from general or industry trends. Thus it is important when contemplating acquisitions (especially when company stock is involved) that sound corporate judgment and the timing of the deal be carefully considered. Prolonged negotiations with the company to be acquired can prove devastating in dilution of the public company's stock. Here's why. Usually, the amount of stock to be issued to the acquired company is negotiated at a fixed dollar or asset value of the acquired company. In the interim, if the public company's stock declines it will have to come up with more of its shares to meet the agreed purchase price. Buyer beware!

IPOs are the most vulnerable when it comes to timing. Public interest at the time of an IPO can mean success or failure, and the public is as fickle as it's reputed to be. Consider the following:

- 1969 saw over 1,000 new offerings for a total of $2.6 billion. (Stocks were doing well that year.)

- 1975 saw only 6 new offerings for just $34 million. (It was a time of recession.)

- 1983 saw 888 new offerings for $12 billion. (The computer boom created a glamour stock market.)

- 1986 saw 719 new offerings for over $22 billion. (The biotechnology boom was riding high, and such stocks were much sought after.)

- 1988 saw the market drop over 500 points in one day. (It proved devastating to new issues.)

The number of IPOs and amounts of money raised are always affected by national and worldwide economic trends. Interest in IPOs changes with interest rates, inflationary or recession trends, general stock market conditions, as well as perceived "hot industry" movements.

During the time an IPO is in the works, management is particularly vulnerable. If the bottom falls out of the market, it may not be possible to complete the IPO. The same holds true if the aftermarket is inactive and trading thin. If the fickle buying public doesn't take to a new issue, its days could be numbered, and management has little or no control over the outcome.

The lack of control in operating a public company can seem overwhelming. But even if management decides they've had it with being a public company, there's little they can do. They could make an effort at getting the company acquired, with the provision that the management stay in place. Or they could try to go private again, which requires considerable cash and lots of agony and patience. Or they could merge with another company—which could end up being the most trouble of all, because of the difficulties in coping with two management teams.

The problem of control also arises in connection with insider stock purchases. SEC Rule 144 establishes holding periods, in effect saying that for 2 years after it comes into their possession, insiders cannot sell company stock they have received, been given, or bought. Other SEC regulations limit the amount and the timing of personal stock sales, as will be discussed in greater detail in chapter 3.

Board meetings are subject to certain requirements. The informal control normally exercised in private companies is not considered sufficient for a public company. Public company operating procedures require more frequent, more substantive, and more formal board of directors' meetings. SEC guidelines require careful preparation of all items offered for board resolution. (More about boards of directors later.)

Expenses

We have already stated over and over again that the cost of going public is high. Be aware, too, that once a private company becomes a public company, the costs don't stop. SEC regulations continue forever. The average layperson may think this a disadvantage, but the sophisticated entrepreneur looks upon it as the cost of doing business.

The CEO, or the accountant of an IPO, who writes the checks, however, will probably react unfavorably to the number of checks that must be written and the amounts that must be paid to accomplish the IPO. Worse yet, a company that has been in business prior to an IPO will have to detail its financial history for 2 to 5 years, depending on how the company registers. A company just starting out in business that applies for an IPO has no backtrack fees.

It may cost more initially, but save money in the long run, to enlist the aid of accountants and attorneys who are specialists in SEC and public company requirements. Their fees usually correspond to their expertise. But they can save you having to do things over again.

On an ongoing basis, the costs of operating a public company are considerably higher than for a private company, primarily because of the SEC reporting requirements. Printing, underwriting, commissions, registration and transfer fees, as well as corporate promotional expenses are necessary evils you really shouldn't try to shortcut.

It would also be advisable to secure the help of a professional financial public relations firm to handle communications with shareholders and the financial community. These are expenses many private companies consider unnecessary, but matters are different for a public company. Public relations is your direct line to the people your company needs to reach to survive. (The importance of financial public relations will be discussed more fully in chapter 11.)

All levels of upper management are affected by the demands of a public company's operations. Much of this time is directed toward complying with SEC and public company reporting requirements which would not be required in a privately held company. Management must constantly itemize its duties in detail. Time is money. Going public gets to be very expensive.

Summary

As should be evident, the process of going public is not a bed of financial roses. Entrepreneurs must comply with a myriad of rules and regulations and surmount many difficulties. One has no control over general economic trends or industry trends, which can turn without warning. Wall Street tells it like it is, without playing favorites.

The disclosure and accountability of a public company may be difficult to accept. A company doesn't like to reveal its corporate practices and strategies. Management seldom takes kindly to revealing remuneration, past employment, or even specific responsibilities. They consider that an infringement.

Sharing ownership of a company inevitably means loss of stock control. Important, too, is loss of management time from company operations. In a public company, much of management's time must be devoted to shareholder relations and communication with the financial community. The time taken by SEC requirements costs money.

There's no getting around it—going public is expensive. With time, these expenses become part of daily operations. While they remain greater than the costs you would incur in a privately held company, the returns outweigh the disadvantages. Ali Baba also encountered difficulties, both in opening the cave doors and then from the onslaught of the 40 thieves. But the riches that followed were worth the effort.

The IPO fantasy can become reality for the entrepreneur willing to face facts and move forward with determination. Following the guidelines and information provided in this book, the Ali Babas of today can become the Apple Computers of tomorrow and gather the treasure that comes with the territory.

2

Going Public

The Cost of Doing Business

No doubt about it—the rewards and benefits that are possible from going public can be incredible. On the other side of the ledger, to the uninitiated, the costs involved to get through the process may seem even more incredible.

Don't let the fear of those costs deter you. As we will repeat throughout this book, it is important to approach these expenses as simply the cost of doing business.

Now, let's take a look at the big picture.

This book particularly addresses the entrepreneur seeking to realize $.5 to $5 million through an IPO. As a rule, an IPO of this magnitude is done on a "best efforts" basis, that is, the underwriting broker has no obligation in the event the shares are not sold. If the underwriter can't sell the company stock, it returns the shares. Whatever costs accrue during the process, remain the responsibility of the entrepreneur whether the IPO is sold or not.

Therefore, it is incumbent upon the CEO or the management group that must make the ultimate decision to proceed with the offering, to be prepared to spend some money. Regardless of the cost, a well-versed entrepreneur knows that more money can come through an IPO than any other method of equity financing. All things considered, it takes money to make money.

It's worth noting that the same basic costs and percentages apply for IPOs up to $7 million. Generally speaking, above that amount, selling commissions and underwriter percentages decrease. However, professional and promotional costs for offerings exceeding $5 million are considerably higher, since they usually require the services of highly skilled national, or even international professionals in the public relations field, and support firms.

There are no hard and fast numbers. Total costs and expenses for smaller IPOs can reach 24 percent to 39 percent of the offering, or total monies raised. *This is not considered excessive by experts in the business.* For example, a survey conducted on 478 IPOs in the late 1980s showed that the general expenses, which included the underwriters, attorneys, accountants, printers, and miscellaneous fees, ranged from 6.4 percent to 41.4 percent.

Costs can vary considerably. In an attempt to be more explicit, we will consider the following areas individually:

1. Underwriter costs

2. Professional costs

3. Up-front costs

4. Hidden and future costs

Underwriter Costs

Commissions

The largest single cost item in a public offering is the underwriter's share or commission. It is also referred to as the *underwriter's discount.* Basically, it's the underwriter's take for raising the money. It amounts to a percentage of each share of stock sold. The generally accepted percentage for an IPO is 10 percent.

In theory, the figure is negotiable; in fact, the underwriter dictates the amount. A 10 percent commission on an IPO has become the accepted practice, though there can always be extenuating circumstances. Since the late seventies, very few smaller IPOs have been done for less than 10 percent.

The factors that affect negotiating commissions are:

• How large is the offering? How many shares are to be sold?

• What efforts will be required to sell the stock—will the underwriter handle the whole package or will it be spread around?

• Type or quality of the offering—will it be an easy or a hard sale?

• Complexity of the offering—how is the company valued?

• What are commissions for similar types of offerings? How comparable is this one?

- What is the "sex appeal" of the company—does the company offer the public something of substance, thus making it a more attractive buy?
- How is the current market environment—is this a good time to offer this stock? Is the economy right for it?

In reference to these points, if the underwriter does the deal in-house, that is, if the stock is sold by brokers who work for the underwriter, the underwriter keeps the full commission. The in-house split is usually 30 percent to 70 percent, which means that the house keeps 30 percent of the commission and the individual broker receives 70 percent. Brokers like new issues because this 70 percent payout exceeds their typical 30 percent to 50 percent share.

In most cases, the underwriter will syndicate an IPO, offering part of the underwriting to other brokerage houses and keeping only a portion in-house. When this is done, the lead, or original, underwriter "reallows" 70 percent of the commission. This means the underwriter retains 30 percent for expenses. The syndicate members, in turn, will pay 60 percent of the commission to their brokers who actually sell the IPO, keeping a 10 percent override for themselves.

Nonaccountable Expense Allowance

The nonaccountable expense allowance is a fee charged to the company by the underwriter. It's called *nonaccountable* because it cannot be construed as an integral part of the offering. It was instituted as a means of reimbursing the underwriter for so-called out-of-pocket expenses. These include things such as postage, phone, printing, entertainment, marketing expenses, and even legal expenses, for example, hiring a lawyer to review the work of the IPO company's lawyer. Although the fees are called nonaccountable, the National Association of Securities Dealers (NASD) requires the underwriter to account for them. The underwriter's legal counsel usually prepares a boilerplate report, which the issuing company accepts as a matter of course.

Underwriters use some of their nonaccountable expense money to offset a portion of the promotional costs of an IPO. This includes paying some of the costs of "tombstones"—ads that appear in financial papers such as *The Wall Street Journal* and *Barron's* or the financial section of local newspapers. They say in effect that here is an approved offering by an appropriate agency, and this announcement is evidence of that.

Another important nonaccountable expense falls under the heading of *due diligence.* This is the obligation on the part of the underwriter to inform the brokerage community about the validity of the issue. It amounts to an investigation of the client, with findings relayed to brokerage houses by formal or informal meetings. (Tombstones and due diligence will be covered in more detail in chapters 20 and 27.)

The nonaccountable expense allowance fee generally ranges from 1 percent to 4 percent of the total monies raised in a public offering. On IPOs up to $3 million, the accepted formula is about 3 percent, or $90,000. It has been standard practice for the company to pay one-third of the fee, or $30,000, at the time of signing a letter of intent (which simply means an intent to go through with the offering). The balance—$60,000—is usually paid upon completion of the offering. It is also generally accepted that the down payment on the nonaccountable is nonrefundable.

It's worth stressing again, that once a letter of intent is signed with an underwriter and a down payment is made on the nonaccountable, the company will probably never see that money again, even if the IPO is later canceled. There have also been reports of underwriters making deals with another brokerage house to take over the letter of intent, with neither completing the offering. (Chapter 22 will deal with this issue in greater detail.)

Professional Costs

Legal Fees

Legal expenses are usually the second largest expense after underwriting commissions. On an IPO of up to $3 million, this expense can vary between $10,000 and $150,000, depending on the complexity of the legal issues that must be dealt with. These issues include the history of the company, how far back it goes, whether other stocks from other companies are involved, whether the company operates in different states or foreign countries, whether patents must be accounted for, how the company will be structured, the new officers involved, ownership, and so on.

Start-up companies, ones with no prior history, are clearly the easiest to set up. The attorney for the company, as a rule, only has to file for incorporation prestructured for public company operation. Follow-up involves no more than preparing a registration statement and filing the actual IPO. Even so, the legal costs can amount to $20,000 to $75,000.

Included among legal expenses of an existing company is *corporate cleanup*. This involves a review of the minutes of directors' and shareholders' meetings. Lawyers must also review all formal agreements and contracts between the company and other interested parties. These contracts could cover anything from leases for copy machines to customer purchase orders. This process of tidying up the corporate loose ends can result in renegotiating contracts, which of course means more legal work. Corporate cleanup can be time consuming if the company has been in existence for a number of years and has a long operating history, but it must be completed prior to any offering. What's more, in all probability the company will have to revise its articles of incorporation and bylaws. And should the company opt to create an Employees Stock Option Plan (ESOP) or incentive stock option plan (ISOP) there will be still more legal fees.

Actually, there are not too many shortcuts when it comes to legal fees on an IPO. In fact, occasionally, depending on negotiations with the underwriter, the offering company may even pay all or part of the underwriter's counsel's fees. Those fees could include a review by the underwriter's attorney of the company attorney's work and the cost of filings with NASD and state *blue-sky regulations*. Most states require that all of the relevant information regarding the activities of the company must be fully divulged. These are called *blue-sky regulations*. They have also been called "hot air" regulations, because they protect the investor from being sold securities that are nothing but hot air.

In most cases, if an existing company has maintained legal counsel on an ongoing basis, much of the required information would be readily available, minimizing the legal fees at the time of going public. (More about legal fees in chapters 9 and 20.)

Accounting for Accounting

As with attorney fees, accounting fees can vary considerably. They're usually at a minimum for a start-up company with no history to justify. The initial costs would include establishment of an accounting system and the audit that must be done immediately before filing an IPO.

The accountant, or accounting firm, reviews and verifies the data in the registration statement and prepares the *comfort letter*. This letter goes over the accountant's responsibilities and says, in effect, he or she is satisfied with the method used to report the company's financial statement.

If the registration process becomes complex, the accountant may find it necessary to prepare a stub statement, or interim audit. This is usually followed by another letter of comfort, confirming that everything remains as reported. A ballpark figure on the cost for a simple start-up IPO could run approximately $5,000 to $15,000.

Accounting costs for existing companies will, of course, be higher. SEC regulations require an audit covering the 2 years preceding the filing for an IPO. The necessary information should have been compiled in the normal course of business. The accountant then will only have to review the audit procedures for compliance with SEC accounting rules. The information is not always complete, however, and the accountant may have to perform a new audit, which could increase accounting costs to $10,000 to $30,000.

If an existing company had no audit performed during the 2 years prior to filing for an IPO, or did not have its inventory audited, the audit accountant's job becomes a monumental project, for it must include items such as major write-downs, where all figures that could seem significant to the transaction must be disclosed. This information can look dubious, and it is up to the accountant to reduce its apparent significance. The work is time consuming, and the costs rise accordingly: An initial audit of this type could range from $15,000 to $60,000. In summary, depending on the complications that arise, the accountant's fees can range from $5,000 to $60,000 or more. Note that the accounting fees must also be disclosed in the IPO prospectus.

Because the right kind of numbers make an IPO look attractive to the financial community as well as the individual investor, it is common for accountants to be key members of the management team on IPOs.

Investment Bankers and Consultants

Investment bankers and consultants are the people who keep an IPO on course. For a management group considering going public, these are the experts who can exert influence, who know the problems, and who can help to bring the process to fruition. Investment bankers usually work for fees or for fees plus a piece of the action, which could include stock or options. Their participation and fees must also be disclosed in the registration statement. (We will discuss investment banking in greater detail in chapter 7.)

Additional Up-front Costs

We have already covered many of the up-front costs a company will face in the process of an IPO, but they seem never to stop. In addition to stamps, paper, phone calls, special forms, entertainment, office equipment, up-front costs include printing and registration fees.

Printing

Printing costs include the typesetting as well as the printing of the initial registration statement and prospectus for submission to the SEC, NASD, and individual state securities commissions. Since these documents must conform to detailed regulations concerning type style and size, it behooves the company to work with a printer that regularly prints these publications.

Some companies or their legal counsel have word processors, computers, or other office equipment compatible with that of the printer. These could prove to be cost savers.

It's important to note, too, that changes are often required after a registration statement or other document has been printed. *Any change, whether a typo, an error, or a change in information requires reprinting.*

The first thing to be printed is usually the registration statement. Only a small quantity will be required—25 or less. Following that, the company will publish a preliminary offering, or what is called, a *red herring.* It is an advance version of the offering that is distinguished by red print on the cover. It provides information in connection with the offering that states all the relevant factors involved are included with the audited statement. This is followed by the *definitive prospectus,* which contains the complete information about the offering. It often includes color photos and graphics and is printed on colored paper. The quantity depends on the requirements of the underwriters, the size of the selling syndicate (a group of brokers, salespeople, and/or investors that facilitate fund-raising for the IPO), and the ultimate distribution of the stock.

An additional cost is printing the actual stock certificates. The old custom of engraving beautiful, intricate designs has given way to modern techniques. Financial printers today keep books of stock designs onto which a company has only to stick its logo. It does the job, and cheaply.

Printing costs can range from $10,000 to $40,000, but the norm is usually between $15,000 and $20,000. (See chapter 10 for further discussion.)

Registration Fees

When it comes to registering an offering, it seems that every regulatory body in existence has its hand out. For individual states, the costs vary from token fees of perhaps $10 to many thousands—whatever the traffic will bear.

Some states create their own individual filing forms, preventing you from filing duplicates of one form. Just coping with the various forms can drive an attorney to distraction, and it drives up legal costs as well. Adding insult to injury, few states will accept private company checks to cover the fee payment. They require certified checks.

Here is a list of the major regulatory and related bodies and their fees:

- *Securities and Exchange Commission (SEC).* When the registration statement is filed with the SEC, fees must be paid at the rate of 0.02 percent of the maximum dollar amount of the securities being registered ($200 per $1 million of securities).

- *National Association of Securities Dealers (NASD).* Upon filing, $100 plus 0.01 percent of the offering's maximum dollar amount ($300 for a $2 million maximum offering).

- *Blue-sky regulations.* These state filing fees vary from $10 to $100 to a percentage or a combination of fee and percentage. (See chapter 26 for details.)

- *National Association of Securities Dealers Automated Quotations (NASDAQ).* For companies that will be trading on NASDAQ (minimum $4 million in assets, $2 million in net worth), the initial entry fee is $5,000. A yearly maintenance fee for continued listing, which is mandatory, is assessed on the company's total assets ($250 to $2500).

- *Miscellaneous Listings.* These are fees for listing the company in financial rating books such as Moody's, Standard & Poor's, and various other magazines, newspapers, and financial publications.

- *Transfer Agent.* This person or service perfects the transaction of closing the sale. When the order comes in for shares, the transfer agent is responsible for issuing them. Very few public companies are equipped to act as their own stock transfer agent, but engage a computerized professional to serve in that capacity. (See chapter 12.) Initial setup fees range from approximately $500 to $1000. Quarterly maintenance fees depend on stock trading activity and the extent of the company's use of services.

Hidden and Future Costs

During the lengthy process of going public, additional unanticipated costs will crop up. These hidden and future costs include extra transportation costs to and from consultants, attorneys, accountants, and underwriters; lunches and entertainment; and revising and copying documents. Postage can mount up, as well as long-distance phone calls, faxes, and messenger deliveries. Other significant expenses can arise in coordinating legal counsel, accountants, underwriters, and printers located in different cities from each other or the company.

An important item is promotion: Many thousands of dollars can be required to make the brokerage community and the investing public aware of the company—through meetings arranged by underwriters and brokerage houses, samples of products or services, brochures, and audiovisual aids. (This area is covered in detail in chapter 27.)

Another cost worth mentioning though rarely considered in today's financial community, is directors' and officers' liability insurance. It's not only difficult to obtain, but the costs are prohibitive—even though it would be desirable, especially for a small company that could use it.

Although the CEOs and the management teams have considerable control over the amount and extent of some of these hidden and future costs, the costs invariably exceed what is anticipated—or rather what is *not* anticipated.

Summary

This chapter is not intended to dissuade the entrepreneur from attempting an IPO. A sound IPO has the potential for being a money machine. This discussion is to make sure the reader enters with eyes open. The cost of going public is high. The costs could easily amount to 25 percent to 35 percent or even 40 percent of the total monies raised. All things considered, however, that's not bad.

The following estimates are averages. But bear in mind that all IPOs are not average. Depending on the actual situation of your company, costs could be higher or lower.

- *Underwriters.* Commissions on the sale of stock average 10 percent of total proceeds, plus another 3 percent for expenses.

- *Professional fees.* Legal expenses, usually the second largest expense, run from $10,000 to $150,000, with an average of $50,000 for a small IPO.

- *Accounting fees.* These vary with the complexity and history of the company. A start-up IPO could run as low as $10,000, or it could cost $40,000 for even a straightforward 2-year historical audit.

- *Up-front costs.* Expect printing the registration statement and prospectus, including typesetting, to run $20,000. Registration fees should be in the area of $5,000.

- *Hidden and future costs.* These costs, some of which can be controlled, could reach $20,000.

The one cost that is difficult to put a dollar value on is *time*—the time and effort it takes for management to complete a public offering. An IPO can become very time consuming, so commitment and perseverance will be required.

If money raising by the rules and regulations that apply to an IPO was a piece of cake, everybody would be doing it. They're not and it's not! The process takes dedication. It takes a willingness to push through all the barriers for what could be an almost unbelievably lucrative reward.

Read on.

3

Timing

No matter how ready your company is, no matter how much in love you are with the product or service you're willing to share with the public, if the market is in the doldrums, if the economy is bad, if the world situation is far from rosy . . . stop a moment and ask yourself, is the world really ready to beat a path to your door, regardless of market conditions?

Even if your answer is a resounding *Yes,* hold off, if you can, until the market and economy say *Go.*

The timing of an IPO, that is, the time an IPO is placed on the market should be well calculated. All too often a company is in position to go public, but for any number of reasons market conditions may not be receptive at that particular time. Proceeding with it as planned could easily jeopardize a good IPO.

Every market analyst and expert alive will tell you that even if your company is chafing at the bit to go public, if the market isn't gung ho at the time—wait! Market makers, analysts, and economists have learned from hard experience over the last couple of decades that the market has been prone to take sudden reversals and leave underwriters and companies high and dry. So it's worth playing it safe, and let the conditions of the time dictate whether or not you should proceed with your offering.

It may seem that we protest too much. But by doing so, we may help you, the entrepreneur, keep intact your dream of going public and subsequently making those marketplace millions. It's important to remember the old adage, "There's a time and place for everything." So it goes with an IPO.

When the timing is right, however, the company contemplating an IPO had better have all its necessary requirements, pieces, and players in place. It should also be prepared to jump in as soon as the situation changes from bad times to good times and the IPO market starts to take off.

The underwriters must also be ready to put the IPO out quickly to take advantage of a booming market, as the value of an IPO stock may shoot up dramatically.

From the company standpoint, a full commitment is necessary by all involved in order to be able to forge ahead without hesitation. This commitment can be focused by the CEO and management team posing pertinent questions for themselves to address. What follows is a checklist that you will find helpful:

- [ ] Is management ready?
- [ ] Are the team players identified and in place, pending additional financing?
- [ ] Are their credentials prepared and satisfactory?
- [ ] Are they prepared for the loss of privacy inherent in going public?
- [ ] Are they up to facing outside investor pressure in the decision-making process?
- [ ] Is planning in place?
- [ ] Has strategic planning been developed to implement both short- and long-term goals?
- [ ] Do these plans include the important areas such as people, products, production, marketing, and finance?
- [ ] Have R&D areas been identified?
- [ ] Have second-generation (follow-up) products or services been determined?
- [ ] Can all public reporting requirements, especially in the financial area, be met with timeliness?
- [ ] Is the company ready?
- [ ] Is the product or service ready to go?
- [ ] Has the product or service been tested?
- [ ] Will the second year as a public company show significant growth?

If you checked off all of the above, your IPO is ready to go. You owe it to your company to keep a sharp eye on the market for an opening. When the market window is open—in other words, when investors' money starts pouring into the market—you'll find prepared companies flocking through.

"When the going gets good, the good go public." So observe the Boy Scout credo and Be prepared. Savvy entrepreneurs can have a field day once the market opens up. Valuations tend to skyrocket, and IPOs can go public at 30 to 40 times earnings. Those are numbers that dreams are made of. At such times IPOs proliferate, and entrepreneurs race to get in before the market window closes. Some make it . . . some don't.

We made much ado about cautioning you not to bring out an IPO until the time is right. In reality, that's good advice. But if you missed the big surge and the market starts turning down, don't lose hope. A company can still gain entry. There are other ways to go in a slow IPO market. The company could seek other capital sources at reasonable costs that will not damage the IPO stock value, such as debt financing, subordinated debt, or convertible debt. These are the cheapest, most popular debts, and the safest way for the company to survive until the market opens up again. (We will examine these choices more closely in chapter 19.)

The CEO of an IPO, of course, hopes to catch a rising stock market and take advantage of good timing. However, bear in mind that the market is fickle. Remember that. Its timing is difficult to judge. Its fickleness is hard to grasp. A company's successful entry in the market depends on many uncontrollable factors. It depends on current and future international trends. It depends on private and government economic forecasts, on current and projected interest rates, on domestic and foreign political developments, on rates of inflation. It also depends on whether the company is engaged in a hot industry—one that's in favor at the moment. Emotion always rules the stock market, be it bullish or bearish. A triumphant entry depends, too, on whether the IPO market is oversaturated with new offerings.

It's true, that seldom do all the factors for assessing the right timing for both the company and the market come out positive. But when they do, the result is a "hot stock."

In order to create activity on a potentially hot stock, underwriters will often purposely price the stock at 10 percent to 15 percent *under* its true value. For example, they would bring out a $20 stock at $17.00—thus giving it an opportunity to go up immediately to create interest. This may mean a quick profit for the underwriter, but it occasionally proves devastating for management, the reason being, it's almost impossible for management to produce results in a short period of time needed by the investment community to justify the artificial price of the stock.

The problem is that management can't put the new money to work fast enough to support its goals. Therefore, the rise isn't sustained, the stock price drops. The big trouble with hot issues is that greed can override the whole market system. People play the market but the company can't really take advantage of it. By the time a stock settles down to a proper value, the quick buck players are usually out of it. Now management is forced to spend a lot of time dealing with the investment community, trying to convince it of the company's exciting potential, taking the time that is needed to manage the company and attain its set goals.

This hot situation doesn't happen too often, and some companies would welcome the opportunity to be in such a predicament. More often than not, entrepreneurs bringing an IPO to market spend their time trying to convince the proper parties that this is a good time to bring this particular company public.

Occasionally on smaller IPOs, the underwriter will make a firm commitment to the company. In essence, it gives the company capital immediately. For example, the underwriter may consider the prospects of the company excellent and give the company $1 million for a million shares up front (less commissions) and take the full risk of selling the offering. Should the price rise, as it usually does in a hot market, the underwriter keeps the difference. Let's say the stock comes out at $1 a share and quickly goes up to $1.40 a share. The $400,000 rise belongs to the underwriter for taking the "risk." If the stock goes down, however, the underwriter assumes the loss. To clarify the difference between *firm commitment* and *best efforts* offerings: With a firm commitment, the underwriter purchases the stock before the offering instead of acting as the company's agent in sales to the public.

It should be obvious by now that the time needed to realize an IPO from inception to fruition is crucial to its success. Now, let's explore some of the details that affect that timing more closely.

Time Planning

You have made the decision to go public. How quickly can you get the show on the road? Expect it to take some time—4 to 12 months—to comply with the requirements of the host of public and private regulatory agencies on local, state, and national levels. You will be dealing with accountants, attorneys, and other professionals whose goals, you may think, are to do nothing but make your life miserable. You can take comfort if your IPO is one in the range of $500,000 to $5 million with which this book is primarily concerned. You'd have a lot more to make you miserable about on IPOs of greater value.

When you go public also depends on how much preplanning you have done. Some IPOs are just *rank start-ups,* also referred to as *ragged start-ups.* The key management people may be committed to the deal, but the whole team may not be. And although some sources of funding are identified, they may not be *committed.* It's even possible the company is not yet ready to operate. That doesn't mean your deal is not viable. Usually, by the time the deal is ready to go, everything and everyone will be in place.

Other companies contemplating an IPO may already be operational, even with a history. For these companies, going public may be like starting over from square 1, because, in all probability, they will need to revamp their corporate structure. Their articles, bylaws, and accounting system may need to be revised, and they may lack a positive cash flow and find difficulty coming up with the monies needed to offset the initial offering costs.

A Two-step Process

The process involved in taking a company public has two parts. First is the preparation for registration, and second is the registration itself. The time involved in the preparation for registration is within management's control. Earlier, we outlined the requirements for registration, which is strictly a management responsibility.

The second part of this process comes after the company has submitted its registration statement to the SEC. It becomes a waiting game that depends on the work load and timing of that SEC regulatory body. It is important for the entrepreneur to realize that the first few months of the calendar year is a traditionally busy period for the SEC. If a company submits its statement at this time, the response will not be quick. This is usually the time the SEC reviews proxy statements for the annual meetings of existing companies. *The best time to submit the registration statement to the SEC is during the second quarter.* As a rule, once the first letter of comment about the registration has been received, its submission goes to the top of the pile and receives priority over new submissions.

Timetable

In the outline that follows we have grouped details for use as a checklist of the key steps of a public offering for you to use as a guide (table 3.1). Each company will, of course, have to adjust the process to fit its individual circumstances. Remember, this is a guide to help a company custom design a timetable for specific offering. For easier understanding, it has been divided into two parts—Public Offering Outline (areas) and Timetable Outline.

Summary

It takes time to complete an offering—not only processing time and waiting time, but *people time. Timing* is the key word to the success of an IPO. It usually depends on a number of favorable developments coming together at the same time, such as general economic conditions, international trends, interest rates, low inflation, and a hot industry or service. All contribute to market timing.

TABLE 3.1

Key Steps to a Public Offering

		Estimated Time (In Weeks)		
		Minimum	Average	Maximum
1.	Business Plans	0	2	6
	a. Corporate master plan			
	b. Underwriter/legal/accounting plan			
	c. Condensed plan (Executive summary)			
	d. Identify pre-private financing			
2.	Identification of Associates	1	2	4
	a. Retain attorneys			
	b. Identify accountants			
	c. Identify underwriters			
	d. Establish pre-private financing			
3.	Form Corporation	1	2	4
	a. File incorporation			
	b. Structure public offering			
	(1) Identify Founders			
	(a) % founders			
	(b) % pre-private			
	(c) % private			
	(d) % dilution			
	c. Negotiate underwriter's letter of intent			
	d. Retain accountants			
	e. Negotiate outside agreements (Patents, sales, licenses, consultants, royalties)			
4.	Private Placement Pre-preparation	2	3	4
	a. Approval of private placement documents			
	(1) Corporation			
	(2) Underwriter			
	(3) State			
5.	Raise Private Funds	3	6	10
	a. Establish escrow account			
	b. Solicit private monies			
	c. Pre-preparation of public registration			
	d. Break private escrow			
6.	Audit and Registration Preparation	2	3	4
	a. Complete initial audit			
	b. Retain printer			
	c. Retain transfer agent			
	d. Approval of SEC registration statement			

TABLE 3.1 *(Continued)*

| | | Estimated Time (In Weeks) | | |
		Minimum	Average	Maximum
	(1) Accountant			
	(2) Corporation			
	(3) Underwriter			
7.	Filings	6	9	12
	a. Submit registration to SEC			
	b. File with blue-sky states			
	c. Clear with NASD			
	d. Initial comment letter from SEC			
	e. Print red herring			
	(1) Send syndication indication request			
	(2) Distribute red herring			
	f. 2nd letter of comment and reply			
	g. 3rd letter (if needed)			
	h. SEC acceleration request (if needed)			
8.	Raise Public	4	8	12
	a. Arrange due diligence schedule			
	b. Sign underwriter's agreement			
	c. Establish public escrow			
	d. Print prospectus			
	e. File with NASDAQ			
	f. Establish syndicate			
	g. Distribute prospectus			
	h. Conduct due diligence meetings			
	i. Place tombstones			
	j. Complete public offering			
	(1) Legal and accounting opinions			
	(2) Closing papers			
	Total Weeks	19	35	56
	Total Months	5	9	13

9. Post-completion
   a. Break escrow
      (1) Corporation, attorneys, accountants, bank, transfer agent, respective counsel
   b. Establish market makers/quotation
      (1) Pink sheets
      (2) NASDAQ
   c. Establish trading
   d. File 8–K

Of equal concern is the *time planning* it takes to instigate a public offering. It's up to the CEO and management to pick and coordinate the many tasks and diverse persons involved in the process.

Some offerings can take as little as 4 months to complete, which is little short of being miraculous. For an offering to take as long as a year to complete is not unusual, especially for a company that is already operating and must complete an audited accounting of its prior 2 years in business. The goal, of course, is to have everything ready, when the magical words are spoken and the market window opens.

For most major business decisions, timing is critical. For an IPO, however, the timing is absolutely crucial to its success or failure, *and that's a fact!*

4

The Business Plan

In today's singles' circles, you would never make a date with someone you know nothing about. The same is true of professional investors. Rarely will they consider a proposal for an IPO by a private or public company unless the proposal is first presented in the form of a cohesive, well-written business plan. Only after evaluating the feasibility of this business plan will they invest the first dollar.

A business plan is a written presentation that carefully explains the business, its management team, its products or services, and its goals together with strategies for reaching the goals. The entrepreneur, or whoever writes the business plan will, in all probability, find it a painstaking process. But keep in mind, this is *the* selling tool, and it requires careful consideration of all the multiple facets of a start-up or business expansion. It cannot be written as an afterthought, and it should not be taken lightly. Check with any underwriter or professional investor anywhere in the country, and you'll hear horror stories about ill-conceived, poorly written, or sloppily put together business plans. As great as the company's potential may be, it is usually doomed to rejection before it can even get a foot in the door, if it has a poorly conceived business plan.

There are two basic purposes to a business plan. One is to present the company in an engaging way with interesting information on how the business will be run for the next 3 to 5 years, or possibly longer. The other, of course, is to raise the money to do so. There's no business without the bucks. The entrepreneur must put all the hows and needs together in one neat package. The human and physical resources must effectively interrelate with the marketing, operational, and financial strategies of the company. Unless an entrepreneur has magical powers of persuasion, this is not the time to try to fake it.

The business plan should be considered a vital sales tool for approaching any financial sources, investors or lenders. They will want to know that the plan has been carefully thought out by the management team. They will want to be convinced that the team has the skills and expertise needed to effectively manage the company and are prepared to seize opportunities and solve all problems that arise. That's why the business plan must be well prepared, professional in tone, and persuasive in conveying the company's potential.

We can't stress too strongly *a good business plan is the cornerstone of successful financing.* If you want their money, you've got to give them a good reason to buy. The business plan is where you lay out the reasons. It doesn't have to be unduly lengthy or complicated. But it must be informative and relevant. It needs to maintain logic and order, and show the company as effectively positioned as a good investment.

More important, the business plan should be specifically directed to the funding source and satisfy its particular concerns. For example, you would orient and write the plan differently for presentation to a banker versus a venture capitalist, an underwriter, or a private investor. The venture capitalist would want to know what risks are involved, whereas the banker cares more about how good the security is. These concerns must be individually addressed. There are no hard-and-fast rules for preparing a business plan. The key word is *ingenuity.* Strive for inventiveness. Strive to be interesting.

Here are some general guidelines covering the basic elements of a business plan. These should be helpful in writing any business plan, no matter who it's directed toward:

1. *Make it easy to read.* There is so much competition for investment dollars today, that if you want to get the jump on the next person, your plan will have to be well formatted and easily understood. Your introductory statement summarizing your operation is one of the most important sections—it must capture the investors' attention and motivate them to read the balance of the plan. If they need a dictionary at their side in order to read, they'll stop.

2. *Your approach should be market driven.* Not product driven. If you want those magic doors to open you must understand that investors are primarily interested in how the product or service will react in the market. They want to see your research demonstrating how the customer will benefit before buying into your plan.

3. *Qualify the competition.* Start by qualifying your product according to cost or time savings and revenue generation. Also show your projections for sales growth. And show how your product or service is

superior to others, and how you intend to exploit the competitive advantage.

4. *Present your distribution plan.* Be specific as to how the company will sell and distribute its product or service. Describe the method and what it will cost to get the product into the customer's hands.

5. *Exploit your company's uniqueness.* Explain what will give your company a competitive edge in the marketplace—special attributes like patents, trade secrets, or copyrights.

6. *Emphasize management strength.* Show proof that the company is comprised of highly qualified people who can cover all the bases. Indicate the incentives that will keep them together, and how they, the directors, and the advisors possess the necessary credibility.

7. *Present attractive projections.* Paint a realistic picture of where your company is going from here. Be detailed and keep it credible. Good validated forecasts are impressive.

8. *Zero in on possible funding sources.* As mentioned earlier, it's different strokes for different folks. Design versions of the plan to fit the idiosyncrasies of each source you plan to approach. A banker's interest lies in stability, security, and sound returns, whereas a venture capitalist is more interested in "early stage" funding, with higher risk and higher returns. Both will want to know how much equity their investment will buy, and how the proceeds will be spent.

9. *Close with a bang.* Drive across the fact that you're offering a great deal. Be definite about how investors will get their money back and when. Specify the return: state how the investor will receive a 30 percent or 50 percent compounded annual return, or whatever you're offering.

The Next Step

You're not finished yet. After you have drafted your business plan, solicit feedback on it. Ask a cross section of people in your business, whose judgment you trust, to review it. Don't fall in love with your words. Make the revisions that are necessary, then prepare a good oral presentation. In fact, you should have ready a 2-minute and a 5-minute oral attention grabber. Follow up with a detailed 15- to 30-minute presentation modeled on your written plan.

A word of caution: When preparing your financial projections, avoid the shortcut of relying on available computerized information—those preset formats in which you plug in figures and percentages. Individualize your financial projections. Think them out carefully. No two businesses are alike. And keep in mind that a new or start-up company won't fit the industry norm.

Your projections should include the financial obligations of bringing out your product: enlisting new management people and workers; taking on more space or manufacturing capacity; purchasing support materials; even the time it will take to receive your accounts receivables.

. It may also be a wise idea to seek out available books on writing a business plan. They can be found at libraries and bookstores. Expect to spend 2 or 3 months to write a business plan, with many more hours to prepare the presentation. Remember, your words not only have to paint a pretty picture, they must be persuasive as well.

It's of little use to approach the writing of a business plan as if it were a necessary evil. Rather look at it as a helpful tool that can be used to exploit the advantages of a product or service. There are many specifics that should be included in a successful business plan. The following outline contains many suggestions which may seem obvious, but one could easily forget to mention them. Again, this outline should be used as a preliminary planning guide.

Outline for Business Plan

1. *Cover sheet*
   Name, address, principal contact, phone, date.

2. *Table of contents*
   Categorize the contents.

3. *Executive summary*
   Very important. This summary briefly sets forth the contents, taking key sentences from each section of the plan to prepare the reader. Devote 2 or 3 pages to it.

4. *History*
   Include a brief description of how, when, and by whom the company was started, and its achievements, acceptance, setbacks, and current status.

5. *Product or service*
   Describe the need for the product or service in today's marketplace, how it will make a difference, the benefits derived from using it, what will make the customer buy it, any other advantages or disadvantages. Explain any special training needed to sell or use it. Include all relevant regulation. Expound on any exclusivity or uniqueness.

6. *Market description and analysis*
   Prepare a customer profile. Describe what persons form your mar-

ket, where they can be found, why they would purchase this product or service rather than another, whether it would appeal to single individuals or to groups. Document quality, warranty, service, and price significance. Pinpoint the buyer and user. Point out political influences, if any. Describe market coverage, whether local, regional, national, or international.

Prepare an industry profile. Discuss pertinent trends, past, present, and future. Offer available statistical data on sales and units. Use charts, graphs, and tables if they seem impressive. Refer to trade associations if helpful.

Prepare a competitive profile. Stress advantages of price, quality, warranties, service, and distribution. Include the operational strengths and weaknesses. Project potential market share, trends in sales, and profitability.

Don't guess. Check your facts and note sources wherever possible.

7. *Marketing strategy*

Specify the company's goals, how they are to be achieved, and who will have the responsibility. Qualify all distribution methods (representatives, dealers, and so forth) and describe any planned advertising. Include sales aids, foreign licensing, and training.

8. *Operations plan*

Disclose all present capabilities as to equipment and facilities, as well as future projections for offices, branches, manufacturing, and distribution.

9. *Research and development*

Explain all past efforts and accomplishments as well as future expectations. Substantiate the patentability of inventions or other advantage the company will have over the competition, and the anticipated market impact.

10. *Schedule*

Describe the timing and sequential steps that will be taken to bring the company up to full speed. Take it month by month for the first year. Thereafter, indicate the progress expected quarterly.

11. *Management*

In the eyes of investors, the quality of the management team often determines the success of the company, so include detailed resumes. These should cover career highlights, accomplishments, positions held, good performance records. Describe how the team has worked together in the past. List directors, consultants, advisors, and other key professionals who will be involved in company operations. Detailed resumes should be appended.

12. *Risks and problems*

These could be a red flag. Indicate them only if the potential investor wants them identified.

13. *Use of proceeds*

Judiciously present a timetable indicating how much money will be needed, when it will be needed, and how it will be used.

14. *Finances*

Present the company's current equity capital structure as well as future plans. Itemize payments made with dates paid. List all outstanding stock options. Include profit and loss statements and balance sheets. Present current and proposed salary structure for those already on board and those who will come on board at a later date. Show projections month by month for the first year, quarterly for the second and third years, and yearly thereafter.

15. *Appendix*

Include a glossary (if pertinent) and all essential pieces of evidence, such as resumes, product brochures, customer listings, testimonials, and news articles.

The Plan's the Thing

Some companies may question the necessity of a business plan, citing successful firms that never had one. Times are changing. When the goal is to go public, it's not only the entrepreneur's own money that's at stake. Advisors, investors, underwriters, and bankers need to be thoroughly convinced. They want evidence that they won't be wasting their time and money. They want to know that company management has a clear sense of direction and is prepared to move toward its established goals. And besides that, they'd be crazy to help a company raise millions of dollars without first seeing what was to be done with the money.

A good business plan is the answer. What's more, much same information would have to be gathered anyway to be made available to potential shareholders, to show them before they place their money in the company that the company is conforming with all the regulatory requirements of a public company.

Pre-private Financing

Information regarding pre-private and private financing prior to a public offering should also be included in the business plan. To explain these terms: If two entrepreneurs each put up a certain amount of money to get a company started, that's pre-private financing. They then go out and seek more money—that's private financing from others. (See chapters 19 and 21.) It's common practice and will not raise any eyebrows when presented in a good business plan.

Special Executive Summary

This summary is not a part of the business plan, however it takes advantage of the high points in the business plan. It serves as an entering wedge by the entrepreneur anticipating a public offering. It's called "special" because it stands alone.

The executive summary discussed earlier usually summarizes the business plan in 2 to 3 pages. The *special executive summary* expounds on the most enticing parts of the business plan for about 6 to 8 pages. In essence, it's a condensed business plan that shows a company to its best advantage. It's an entree when seeking help to locate and identify potential financial sources. It can also be used as an overview for persons who do not need to know all that much about the company, or for those from whom management wants to to keep proprietary information. It can be changed and adapted to any particular audience. The special executive summary also serves as an informational document to create enthusiasm among brokers involved in selling the stock at the time of public offering. It certainly will make more interesting reading than a formal SEC document. A company should not go into an offering without it. Above all, a Special Executive Summary should not be taken lightly. It is indispensable, and should be kept updated. It could very well be the key to reaching the right source, the "Open sesame" to the magic doors.

Follow-up

A business plan requires regular updating. This should be given top priority. After a company has gone public and has raised the needed capital, the business plan should not be cast aside, but rather converted into an operating plan. It should also be used to reflect on and to assist the management group in keeping the company focused on its goals. Refine it; adjust it; refer to it. Use it. Use it. *Use it!*

Summary

If a company's goal is to go public, it must have a business plan. Preparing it may take months, but you won't make it to first base without it. The outlines we presented in this chapter may not fit every company's particular requirements, but should contain enough general information and suggestions to provide a solid base for preparing your business plan. Other materials and information on writing business plans can be found in bookstores and public libraries.

A company should give its plan its very best effort. You will discover that a well-prepared business plan will prove to be a vital sales tool when approaching any financial source, investor or lender.

A final note for anyone planning to go public: Failing to plan, is planning to fail.

PART II
ASSEMBLING THE IPO TEAM

5

The Management Players

In the game of baseball, it takes a team effort to get a player out. In the game of football, a tailback would be hard pressed to cross the line of scrimmage without having the way paved by teammates. In the game of hockey, the puck is passed from player to player until it is finally slammed towards the goal. In the game of business, it takes the same kind of teamwork to make a public company operate successfully. But as with any sport, it takes leadership to make the team work as a unit. This is management's role—to provide the vision, the direction, and the motivation to make the *team* a winner.

Let's take a look into the relationships, responsibilities, and qualities that can be expected from those members of the team in key management positions in a public company. These people are responsible for carrying out the directions of the CEO for the operation of the company. The CEO is the information and communications architect of the company, communicating to the team what must be done, while, by working together, they make it happen. Another responsibility of a public company's management team is to make certain that the company operates within the rules of the SEC. We all know that teams perform better when they're well motivated. In a public company, the motivation for management is usually the rewards of salary, stock options, and bonuses. These motivate individual players to play well, and ultimately makes the team perform well.

When reviewing a prospective offering, underwriters view the quality of the management team as one of the most important factors. They expect management, under the direction of the CEO, to foster growth and establish a leadership position in the market. The reason is obvious—a good market position results in the public purchasing more of the company's stock, which increases the stock's value, which increases the value of the management team's stock holdings. Underwriters are especially pleased if one or more persons on the management team has already gone through an IPO. It adds credibility to management's role. That's a good rationalization for the entrepreneur to be selective in the choice of management people. But then, of course, most entrepreneurs will do whatever is necessary to make their business a success.

In today's business world, entrepreneur/CEOs are the primary creators of all new businesses. They were responsible for over 80 percent of new jobs created in the United States in the 1980s. The decade of the eighties has been heralded by the financial press as the era of the entrepreneur. In *Entrepreneurial Megabucks* (New York: John Wiley & Sons, 1985), A. David Silver states, "An economy is governed by its entrepreneurs, entrepreneurs set economics in motion; start the game; bring the ball, bat, and gloves."

The influence of the entrepreneur of the eighties is without parallel in our history. At the turn of this century, 80 percent of all Americans were self-employed. By 1950, this figure dropped to 18 percent. By 1970, just 20 years later, it dropped to just 9 percent. The 1980s saw a reverse in that trend as entrepreneurs moved to the forefront of a free enterprise–driven society. The results of their entrepreneurship and creativity have not only increased our quality of life, but caused revolutionary changes in our daily living.

Here are just a few examples of the impact made by entrepreneurs: Ray Kroc, the founder of McDonald's Corporation, was one of the prime contributors to the concept of fast foods in this country. His franchise operations opened the door to thousands of entrepreneurs who dreamed of self-employment and in the process expanded the job market. Mary Kay Ash, of Mary Kay Cosmetics, was responsible for millions of dollars being earned by second-income families, but more importantly, she helped thousands of women launch entrepreneurial life-styles. The Block brothers, Henry and Richard, not only changed the practice of income tax preparation, but in the process built a $500 million company, and opened the door to thousands of new jobs. David Packard and William Hewlett created Hewlett-Packard. Today it's the largest manufacturer of electronic test and measurement equipment in the world. They trained and encouraged many people who now are among our most outstanding electronic entrepreneurs. And the list goes on.

In the past decade, thousands of entrepreneurs have created millions of jobs all over the world. Many thousands of new products and service ideas have been spawned in hundreds of industrial classifications. Few of these entrepreneurs could have accomplished their goals without the expertise of their management team.

While the value of a good management team is undeniable, deciding upon the right people to constitute a particular team can be a genuine challenge for CEOs. It requires careful evaluation of their own skills to determine the supplementary skills that will need to be provided by others on the management team.

The CEO's decision should be based on a thorough understanding of the business and what the members of the management team can bring with them to further that business. Their education and experience in business is essential to the company. It is also crucial for the entrepreneur/CEO to consider the personality of each team member, and his or her ability to deal with management problems that will be aired in public, to adapt to the frustrations and compromises involved in accomplishing short- or long-range goals, and to handle the continuing time diversions to accommodate public investors—let alone the burdensome reports constantly required by government agencies such as the SEC. In other words, besides having special abilities, the team members must be prepared to live in a goldfish bowl, even to the point of having their salary made public. These are only some of the factors that affect the important decisions an effective entrepreneur/CEO must make regarding the management team, but they are particularly important for building a strong team to run a public company.

The entrepreneur/CEO must understand, too, that the credentials and experience of the management team will be closely scrutinized by those involved in the investment process, including regulatory bodies, public investors, private investors, underwriters, consultants, attorneys, and accountants. The management team must be able to enhance the company's ability to raise needed money. Because, simply, that's what the game is all about!

Of course, the functions of the management team differ for different companies, depending on the nature of the company. For instance, some companies may require a research and development department, whereas a service company may not. An engineer-to-order manufacturing company and a fast food company require different kinds of management. Specific management abilities function in specific designated areas. Here we have prepared a general list of guidelines, qualifications, and fundamentals outlining abilities needed by members of the management team for a variety of public company environments:

Administration and General Management

Planning. Ability to identify obstacles, establish attainable goals, develop and implement action plans

Problem Solving. Ability to gather and analyze facts, anticipate trouble and know what to avoid, implement solutions effectively and follow up thoroughly

Making Decisions. Ability to take input from the team and implement changes

Project and Task Management. Ability to properly define and set goals, organize participants, and monitor a project to completion

Negotiating. Ability to solicit differences from all sides, balance opinions, and fairly arbitrate for mutual benefit

Communication. Ability to communicate clearly and effectively to all parties and the public in both written and oral form

Operations Management

Purchasing. Ability to seek out the most appropriate sources and suppliers, considering cost, delivery time, and quality; and to effectively negotiate contracts and manage flow, balancing current need and dollar resources

Manufacturing. Demonstrated experience in the process; open to continuous improvement techniques, people-power, machinery, time, costs, and quality needs of the customer

Inventory and Quality Control. Ability to establish suitable inspection standards, maintain accuracy, and set realistic dollar benchmarks for raw, in-process, and finished goods

Financial Management

Ratios Applications. Ability to produce detailed pro formas for profit and loss (P&L), cash flow, and balance sheets; and analyze and monitor all financial areas

Money Controls. Ability to design, implement, and monitor all money management and to set up systems for overall and individual projects

Capital Raising. Ability to determine the best approach, form, structure debt/equity, short versus long term, and familiarity with sources

Marketing Management

Evaluation and Research. Ability to conduct thorough studies using proper demographics and to interpret and analyze the results in structuring viable territories and sales potential

Support. Ability to obtain market share by organizing, supervising, and most important, motivating a sales force

Planning. Ability to provide promotion, advertising, and sales programs that are effective with and for sales representatives and distributors

Selling. Ability to effectively demonstrate a capacity to identify, open the door, and develop new customers by closing the sale

Product Distribution. Ability to manage and supervise product flow from manufacturing through the channels of distribution to the end user, with attention to costs, scheduling, and planning techniques

Product Continuation. Ability to determine service and spare parts requirements, track customer complaints, supervise the setup and management of the service organization

Engineering and R&D

Research. Ability to distinguish between basic and applied research, keeping a bottom-line balance

Development. Ability to guide product development so that a product is introduced on time, within budget, and meets the customers' basic needs

Engineering. Ability to supervise the final design through engineering, testing, and manufacturing

Personnel

Listening. Ability to listen without prejudging, really hear the message, and make effective decisions

Help. Ability to determine situations where help is needed

Criticism. Ability to receive feedback without becoming defensive and to provide constructive criticism

Conflict. Ability to confront differences openly and determine resolution with teamwork

Development. Ability to select and coach subordinates and pass this ability on to peers

Culture. Ability to create an atmosphere and attitude conducive to high performance, rewarding work well done either verbally or monetarily

Legal

Contracts. Experienced in and knowledgeable about the broad procedures and structure for government regulation and commercial law, including warranty, default, and incentives

Corporate. Experienced in and knowledgeable about the intricacies of incorporation, leases, distribution, stock issues, and patents

This list covers the qualifications, abilities, and characteristics the entrepreneur should take into account when assembling a management team for a public company.

A final word. It is not necessary to have the full team assembled and in place at the time of submitting the IPO registration statement. It is perfectly acceptable to simply list the titles of positions not yet filled, followed by a statement that the persons will soon come on board or the company is still searching for qualified candidates. List the qualities and qualifications desired and include the positions in the officers' compensation table. Thus you will show that management is aware of a personnel deficiency and intends to fill the vacancy with a highly qualified candidate.

Summary

One of the most important decisions of an IPO CEO is the selection of a qualified and experienced management team. Each management position serves a specific function, and it's the responsibility of the CEO to make certain that the persons chosen to fill those positions possess the skills to do the job. Equally important to the company's success is a commitment by the management team to the company's goals. Underwriters, investors, and others in the financial community regard the management team as a crucial element when considering a prospective offering. As we will see, this same kind of commitment to the company's goals should apply to the other IPO team members such as the members of the board of directors, advisors, attorneys, and accountants.

Choosing qualified, compatible people can be a long and laborious process, but the time is well spent if the end result spells *success.*

6

The Board of Directors

There's an old story about a "smart" entrepreneur, the chief executive officer (CEO) of a company, who was advised by underwriters to be sure to get a highly qualified board of directors to help make important company decisions—people of integrity, who could be objective and had good judgment.

The CEO told the underwriters there was no need for outsiders to tell him how to run his business—he would make a killing with his company on his own. Well, he made a killing all right. He killed the company.

The point here is that IPO CEOs need and should seek the best help they can get in making important company decisions. They should begin by assembling a strong board of directors.

Good and Bad Boards

A good board of directors is composed mainly of outsiders. There you have it. Telling that to some CEOs is like trying to tell it to the marines. Selecting outsiders for the board often goes against the grain of the CEO. It's true that no one has the CEO's stake in the company. It's understandable if one dislikes involving outsiders in important decisions. Thus CEOs tend to enlist people who are involved in the day-to-day operations of the company, such as the management team. That is a *bad* board of directors.

They'll deny it till hell freezes over, but employees and managers tend to rubber-stamp the CEO's decisions and to inhibit rather than encourage frank comments by outsiders. It's called self-preservation. It's hard to be objective when one's job could be in jeopardy. Therefore, it's in the CEO's own interest to choose board members who will give independent, unbiased feedback, and who will not be afraid to disagree or say No.

Another good reason to limit insiders on the board is to preserve the CEO's own fallibility. No one has all the answers, but when CEOs can't come up with answers it can weaken their leadership position in the eyes of management. It's just not a good idea for subordinates to know when CEOs are frustrated and unable to come up with the solution to a problem, or to discover they are not the great leaders they seemed. We are all of us, at one time or another, faced with decisions we just don't know how to make. Strong boards of directors can serve as psychological support teams to help CEOs make the important decisions only they can make.

Outside board members serve a very important function in a company. They are outsiders only in that they do not actively work in the company as an employee or in management. A board member could be a major shareholder (most valuable), a business associate (valuable), a retired chief executive (valuable), an investment banker (good). Also acceptable, but ranked lower on the ladder, are lawyers, accountants, and suppliers with a financial stake in the company. The common feeling is that they should be reviewed very carefully, since they may have personal interests at odds with the company's best interests. Other excellent candidates for the board are persons engaged in businesses different from the company's, who can appreciate and understand the risk of running a company or who manage, or have managed, a public company.

A good board member plays many roles—from assisting in formulating long-term policies and plans, to critiquing existing financial, production, or marketing practices. But the board's most powerful role is that of confidant, mentor, and peer to the CEO. With a good board, rather than the president making the decisions alone, the directors become involved in setting company policies and strategies and reviewing operating results.

Overall, the board of directors should demonstrate respect for the CEO. They should like the CEO and want him or her to succeed. They should have unquestionable integrity, good judgment, relevant experience, problem-solving skills, and a capability for action and risk taking. That's why a good board is hard to find.

Changing the composition of the board of directors may prove embarrassing to the CEO, especially if the board existed before the company went public, and it can be even more embarrassing if the board consisted of friends and relatives lacking real credentials. But the CEO must understand that in going public the board will assume greater responsibilities. Their credentials must be acceptable to the public, and the public must have confidence in them. So, to paraphrase a well-known statement, CEOs must do not what is best for them, but what is best for the company.

An Informed Board Is a Helpful Board

One of the prime responsibilities the CEO has to the board of directors is to keep it informed. Directors must be given information on a timely and continuing basis. They must have meeting agendas and pertinent background information sufficiently in advance of a board meeting to allow them time to prepare for the meeting. They must be furnished with monthly financial statements, including comparisons to budgets. At all board meetings, they must be given detailed reports on the company's progress.

Although most directors know what is expected of them, it would be a good idea for the company's legal counsel to furnish each board member with a copy of the *Corporate Directors Guidebook,* published by the American Bar Association. This book provides a general overview of the functions and responsibilities of the corporate director and will help the directors to perform their directorial functions responsibly as well as to adhere to the board's bylaws and the regulations of the SEC and other governmental agencies. Consider it *must* reading.

What to Expect from a Board of Directors and What Not

The Board of Directors Does Not Run the Company

The board of directors does not run the company, management runs the company. The board sees to it that the company is well managed.

The Board of Directors Does Not Develop Company Strategy

The CEO and management develop company strategy. Board input can be indispensable, however, in coming up with ways to test and evaluate management strategy.

The Board of Directors Enhances Company Performance

The attention of the board of directors can be turned to immediate needs, such as controlling costs, or it can apply its expertise to planning ahead to future needs, such as defining and penetrating a new market. The board must be flexible enough to deal with all matters in the best interests of the company.

Directors Should Be Experts in Their Fields

It's up to the CEO to assess the management team's strengths and weaknesses and the company's direction and then select the best candidates for board positions to fill the voids in the management plan and thereby help improve the company's performance. The entrepreneur/CEO will probably be pleasantly surprised to find the high caliber of outside people who not only are flattered, but would give their eyeteeth to be asked to serve on a board of directors. The ideal board is composed of top-notch people who are experts in the industry, such as a scientist with an interest in business dealings who would benefit from the experience, a former CEO of a public company, or a former politician with a business background.

Directors Must Attend Meetings

At the very minimum board of directors' meetings should be held quarterly. The frequency of meetings depends on the needs of the company. According to surveys conducted annually since 1971 by Korn/Ferry International, the world's largest executive search firm, the national board meeting average is 8 times a year. Small public companies, start-up companies, or those in the early stages of going public may find it necessary to schedule meetings 10 to 12 times a year. The Korn/Ferry survey also determined that the average outside director devotes more than 150 hours annually to company business.

By contrast, a survey by *Venture* magazine found that 38 percent of private companies held board meetings only when needed, 29 percent held monthly meetings, 25 percent held quarterly meetings, and 8 percent met semiannually.

Directors Get Paid

As far as compensation goes for directors—no two companies do it the same. Compensation can take many forms, including annual retainer fees and hourly or per meeting fees plus expenses. In a recent Korn/Ferry survey of 31,000 companies, meeting fees for outside directors ranged from $100 to $1000 with an average of $534. In addition, many firms have established annual retainers of $5000 to $10,000. For smaller companies there may be no fees at all, although $100 per meeting seems to be common practice.

Another form of compensation, especially suitable for cash-short companies, is the issuance of stock in lieu of money. This practice can prove to be a disadvantage over time, as it makes outside directors insiders. Let's say, for example, that a director is also a shareholder. If the board is contemplating a decision that may adversely affect the value of the shares, that board member may not come up with the desired objectivity. Also worth thinking about is that when directors become shareholders they open themselves to directors' liability lawsuits.

Directors Can Get Sued

By way of explanation, in 1977, the Foreign Corrupt Practices Act (FCPA) was passed by Congress. It stated that officers and board members should create an environment whereby middle and lower levels of managers and employees understood the nature of corporate accountability. It urged board members to be cognizant of their responsibility to monitor the totality of corporate performance. (Chapter 32 deals more fully with FCPA.) This well-intended legislation was probably the forerunner of many current lawsuits.

Most lawsuits filed are nuisance suits, but they are very expensive to fight. There were hundreds of such lawsuits filed in the mid 1980s against public companies, and liability insurance premiums skyrocketed. Many insurance companies stopped writing policies, and many fine prospects turned down offers to serve on boards of directors.

In response, many states passed legislation that limited liability, SEC compliance became stricter, tighter financial accounting rules were instituted, companies policed themselves more carefully, and court awards were reduced. These cases were no longer plums for lawyers seeking to make quick bucks; plaintiffs had to prove that the company, its management, and more particularly, individual directors, were purposely negligent in performing their duties, party to insider trading abuses, or committed willful acts of omissions, especially fraud. By 1988, the volume of suits subsided, but much damage had already been done.

Makeup of the Board

There is no standard operating procedure regarding the number of members that must constitute a board of directors or the mix of outside directors versus management members. It depends on the scope of the company, egos, and personal preferences of the CEO.

Five directors on the board is a good number for several reasons. It's an odd number, which avoids tie votes, the taking of sides, and bitter personality battles. Three members may not allow for sufficient diversity of opinion or fill weak areas in management. Two outside directors seems to satisfy the vague FCPA rules and courts' feelings about the need for outside objective input. And, of course, on the inside, managing directors have a high stake in the success of the company. Rounding out the board could be a major shareholder. For a small IPO company five directors is ordinarily sufficient and, as the company matures, can easily be expanded to seven. Thus a company can add expertise from either the inside or outside to fit expanding needs without the board becoming cumbersome and overly expensive.

Committees of the Board

Because of the proliferation of liability suits against companies, management, and boards during the late seventies and early eighties, as mentioned earlier, companies were compelled to become more accountable. Committees were established to validate accountability. Most OTC companies today maintain committees composed of board members, management, and outside experts. These include:

Audit Committee

The audit committee is found on most boards. Comprised entirely of directors who are not officers of the company, it supervises and directs investigations into matters relating to audit functions and is responsible for a general review of the annual report. The audit committee recommends to the board of directors the retention of independent auditors and approves their work. This includes the fee arrangement, the scope of services, and a confirmation of the independence of the auditors. The audit committee also reviews the company's internal accounting procedures and controls.

Nominating Committee

The nominating committee reviews the performance of the directors and recommends management nominees for directorships.

Conflict of Interest Committee

At least two-thirds of the members of this committee should be outside directors unaffiliated with the company or its subsidiaries to avoid the potential for favoritism. The committee's function is to oversee the company's conflict of interest policy and to keep track of significant transactions between the company, its subsidiaries, and members of management.

Compensation Committee

The compensation committee reviews the achievements of executives and officers of the company and makes recommendations to the board concerning their compensation. This includes the awarding of bonuses, perks, and stocks.

Executive Committee

The executive committee is less common than the others that were mentioned. Its primary function is to assist management to implement corporate policy established by the board of directors. For instance, the board may decide that certain procedures could benefit or expedite the company's operations. The executive committee would have the power and authority to act on behalf of the board in working with management to see that the board's directives are implemented.

Board of Advisors (Advisory Committee)

The board of advisors is not set up as a committee of the board, although in some corporate structures it is considered to be one. One or two board members may head the advisory committee and act as a buffer between the advisors on the outside and the board itself.

As a rule, the formal setup of the board of advisors is accomplished through an amendment of the bylaws. The advisors are appointed by the board of directors, but they are distinct from the board. In most companies advisors may not be officers, directors, or employees of the company. They are experts in various fields whose function is to consult with directors and officers of the company on technical, management, and economic factors that affect the company. Well-chosen advisors add prestige and credibility to an IPO.

It should be noted, too, that members of the board of advisors serve at the pleasure of the board of directors and receive compensation as determined by the board. They are also provided with indemnification by the company.

There are no requirements for formal group meetings by the board of advisors, although the custom is for them to meet as a group at least twice a year, with, individual members of the board consulted as necessary in their areas of expertise.

For Directors Only

Directors of OTC companies and entrepreneurs contemplating an IPO should consider membership in the National Association of Corporate Directors, a nonprofit organization serving the needs of corporate directors and boards. Member benefits include an informative newsletter, *Director's Monthly*, and the *Directors' Register*, a unique service to help companies search for appropriate candidates to fill board vacancies. The association sponsors seminars featuring timely directors' topics. It offers liability insurance and other services of interest to corporate directors. It's an organization for all companies regardless of business size, structure, or sector. What's more, membership fees are reasonable. For information write to: Association of Corporate Directors, 450 Fifth St. NW, Suite 1140, Washington, DC 20001. The phone number is (202) 347–3123.

Officers' and Directors' Questionnaire

All executive officers and all directors of an IPO, including outside directors (but excluding members of the board of advisors), are required by the SEC to complete a very extensive questionnaire. It includes some of the personal information required in the registration statement and in the annual proxy statements. Many of the questions are of a technical nature and require lengthy answers.

The questions place special emphasis on relationships among the company, its suppliers, lessors, lessees, purchasers, consultants, principals, and even their relatives. Other subjects deal with fraud, misrepresentation, education, employment, legal and illegal acts, past history (with specific dates), outside stock or equity ownerships (present, past, public, and private), and any dealings with the SEC or NASD. It's not a pleasant task to fill out one of the questionnaires, but it's amazing the things you find out about yourself in the process.

Summary

The main purpose of a board of directors is to help the CEO make sound company decisions. They can best help by giving independent unbiased feedback. Management and employees of a company tend to rubber-stamp their CEO's decisions, and that is why it is so important to appoint outside experts as board members.

The board's most powerful role is that of confidant, mentor, and peer to the CEO. It acts as sounding board or devil's advocate and stimulates strategic thinking. Therefore, it is the IPO CEO's responsibility to select people to serve on the board who can help him or her gain the corporate credibility the company needs. The task is not an easy one, but it can be full of rewards. When an IPO is successful, the board of directors may not take the bows, but you can bet your valuable shares it deserves a lot of the credit.

7

Consultants and Advisors

Too many cooks spoil the broth. That ain't necessarily so—especially when it comes to hiring consultants for small companies, or even large companies for that matter. No matter how professional a management team may be, and no matter how well staffed the company, there are usually areas of the business where it can use outside expertise. That's why consultants were born.

A *consultant* is a person with specialized expertise. Consultants are often retained on a onetime basis for a specific problem. *Advisors,* also discussed in this chapter, may also serve as consultants, but are expected to have a broader knowledge of the business. Advisors are usually retained to advise the company's management team for a longer term. They can be especially useful working through the IPO process.

Consultants

Bringing in a consultant is not the same as hiring another person on the staff of the company. Consultants should be retained only for the period of time required to assist the management team in identifying, isolating, and solving problems or deficiencies. The consultant's function is to bring a particular problem into focus and zero in on the solution.

If there is a marketing problem, for example, the consultant may advise the company when to put a product on the market, whom the product should be directed to, and where the product is likely to receive a good reception. Or a consultant can provide expertise on product improvement or production techniques. There are countless situations where management could be served by help from a professional on the outside.

A consultant or consulting firm is *not* someone management turns to in desperation; rather they should be used as a source for helpful guidance. Many consultants, where an IPO is concerned, like to get involved during the conception phases of the company. If they really know their craft, they can be very helpful in starting a company off on the right foot.

Consultants Can Come from Anywhere

Anyone can call himself or herself a consultant. Some people who call themselves consultants are self-promoters. Some work at it on a temporary basis. They are often people with good management skills who are between jobs, or they can be former CEOs who offer expertise in their particular fields.

There are over 50,000 private consultants in the United States today. Most work on their own, but there are also consulting firms that employ as many as several hundred people. These range from national to international in scope. Their clients are usually major companies. They prefer long-term projects and their fees are commensurately high. Many major companies operate on the premise, the higher fee, the better the consultation. The question is whether the consultant's experience fits your company's needs. Look for proven professionals in their field, who have successfully helped others with similar problems to those facing your company.

Hire When Ready!

When enlisting the aid of a consultant or consulting firm, the company should first be convinced of the need. According to a recent *Harvard Business Review* article, "Management consultants are generally hired for the wrong reasons. Once hired, they are generally poorly employed and loosely supervised."

Therefore it is important that the company does its homework before hiring a consultant. Most consultants have an area of specialty. Some may claim broad expertise, but their experience may actually lie in a special industry or technical area. The company should find out this information in advance. The fact that a consultant has an excellent background in one field does not make him or her an expert in another field. The company should also determine in advance the precise problem needing a solution— thus eliminating some consultants from the running.

Consultants Are Not Always Necessary

Properly utilized a consultant can appreciably help a company's operations, but too often management may already have the answer to a problem, and only need to convince key people. The consultant can serve that purpose, but at a price. Consultants also are often asked to explore areas the company has no intention of pursuing. Yet another misuse of company money is to hire consultants to research information that is readily available.

A sharp management group can solve many consulting chores without paying unnecessary consulting fees. For instance, suppliers can usually advise a company whether it is more advantageous to buy or lease certain assets, or how best to go about computerizing a business with the right kind of hardware and software. Insurance company agents are trained to determine the most efficient insurance and employee benefit plans. Advertising agencies and marketing companies interested in working with the company will usually provide sound, useful information for free. All it takes is a little talking to the people a company does business with or plans to do business with. Remember, a consultant is not the only one who can supply answers.

Consultant is not a magic word. Consultants should not be left to their own devices. Management has an obligation to stay on top of consultants' activities as well as to make certain they get the necessary support from the company's staff. Consultants should be encouraged to bring in solutions within a reasonable period of time. As mentioned in an earlier chapter: Time is Money.

Fees

Consulting fees can take many forms. They are often open to negotiation, but some consultants are firm in their charges. Much depends on the complexities involved. Fees can be based on hourly time or a weekly amount. Some consultants ask for a fixed fee or retainer. Some companies prefer to have consultants work in-house, but some consultants will only work off site.

The ideal way for the company to approach the consultant situation would be to contact several possible consultants. Brief them on the problem. Secure proof of their expertise and information on similar projects they have worked on. Besides asking for their credentials and resume, request specific proposals on how the project could be handled.

Before the final decision is reached, management should feel confident of working with the consultant and satisfied of receiving:

1. A realistic and reasonable charge for services

2. A determined attempt to produce results

3. A cooperative attitude toward the people involved

4. Maintenance of a continuing relationship

The effort and time involved in securing the services of the right consultant for a particular need will pay off handsomely. The chemistry must be there, for with it comes the confidence and security the job will be done right.

There are many sources for locating consultants. They can be found through the Small Business Administration, colleges and universities, and even professional placement services. Some of the best sources may be recommendations from other companies.

Advisors

Don't even think about going public without the backing of knowledgeable advisors. There are more obstacles to be encountered in the IPO process than in the game of Monopoly, from finding the right underwriter to submitting the proper forms to the SEC at the proper time.

The best advisors—the most dependable advisors—are those persons or consulting firms that have been through the IPO battle from beginning to end more than once. You may have to search, because there are not very many of them out there, but they are the only sure way to go. What's more, even though the advisors may have been through the process, they'll find it different every time. The rules change from day to day with the never-ending changes in federal and state regulations and the fickleness of the financial community, which wants every speculative investment to be a sure thing.

Young's Study

Dr. John E. Young of the College of Business and Administration of the University of Colorado at Denver questioned hundreds of CEOs who had gone through the IPO process on the subject of outside advisors. Those shown to be most important were legal counsel, CPAs, underwriters, bankers, and printers.

Other advisors not specifically covered in the study, but who should be considered important, are people who have been through the IPO process and who could apply their knowledge and experience for the benefit of the company—people such as a member of the board of directors or someone in the management team who has been involved in the IPO process before, or an experienced outside investment banker with prior dealings with IPOs. What matters is having a broad perspective of the process and being objective about what the CEO must contend with in confrontations with other professionals, such as attorneys, CPAs, and the SEC and other governmental agencies.

Young's CEOs rated legal counsel as being "very important" before, during, and after the company became public. This was not surprising, as lawyers play a key role in almost every aspect of a company going public. It's especially advantageous to have legal counsel with a strong working knowledge of the IPO process.

Young's CEOs continued to find underwriters important advisors, but they have lost some of their mystique. While it's true that underwriters are a direct connection between the entrepreneur and the money to be raised, the entrepreneur is more and more becoming aware of the human frailties that the underwriter is subject to. It can soon become obvious that underwriters' main incentive for working on an IPO is to make commission revenues by selling the company's stock. That motivates them to keep the stock in the public eye, but they usually lack any deep or abiding interest in the operations of the company. This need not diminish their effectiveness as advisors, providing they put in the time it takes to give the company its best shot at going public.

CPAs who have been through the process can be invaluable in showing the company to its best advantage. The end result of any business has to do with accountability—profit and loss. CPAs with a working knowledge of IPOs can evaluate how well the company's earning stream will hold up. They can put the company in touch with interested investment sources through banking and underwriter contacts. They can also act as a bridge between the CEO and the SEC legal department and advise the entrepreneur whether the company can be competitive in the market.

Although bankers seldom play a lead role in the IPO process, they lend a note of credibility and longevity for a company involved in the IPO process. They can advise the CEO how to deal with the banking community, how to get the most for the company's dollar, and where to get it.

Printers' contributions to an IPO can be critical, for they are involved in the process from beginning to end. On their shoulders fall the supervision of the preparation and issuance of documents, including the prospectus and registration statement, which must be flawless. Also, the printing of all the documents can be very costly. As an advisor, the printer can help the company obtain quality work at the best price.

Plan Ahead

The purpose of this book is to help the entrepreneur/CEO through the stages and processes involved in taking a company public. Young's study substantiated the importance of pre-public planning. After asking hundreds of CEOs, "Now that your company has gone public, to what extent do you feel that your company should have engaged in pre-public planning?" he concluded, *"Most CEOs, after having gone public, believe that they should have engaged in even more planning for the IPO process."* For the uninitiated it's something worth considering. It's also something the responsible advisor should suggest.

Because his study was broken down by industries, Young was able to determine that *industry dynamism* was a factor in the purchase of stocks as far as investors were concerned. Industry dynamism refers to "hot" industries—those favored by the stock buying public. At the time of Young's report, the hot industries were oil and gas, electronic equipment manufacturers, instruments manufacturing, and computer software. These are industries that react to market fluctuations, unlike ostensibly stable industries. Young concluded that "industries characterized by rapidly changing market conditions and increasing competitive entry cited a greater need for pre-public planning."

Advisors well versed in the IPO process should have a handle on progress being made during the pre-public planning. They should be able to temper the eagerness of the CEO and the management team, ignore minor pitfalls, and get on with the show. Problems, whatever they are, that were not solved in advance, have a way of snowballing into almost insurmountable difficulties that require inordinate time and effort to correct.

Young's study confirms the importance of advisors and of settling for nothing less than the most qualified and highly experienced advisory people available. Once these are found, the CEO should give them good incentives to maintain ongoing relationships with the company.

Summary

Entrepreneur/CEOs contemplating an IPO are well advised to surround themselves with experienced, professional, outside people. While there are many highly qualified consultants and advisors who have been through the process and can advise on all phases, not just anyone with the title of consultant or advisor will suffice. All persons can't be all things to all companies. If an operation is for brain surgery, it would be ridiculous to ask an obstetrician to do the job. It's imperative to seek out people with expertise in the company's specialty. It helps also if the experts have a cooperative attitude and contacts in the financial community.

For a company going public, the right consultants and advisors can help a company *make* history rather than *become* history.

8

Accountants

One of the key figures in a company going public is the accountant. If the books aren't in order, if the figures don't check and balance, the company doesn't stand a chance of satisfying the SEC requirements for public companies. Therefore, the role of the accountant is most crucial to the completion of any IPO.

For an existing company, the SEC rules for registration require a company to have at least 1 year of audited balance sheets and 2 years of audited income statements. Although a start-up company does not have to furnish such financial information, it would be ill advised to proceed past square 1 without the services of a highly qualified accountant, preferably one well versed in the IPO process.

A Brief History Lesson

Accountants were not always considered an integral to a public company. The historical impact of the accounting profession on public accounting practices and the evolution of the rules now in effect were long in coming.

Until the 1929 stock market crash, the U.S. accounting profession did not adhere to rigid accounting practice standards. Even though history proves it should have shared in the blame for the crash and the subsequent Depression, accountants escaped any direct responsibility. Except for mild chastisement, the accounting profession was ignored in Roosevelt's New Deal 1933 securities act, and this "held harmless" attitude continued into the 1970s, until post-Watergate political pressure called for corporate accounting reform.

In 1976, a House subcommittee reported that scandalous episodes of corporate illegality, unaccountability, and the use of questionable business practices raised questions about the effectiveness of our system of corporate accountability. The Financial Accounting Standards Board (FASB—the profession's internal rule-making body) made virtually no progress toward increasing accountability in the accounting profession for the continued accounting abuses especially in large corporations. (These corporations mainly utilized the services of the Big Eight accounting firms, now referred to by some as the Big Five, due to mergers and acquisitions.) The House report further stated, "the SEC's continued reliance on the private accounting profession is questionable."

A Senate subcommittee agreed with the House report and advocated more federal control, which resulted in Congress passing the Foreign Corrupt Practices Act in December 1977. One purpose of this act was to make a foreign bribe by a U.S. company a federal crime, but more important, it strengthened Section 13(b) (2) of the '34 exchange act, which regulates the accounting controls and financial record keeping of U.S. companies that are registered with the SEC.

The strengthening of the accounting standards effected by the FCPA created a whole new ball game. The Big Eight firms were now forced to attest to a company's inventories, purchases, and financial status. As one result, to cover their new liability exposure, they increased their fees substantially.

Companies that experienced financial difficulties or bankruptcy had caused much shareholder disenchantment, and suing the accountants who, it was felt, did not conduct proper audits, became fashionable. During the late 1970s and early 1980s, juries often found accounting firms negligent in their auditing of client companies and made substantial awards against them. The verdicts might have seemed justified by the fact that the accounting firms raised their fees and therefore made more money, which allowed them to purchase high liability insurance.

During this same period, the large accounting firms were pricing themselves out of the lower-priced OTC company market. Fees for a simple start-up company audit began at $10,000, and even at those prices a small account was usually delegated to a junior accountant of the firm. Companies in the process of IPOs found it extremely difficult to get timely responses during the critical registration process. The regular procedure was for a partner of the accounting firm to sign off on an audit. But the partners were often too busy with their larger accounts. Small IPOs experienced as much as 2- to 8-week delays in their underwritings. Many of them rebelled at being treated like country cousins by the prestigious Big Eight firms.

This attitude helped to open the doors for many regional accounting firms, and helped them gain a toehold in SEC audit accounting, especially for IPOs. The market's thinking changed as more and more people came to realize that the Big Eight firms were not infallible and that smaller accounting firms could often furnish superior and more timely product at considerably less cost.

The eighties also witnessed the coming of age of the entrepreneur. With it came a strong IPO market and a steady increase of venture capitalism and investment banking. The Big Eight firms soon found that they were missing out on many new, fast-growing, potentially valuable clients. By the mid 1980s, the large and the small were in a head-to-head battle for the audit account business of smaller companies and IPOs. The competition not only benefited the OTC IPOs, it brought the fee structure more in line.

On Selecting Accountants

According to law, every IPO and public company must have audited financial statements. Not only that, but when going public, the company must have an SEC-qualified accountant perform the audit. To be considered qualified, the accountant or accounting firm must be a member of the SEC Practice Section of the American Institute of CPA (certified public accountants).

For the small company, hiring an auditing accountant to verify the bookkeeper's figures may seem like having to pay to have the same job done twice. Generally, start-up and early stage companies do not have a need for a detailed or complex accounting system. In all probability, a part-time bookkeeper or comptroller could easily handle the accounting. The situation is different in the larger IPOs. They often do better with a prestigious major accounting firm, because those firms usually have contacts with SEC legal counsel, underwriters, and investment banking firms. It's also worth noting that in the past the Big Eight firms were reluctant to represent "best efforts" underwritings (see chapter 3), still done for most small IPOs.

Since, by law, every business has to prepare financial statements, sophisticated entrepreneurs seek out the services of a certified public accountant (CPA) to prepare the different required reports.

1. Compilations

A *compilation* is the simplest of the CPA reports, generally performed for internal company use only. The purpose is to give the accountant a general understanding of the nature of the company's business, the accounting records, and company policies. The CPA reads the company's financial statements and makes sure they are in appropriate form and free from clerical errors. The figures are supplied by management, and the CPA does not express any opinion about them.

2. Reviews

A *review* is a report that goes beyond the compilation. It provides some assurance about the reliability of the financial statements. The company accountant or CPA reviews the accounting principles and practices of the company and its industry, and analyzes and compares expected trends, past results, industry data, and internal projections. The review may also contain some of the specific procedures that would ordinarily be performed in an audit.

3. Audits

An *audit* is a confirmation of the credibility and reliability of the financial statement of a company. Every IPO and public company has to have an audited financial statement performed by an outside audit accountant (CPA) to guard against company manipulations in the report. The accountant reviews and evaluates the effectiveness of all the accounting procedures and internal controls that are necessary to meet SEC accounting standards for public companies. The accountant must also attest to the correctness of the company's financial statements and to the company's financial position for the period covered.

It is the responsibility of an existing company going public to present the auditing accountant with as complete and correct financial records as possible to verify the income statements. If the balance sheets and inventory verification are not possible to reconstruct, a cloud on the audit could result: a "qualified" financial opinion on the part of the audit accountant that could delay the offering by the SEC until a full year of auditable inventory has taken place.

Be Prepared

It bears repeating: Companies in the early stages of doing business should make preparations for the eventuality of going public. They should start by assembling an accounting team. The team should consist of inside (often called in-house), outside (usually a CPA), and audit accountants.

An in-house accountant should have bookkeeping and accounting experience, but need not be a full-fledged accountant. The position includes responsibility for day-to-day routine bookkeeping functions and coordinating with the outside accountant. As the company grows, there may be an increasing need to bring in a full-fledged accountant.

The outside accountant is independent, not personally involved with the company, and preferably a CPA. It's important that the CEO has respect and confidence in this person, who represents a link between the company and the SEC accounting world. This accountant usually prepares or at least reviews the monthly financial statements and supervises the company's quarterly and annual reports. The position requires someone familiar with and knowledgeable in SEC accounting procedures, as well as being able to serve as liaison between the company and audit accountants.

Audit Accounting

Audit accounting is a subject warranting a close look. Auditing accountants must be completely independent. They must not have any financial interest or ownership in the company. SEC auditing accountants work in teams. Their job is to look for trouble in the books, so they tend to be suspicious. They seem to trust no one, especially no one in the company. They can be expected to check and cross-check every item. That's what they're paid to do.

Audit Guidelines

SEC Regulation S–X deals with the form and content of financial statements and their ultimate certification. It spells out the importance of independent auditing accountants and details the rules and regulations that must be adhered to by audit accountants in order to establish their independence. It further sets out qualifications to guarantee that independence, including:

- Independence during the full period of audit
- No financial interest in the company
- Cannot be a promoter, officer, director, or employee of the company
- Cannot certify another auditor's work
- Must avoid interrelations with employees or relatives of employees of the company
- Must perform the audit personally, without subcontracting it to others
- Cannot "write up the books" (post the general ledger) (Must be done by in-house accountant)

Also, SEC rules state that the company cannot owe the independent auditor for past audit fees.

SEC Regulation S–X seems to infringe upon the auditor's basic rights in making any contact with management or employees strictly taboo. However, the SEC looks upon these rules as a way to assure the independence of the auditor and to make certain that favoritism in any form towards the company does not take place.

Qualifying the Auditing Accountant

There are many ways to qualify an auditing firm. One way is to get recommendations from a trusted person, someone knowledgeable about the IPO process, or from the company's IPO advisor or attorney. Although heavy SEC experience is not critical for the accounting firm, since set guidelines are followed by all accountants, it is nonetheless essential that the firm have some experience in SEC accounting. This holds true for existing and start-up companies. For an IPO, you shouldn't make a move without an audit accountant who has been through the registration process more than once—and recently! Any CPA firm can work the numbers game, but not all CPA firms can play the SEC numbers game to the benefit of the client. Also important to remember, the managing partner in the accounting firm should be the sign-off person, as someone fully accountable for the detail work of subordinates.

Another good way to qualify an auditing firm is by interview. Select several promising contenders and request proposals for final evaluation. Ask questions such as:

- What are the firm's areas of expertise?
- What is its recent SEC filing experience?
- Who will work with the company day to day?
- What are the billing methods? By hour? By job?
- What is the billing cycle?
- When can someone begin?
- How long will it take?.
- Does the firm have underwriter or investor contacts?
- Will it give an estimated total cost in a written proposal?

Familiarity Is a Must

Every effort should be made to hire audit accountants familiar with the company's type of business and industry. It is also beneficial if they have experience with competitors—as long as their other client is not presently in direct competition with your company.

Familiarity helps because audit requirements differ vastly from industry to industry. For example, an oil pipe supply company's inventory occupies many acres of outdoor storage whereas the inventory of a fast food franchise is turned over by being eaten every day, and a manufacturer of high-tech small parts may fit 3 months' inventory in a few fireproof file drawers. Bookkeeping, payable, and receivable methods vary from company to company. This results in special rules being applied to different types of companies and to their various stages of development. The auditing accountant must have the skill and knowledge to work through these differences. That is why familiarity can be a plus.

Actually, audit accountants are bound by an ethical code to turn down companies that may represent a potential conflict of interest. Nevertheless, a base familiarity with the company's business should be considered very valuable indeed.

GAAP Must Be Observed

GAAP is an industry term. It means *G*enerally *A*ccepted *A*ccounting *P*rinciples. GAAP dictates the principles for presenting audit information. As an example, accounting methods of private companies are generally aimed toward decreasing taxable income and depreciation. Inventory booking and write-downs are adjusted accordingly. Private companies frequently switch back and forth from cash to accrual accounting methods to assist in tax adjustment. These practices are not allowed for public companies which function under GAAP. *All* accounting for public companies must be done on an accrual basis.

In a case where an existing company has operating subsidiaries, the subsidiaries must also have financials audited under GAAP. This makes for auditing headaches, especially if offshore subsidiaries are involved. Separate audits must also be prepared for subsidiaries that may be sole proprietors or partnerships. Even if the company is considering an acquisition on a pro forma basis in conjunction with an IPO, if the acquisition amounts to more than 10 percent of the combined total assets, it too must be audited. The SEC considers as "material" any assets representing 10 percent or more, and they must be audited.

Although the process of auditing an existing company that has not previously been audited can be costly and time consuming, it can be done, providing the company has maintained fairly complete financial records. However, getting into the area of inventory may be a different matter.

Inventory verification, within GAAP, can become very complicated. It must include historical (prior) audited financials, which can present a sticky problem for the auditor who was not around when the inventory items were first counted. Consequently, many companies may find themselves in the awkward position of writing off large amounts of inventory with the audit opinion qualified regarding past inventory procedures. In essence, the auditor says, "Since I wasn't involved in taking the inventory count, I can't truly say that all the statements are absolutely correct. But I assume they are."

For inventory accounting, the auditor must know whether the inventory valuation has been applied on a consistent basis—was the method used last in first out (LIFO) or first in first out (FIFO), as there is often a price variation in the interim. What, if any, tax adjustments were made and how they affected the tax reporting are other possible variables, as well as the inclusion of overhead in finished goods inventory (a requirement of the SEC). And, of course, the method used for inventory accounting must be acceptable to GAAP.

Prior to the new SEC regulations, the audit accountant could simply state in effect, "I was not present to physically observe the taking of the prior year's inventory; however, I did physically monitor the most recent inventory. Consequently, it is my opinion that all past inventories were properly conducted, and I believe all accounts are reasonable." Because this type of statement occasionally proved to be incorrect, the SEC has disallowed the practice, and now insists on a clean, fully satisfied, "I did physically observe all inventory."

Time Costs Money

A forward-looking entrepreneur/CEO with the goal of eventually taking the company public should seriously consider enlisting the services of an accountant to monitor and audit inventory procedures from the start. The cost will be considerably less than a fully audited financial statement, and so will the aggravation. It won't eliminate the necessity of an audit when going public, but it will save time and dollars, even if a different accounting firm becomes involved with the IPO. What's more, even if a company's inventory has been audited regularly, prior audits must be reviewed to assure compliance with SEC regulations.

An audit for a small existing company can take from a few weeks to possibly 6 months. It depends on the problems the auditing accountant may uncover. Previously unaudited companies are typically beset with such deficiencies as poor accounts payable systems, uncollectible accounts receivable that haven't been written off or down, unreconciled bank accounts, notes payable with doubled assets pledged as underlying collateral, and incorrectly recorded depreciation expenses.

Accounting ethics require strict adherence to due diligence procedures.

For instance, if the company purchased a major piece of equipment, the accountants will have to see copies of purchase orders, invoices, and canceled checks. They will be expected to inquire about possible securities fraud violations and bankruptcy filings.

Areas that can present very complicated problems for previously unaudited existing companies include personal financial dealings by officers and directors that were placed through the corporation. Even advances or loans made to officers by the company, especially in recent accounting periods, require special schedules to be filled out and reported. Most likely, too, they will have to be declared in the IPO prospectus.

All of these issues take time to resolve, and the cost varies according to the time involved. It's not unusual for an auditing firm to charge as much as $25,000 for a noncomplex audit.

Audit Accountants Are Accountable

Audit accountants today must take full responsibility for their work. SEC CPAs can be held liable for misleading or false financial data in a prospectus. If they were misled by company falsification but cannot establish that they conducted their work with sufficient diligence, they are accountable under the Securities Act of 1933 through the comfort letter we spoke about in an earlier chapter. This leaves them vulnerable to lawsuits by both the SEC and investors.

Experienced auditors know that the financial statements they submit will be used in the prospectus of a company going public. They know that the prospectus basically serves as a selling document. Therefore, they can be expected to make every effort to express their findings in clear, concise, and easily understood language, down to the thoroughness of the footnotes in the financials. Their reputation rides on the effectiveness of their presentation. And so does their next job.

Summary

A company anticipating an IPO should make every effort to create a good working relationship with an SEC-qualified and knowledgeable accounting firm, preferably one versed in the IPO process. It's also advantageous if the accountant is familiar with the company's business and can efficiently perform all the required SEC accounting procedures for that particular company. The right firm will provide continuing counsel and guidance as well as assist the company in all its financial statements and proceedings that require SEC approval. It would be especially desirable for the accounting firm to have working contacts with SEC legal counsel, underwriters, and investment banking firms. When it comes to selecting an accounting firm for a company going public, it should not only be *what* you know, but *who* you know.

Today's regulatory environment requires an opinioned audit from an accredited accounting firm. It is therefore important that the management of the company going public understand completely the specific rules that apply for public company operations. Most important is that their audit accountant remain independent of all company involvement.

9

Attorneys

Highly specialized. Past and current IPO SEC experience. Successful record in IPO filings. Compatible, intelligent, knowledgeable. Friendly, if possible. Good contacts with underwriters, investors, bankers, and brokers. Reasonable fee.

Well, the last may be asking too much. But that's the kind of counsel that makes an IPO a happy experience. The services of qualified SEC counsel in an IPO cannot be overemphasized. In fact, they can be crucial. The company must depend on legal counsel to see it through compliance with a multitude of federal and state securities laws and regulations. If all is not done according to SEC rules, which require a keen legal mind to decipher, the IPO can be stopped in its tracks.

Letting Go

Unfortunately, it's not easy to let go of the friendly legal counsel that has seen a company through thick and thin. However, as private companies grow, and contemplate going public, they must be prepared to make changes—unless their old attorney has SEC experience. Most competent attorneys will realize their limitations and even suggest bringing in a highly competent, recognized specialist in the IPO process.

Every effort should be made to select counsel with current IPO SEC experience in an industry similar to yours. Although many legal firms have an active SEC practice, their experience may have been in dissimilar industries, and their involvement may be limited to ongoing companies, as opposed to new filings.

There are what are called generic filings. They are categorized as S–18 and S–1 by the SEC, and apply to general types of industries. There are also filings that apply only to oil and gas, and also to gold mining, under the heading of S–4. Some attorneys specialize in oil and gas, or gold mining filings; others have expertise in high-tech filings. Large, prestigious law firms are usually geared to handle more complicated SEC filings, whereas smaller law firms may not be. The secret is to select an attorney or firm familiar with the business of the company going public and, we emphasize, experienced in IPO filings.

The Difference Between Large and Small

Like shoes, legal firms come in different sizes and styles. Many of them specialize in various types of services. It's up to company management to choose the firm that best fits the company's requirements as to size, compatibility, competency, and contacts in the investment community.

A large legal firm is not the answer for all companies. True, a large firm may have several hundred lawyers with many areas of specialties. On the surface that may seem advantageous. Many large corporations prefer such firms, as they can call upon the services of different specialists in one office. That arrangement may serve the purpose of a diversified, multidimensional company with many different companies under one umbrella—say a manufacturing company, a mining company, a food company, and a service company—each requiring different legal input. A small IPO lacking that corporate makeup wouldn't need a firm with all those attorneys and faces the possibility of getting lost in the shuffle.

Large legal firms with many partners and associates traditionally also have many young, inexperienced junior associate attorneys. These are usually assigned to work with small companies on a day-to-day basis. Since the associates must often clear their advice with a managing partner, dealings can become frustrating for the company management as well as inefficient, time consuming, and costly. Those new, bright, young lawyers, although capable and intelligent, lack experience, and they can make a lot of mistakes. It's a learning process for them, but it's usually the client who pays for their mistakes.

Depending on the benefits and prestige derived from engaging large law firm versus a small firm, it may be preferable for an IPO to work with a small, SEC-specialized legal firm. For one thing, the company will get closer attention. Junior associates or paralegals become involved usually only to help out in routine matters. Small firms can be fully competent to handle all the corporate information, including all the SEC rules and regulations. Specializing in companies going public, they are usually more cognizant of the nuances of prospectus writing and more aware of the current SEC environment; that's their whole business.

Getting Along

Too often the attorney's image is that of a necessary evil. Attorneys have been typecast as arrogant, nonresponsive, and overpriced. In fact, some are really nice. But rarely do they come cheap. However, in the eyes of reasonable entrepreneurs, the price is right if it gets them through the IPO.

Setting Parameters

It's up to management to set the parameters when selecting counsel for an IPO. Management should be clear about what it expects—whether it's hand holding, assurances that the company's goals to go public are attainable, or even alternatives on how the IPO can best be achieved. Management must also cooperate fully with counsel. It's the attorney's responsibility to write a full disclosure document describing the company, its markets, the competition in the market, and its product or services.

There must be no secrets kept from counsel. The more the counsel understands the company's industry, its management team, and its aspirations, the more helpful he or she can be, and less frustrated. Forthrightness will also save time, which translates directly into dollars.

Questions to Ask

When interviewing for IPO counsel, it's advisable for management to prepare a list of questions for a potential law firm or attorney to answer to assist the CEO in the selection process. The following questions can prove helpful in making the decision:

- What types of registration has your firm worked with in the past (S–1 to S–18)?
- Do you have recent filing experience?
- Do you have particular areas of specialty, and are they compatible with our company's industry?
- Who will be our day-to-day contact?

- What is your billing procedure? Hourly, monthly, by segments?
- Can you give us your estimated total cost, including expenses and fees?
- Do you have any useful investment contacts? Underwriters, brokers, investors?
- What is your projected timetable? How long do you expect the process to take?
- When will you be able to start on the project?

Billing and Fees

IPO attorneys typically bill by time and they count not just hours, but minutes. Their rationalization is that they do not sell products or services, they sell knowledge and past experience, which can be invaluable to a client.

Although hourly rates can vary from less than a hundred dollars to several hundred, a good round figure for the primary senior contact member of a law firm would be about $150 per hour. Junior associates' time could bill in the area of $75 an hour, and administrative functions (typing, copying) could range from $30 to $40 per hour. These are give-and-take figures.

Total fees can vary considerably. A simple start-up through the public offering could be in the range of $8000 to $10,000. The more complex process for an existing company with past history is usually more costly. It requires going back into the company's past and reviewing the minutes, article and bylaw changes, patents, employment, license agreements, financing, and clarification of anything that may put a cloud on the company's operations. Depending on the complications, the fees could be as much as $50,000 to $60,000. On the average, in a complex situation, the costs would approximate $25,000 to $30,000.

Ethical law firms usually provide an estimate of the total costs. It's a safe guess that the final amount will seldom be less than the estimate. Although some firms are willing to put a cap on the project, they will usually leave an out for themselves for unanticipated exigencies. These could be article or bylaw changes, unexpected litigation, state law changes, unresolved lawsuits, or new SEC requirements. The entrepreneur can make book there will be something.

It is also unrealistic to assume that legal counsel will work on the contingency that the fee will be paid after the IPO is completed, regardless of the negotiated amount. It's best to plan on a deposit or advance. A reasonable figure would be a percentage of the total estimated fee, or an estimate of the first month's work or of the first stage of work. Rarely will any substantial work be performed by an IPO law firm prior to an initial payment, usually made at the time of signing an engagement letter.

Other Forms of Payment

Generally speaking, the legal profession is not averse to taking a flyer with the company. Many attorneys like IPOs, not only because they generate handsome fees, but because they like the idea of taking a portion of their fees in stock. The structure of the legal business in itself does not generate capital appreciation or equity buildup. Consequently, accepting stock as part payment allows lawyers to become more intimately involved with the company and gives them an opportunity to invest without actually putting out any hard cash.

Paying stock in lieu of money can create problems. For one thing, it can dilute ownership among stockholders in the company. It can cause disagreement among the partners in the law firm, too. Especially in larger firms, it often happens that partners who are not directly involved in the project may not feel as positive about the company's potential. They would prefer the cash to restricted stock that has no guarantees.

The strongest argument against stock as payment is the potential conflict of interest. Some company managers may question whether the advice they are receiving is in their interest or their advisor's interest. Attorneys in the law firm may question a conflict of interest regarding outside parties' involvement and whether it would be condoned by the SEC. The ability to remain objective when negotiating non-arm's-length transactions may also be questioned. These may seem extreme concerns, but should not be ignored in a decision whether to offer stock for the services of legal counsel.

Double-check the Cost

As mentioned earlier, the cost of doing business with an IPO law firm is high under the best of circumstances. Therefore, it's just common sense to make a practice of regularly reviewing counsel's billings. To err is forgivable. To not check the error can be expensive. Time and again, good relationships between management and legal counsel have dissolved because it seemed counsel was taking advantage regarding billings. This assumption, more often than not, turns out to be unfounded. But that is why professional legal counsel is always ready to discuss, substantiate, and if necessary, adjust billings. It's up to the company to keep the lines of communication open and frank. Establishing a good working relationship is of benefit to both company and counsel.

Legal Responsibilities

The role and responsibilities of legal counsel is covered more fully in subsequent chapters involving:

- Pre-public planning
- Corporate record cleanup
- Review of all contracts and agreements
- Amending articles and bylaws
- Capital structure

Other areas that involve legal counsel are preparing information for the SEC, advising on exemptions and their impact on the company, and developing stock incentive plans that meet SEC regulations. These are all part of the process of making the company ready to go public that leads up to the actual presentation of the registration statement and the filing.

The '33 and '34 securities acts (discussed further in chapter 17) established the parameters for the legal profession's role in an IPO and the company's role as a public company. It's worth noting that these acts were conceived and written by lawyers. The interpretation, as for all U.S. laws, was left to the discretion of the courts, which only helped to line the pockets of the legal community.

Judicial decisions have played havoc with the accounting profession, resulting in accounting firms being named in shareholder lawsuits. Accountants were the first to be blamed for "improper" company financial records. Judges soon discovered complicity on the part of the legal profession, which increasingly became named in these suits after companies faltered. Today, accountants and attorneys, as well as management and directors are jointly sued by disgruntled shareholders. As a result, the fees of all continue to rise.

The Multiple Counsel Approach

It is common practice today for entrepreneurs going public to continue the employment of lawyers they worked with in the past or are currently working with. Existing companies frequently remain with the corporate counsel they have felt comfortable with, even lacking SEC experience. They may also use outside counsel in areas such as patent, trademark, copyright, real estate, or other specialties. The SEC attorney is another specialist who will supervise the IPO undertaking. Working with the company's corporate attorney should present no problem, but rather be of help in general business issues.

Retaining the company attorney could very well save the company hefty legal fees. For many items, instead of paying the high hourly rate of the SEC counsel, the company can pay its regular counsel, usually at a much lower rate, to clean up and update company records needed in the IPO process. The two lawyers can complement each other as well as realize a savings for the company. In the final analysis, it's a "save and sound" idea.

Summary

For small IPOs, small legal firms or individual attorneys with SEC expertise are often preferable to large legal firms. Of course, it depends on how complex and involved the IPO is. Choosing counsel should never be approached as a crapshoot by management, as SEC attorneys play a major role in the final resolution of a public offering.

Personal compatibility is a paramount consideration. The relationship of management and counsel is often likened to a marriage, as they will be practically living together. Legal costs for a highly qualified SEC counsel also need continuing evaluation. These costs can be the second largest item in an underwriting, but cost should never be the overriding factor in the selection of an attorney. More important is current and repeated experience in IPO filings, and familiarity with the company's business is especially helpful. Remember, it is the responsibility of legal counsel to make sure the company going public complies with the federal and state securities laws.

Payment in stock for legal services, although seeming inviting, should be carefully considered, as it may lead to long-term complications. But it can be reassuring to know that SEC attorneys are human. They're not ogres or gougers, and their success with an IPO means better recommendations and more jobs for them. Remember, they want that golden ring as badly as the company does.

10

Financial Printers

Financial printers are a breed unto themselves. They are specialists in the printing of financial documents, including registration statements, prospectuses, even stock certificates. On the surface this may sound like nothing out of the ordinary. Not so. It calls for complete involvement with the client.

As mentioned in chapter 2, the initial registration statement and prospectus must be submitted to the SEC, NASD, and the state securities commissions. The preliminary prospectus, called *red herring* because it is printed with red ink, accompanies the registration statement and is distributed to the brokerage community to solicit indications of interest for the underwriting. The final or definitive prospectus is the completed approved offering document that is used to solicit prospective shareholders and interested persons in the financial community. It's a showpiece and can include photos, graphics, colored paper, and multicolored printing. These are all unique documents and call for special attention by the printer.

These documents cannot be distributed if they are not letter perfect. There can be no typos or errors. After proofreading by all key parties, the printer will make an additional review to make sure all necessary elements are included and correct before going to press. No one concerned can consider these to be run-of-the-mill printing jobs.

Not just any printer can do financial printing. Recognized financial printers must stay current with the strict SEC rules, regulations, and printing requirements regarding size of type and paper, format, and other technical specifications. Nothing short of 100 percent accuracy is acceptable.

In addition to accuracy, timeliness is critical. After layout, typesetting, and submission—then come the changes. There are always changes in a prospectus. These changes are determined according to a letter of comment from the SEC. The changes can be typographical. They can concern a new SEC ruling or a requirement that had not been included in the prospectus. The changes must be made quickly and accurately—usually overnight or within 24 hours. Once the SEC gives its final approval, no time should be lost in getting the prospectus out and into the hands of the underwriter and selling group for distribution to the public.

To expedite the printing, management needs to assure that each proof is promptly reviewed by all the key parties. It is usual for management to authorize one person to communicate and coordinate the project with the printer. Many companies rely on SEC counsel to handle that chore. Another time saver is to assign one person—a secretary or the central editor—to submit corrected copy to the printer with all the correct spelling, punctuation, and content. It will avoid a lot of confusion and allow the printer to move fast.

You need 100 percent cooperation, dedication to the job, and know-how from the printer, which probably explains why there are only about 20 qualified financial printers in the United States today. (Lists are available through most brokerage houses and underwriters.)

Secrecy is another reason for using experienced, qualified financial printers. They are well aware of the importance of keeping inside information from leaking. They are accustomed to working behind a veil of secrecy and are cognizant of the implications. They know that companies they work for must be able to trust them and feel comfortable with their security precautions.

Costs

Financial printing is not cheap. As of this writing, a one-color run of 30,000 to 40,000 copies could cost approximately $10,000. Four-color runs can easily amount to $50,000. It takes a lot of paper to cover the territory: Copies of the prospectus must be furnished to all prospective purchasers of stock, whether they buy or not.

It's also customary to keep a supply on hand for at least a year after public trading starts. The prospectus can be used as a public relations tool also. Copies are sent to brokers, financial publications, magazine publishers, and they are used as media kits. The quantity required is usually determined by the company's attorney, the underwriter, the printer, and the PR firm hired to promote the company.

Qualifying the Financial Printer

The company's attorney usually has the best access to qualified financial printers. Recommendations can also come from the IPO advisor, the underwriter, and the financial public relations firm. Because the outlay for financial printing is substantial, a wise management team will ask for several recommendations. There are not that many printers to choose from, but it's important to find the one that can offer the best deal as to price and performance. Printers with computerized equipment may be capable of accepting floppy disks and other word-processing input directly from the attorney's office, saving time and money.

Here are some pertinent questions a company should ask a potential financial printer:

1. Could we have a list of your recent clients?
2. What type of facilities do you operate?
3. May we have samples of recent similar jobs?
4. How long have you done financial printing?
5. Do you expect computer, hard copy, or both from us?
6. Can you give us an estimate of the cost of the complete job, breaking out any extras?
7. Who will be your contact person?

Management should carefully evaluate the responses to select a printer who will fulfill the company's requirements and with whom company personnel can work comfortably.

Ancillary Services

Stock certificates are also printed by financial printers, though no longer exclusively. Few public companies any longer use the elaborately engraved certificates of earlier days, but now opt for preprinted certificates, simply inserting the company name and logo for a customized look.

Financial printers are also geared for handling the distribution of both preliminary and final prospectus to broker/dealers, and other members of the financial community. The printer will sort and deliver copies to the various places and people specified by the lead underwriter—the service isn't free, but it relieves the company from a burdensome task.

Most financial printers also provide full conference room facilities, complete with bar and kitchen, to offer clients comfortable surroundings where they can proof their documents and make last-minute changes before going to press.

Summary

Financial printing is a specialized field. Only some 20 firms throughout the United States can meet SEC standards in printing the documents required by a company going public, from the registration statement to the prospectus. They will cost you money, but you should get your money's worth in a printer who will remain involved in the distribution of the documents, working closely with the management of an IPO; and confidentiality is part of the job.

Although there are few financial printers to choose from, they are competitive. It pays to shop for one that fits your budget, delivers the product on time, and most important, guarantees accuracy.

Remember, if it's worth doing at all—it had better be done right!

11

Financial Public Relations

Financial public relations, as it pertains to public companies traded over the counter, and especially to small ones, is usually sadly lacking. The reason is that, unfortunately, management of too many small companies just don't comprehend the value of financial public relations. In fact, it's often a totally foreign subject to them. They don't understand how important it is to get out information about the company to brokers to keep them hyped up, to members of the public so that they will buy the stock, to shareholders to keep them from selling their stock, and to the media generally. Too few people in management think "Out of sight, out of mind" could possibly pertain to their company.

A wise entrepreneur knows, "You gotta sell the company to sell the company." Entrepreneurs astute enough to include financial public relations in their business program, even on a limited basis, stand a greater chance of success than those who neglect it.

The Public Relations Mystique

There's really no mystery about public relations except perhaps in the minds of some members of management teams. Financial public relations is simply a means of informing the public what a company is doing, in such a way as to make the public take notice and take the kind of action that enables the company's goals to be reached—that is, buy the company's stock.

Public relations begins within the company in the day-to-day conduct of business. It's the shine on a salesperson's shoes, the smile on a face, a friendly greeting. A welcome attitude by a receptionist. A telephone call put through promptly by a telephone operator. It's a cordial letter by the company president. It's employees who think and speak well of the company. Public relations is, in essence, a state of mind with a positive attitude toward anyone who hears about, reads about, or comes in contact with the company.

Four Steps to Effective Corporate
Financial Public Relations

Embarking on a financial public relations program can be divided into four basic steps:

1. Analysis

PR people will first analyze the public's attitude toward the company: Is it positive? Negative? Indifferent? They may resort to a public opinion poll or an attitude survey. They may randomly ask people what kind of feelings they have toward the company or industry. Or the PR people may have enough research on hand to proceed with the next step.

2. Interpretation and Policy Making

After an understanding of public opinion regarding the company has been gained through formal or informal means, the next step is evaluating these opinions in order to formulate policies and objectives. Then PR must prepare plans to achieve these objectives.

Effective corporate financial public relations revolves around this interpretation, planning, and decision making. Plans should cover existing conditions—products, markets, sales performance (if significant), competition, policies, dealers and distributors, and the various people the company wishes to reach. The objective is always to create an interest in the company as one that should be invested in. Specific needs and goals must be set forth to reach this objective. Methods include human interest stories, news releases, or other forms of communication such as broadcasting, TV, or printed material. They should take into consideration the results of research, including attitudes and public opinion. The goal is to reach *all* interested parties—shareholders, investors, underwriters, and the financial press.

3. Communication

The basic message to be communicated should be established and agreed upon. The target audience should be clearly defined in order to reach the greatest possible number of the persons the message is aimed at. Appropriate media should be used, whether brochures, newsletters, newspapers, even broadcasting. The more people who can become interested in the company, the greater potential there is of the stock going up in value.

4. Continuing Evaluation

PR should not be considered a onetime effort. The results of programs and the effectiveness of techniques should be constantly evaluated. Although the corporation may have gained approval today, there is no assurance it will continue through tomorrow. Attitudes and opinions of individuals change with time, with new points of view, and information from competing sources.

Markets also change. New markets develop. Income levels and populations shift, which may necessitate company diversification. Technology may change. The need for venture capital may arise. All of these factors require a company to be prepared to alter its strategy. It will pay off in increased profits and future growth for a company to constantly reevaluate its public relations program.

To reiterate: A financial public relations program begins with building a favorable image and a friendly climate of opinion in which to operate. Maintaining them is critical to a company's success. It stands to reason, if a company is perceived to have growth potential, chances are it will have more stock buyers.

The Public Relations Difference

There is a difference between financial and other public relations. In "other," the company is mainly concerned with its community image, its customers, its suppliers, its employees, and its standing in the industry. In financial public relations, there is a focus on those areas that affect the public's impression of the company financially. Of key concern are existing and prospective shareholders. The goal is to attract new shareholders while retaining the old ones, because the more a company has of both, the greater chance its stock has of going up in value.

The CEO of a company is rarely involved in the sale of its stock. Sales are usually handled by market-maker contacts, printed material, news releases, and *the efforts of financial public relations.*

The Rewards of Financial PR

In most companies, the CEO or a key member of the management team will have the responsibility for implementing and overseeing the financial public relations program, which makes it even more important that they have an awareness of all the areas financial PR encompasses. It's through financial public relations that management is able to maximize the company's progress and development, not only for itself, but for all shareholders.

Take the price the company's stock sells for. The higher the current price, the fewer additional shares must be issued for company transactions, such as expansion or acquisition. That translates to less stock dilution. It's simple arithmetic. Instead of selling 20 percent of the company for $20 million to consummate a deal, you may only have to sell 10 percent for the same $20 million, if the stock appreciates in value. That means more shares remaining for the company, and higher value per share for the shareholders.

Also to be considered is that with the increase of the trading price of the company's stock, management's *personal* net worth increases, which naturally makes for a more contented management.

All starts with the fact that any stock on any exchange or market faces a potential demand every day it's traded—and that demand usually originates in the concerted efforts of financial public relations. Stocks go up when there are more buyers than sellers. Stocks go down when there are more sellers than buyers. If a company is perceived to have growth potential, chances are that it will have more buyers. It's the job of the financial PR firm to let the public know that the company is there and that good things are happening to it.

Unfortunately, a common cry among financial PR people is that many corporations think of them only as a means to put out fires, and too often the PR people have good reason for complaint. But hiring a qualified financial public relations firm is one of the best investments an IPO can make. PR can set the fires that an IPO needs to gain the recognition and acceptance that it seeks.

Today's investors are more sophisticated. With the new stock disclosure laws, there is little, if any, manipulation of stocks. There are also many other choices available to investors, such as bonds, money-market funds, and real estate. For a public company, especially an IPO, to get the investor's attention requires a serious attempt to reach the target audience. You can't just sit back and wait for market analysts to find buyers and hope to make an impact on the market. Financial public relations can help make your day.

What to Expect from Financial PR

- Financial public relations can develop exposure for a company's business. It can make the potential investor aware of the company's product, marketing approach, personnel, philosophy, and benefit to the industry. This is not to negate the advantages of advertising, but the costs could be considerably less than the cost of a full-page advertisement in a newspaper or magazine.

• Financial public relations can provide information to clients, investors, brokers, and analysts, influencing their decisions to purchase or retain a stock.

• Financial public relations can, over a period of time, develop a favorable reputation for a company, especially if it accurately reflects what the company is doing.

What Not to Expect from Financial PR

• Don't expect financial public relations to communicate ideas or information about a company's performance, plans, attitude, or potential that don't exist.

• Financial public relations cannot guarantee that a company's publicity message will appear in a specific media at a specific time.

• Financial public relations cannot persuade media to run anything but accurate, newsworthy information.

Making a Commitment

Financial PR requires the same kind of commitment on the part of the president and management of an IPO that they give to manufacturing, distributing, and selling the best quality product possible. PR can't be treated as a stepchild. What's more, company management must get involved in the decision-making process of financial public relations if they want it to work. And they must regard the cost, which won't be cheap, as an integral expense of doing business. They must also be able to communicate that positive attitude to the entire company staff.

Let's look at how a few of the major companies regard financial PR. At Reynolds, the public relations staff is designated as an arm of the president's office. At AT&T, the public relations director reports directly to the president. At Standard Oil, the public relations manager reports to the executive vice president. If those successful companies, that some people may feel don't need financial PR, wouldn't make a move without it, shouldn't that serve to convince IPOs and smaller public companies of the value of financial public relations? We think so.

Choose a Professional

A professional financial public relations firm is the only way to go. You will get experts at getting the attention of the right people—the brokers, underwriters, and investors who can make a difference. Even if a company is large enough to have a full-time person assigned to "investor relations," it's not enough. There aren't enough hours in the day, what with other obligations full-time people get involved in, to implement a comprehensive financial public relations program without outside professional help.

Why short-change the program? Management wouldn't think of doing legal work without engaging professional counsel. It would not, and could not audit its own certified accounting. By the same token, it's much more cost effective and time effective to engage professionals in financial PR. They have established contacts with media and investors; they know how to set up a continuing, consistent, and reliable program.

To make the program work, there must be a commitment between the financial public relations firm and the company. Because what comes out of it reflects corporate policy, insight, and planning.

Start Early, Stay Late

The importance of establishing an early relationship with a financial public relations firm cannot be overemphasized. In fact, if at all possible, it should be done prior to going public. There's too much at stake for management to put the matter off until later. Hiring professional financial PR can be expensive, but worth every penny in selling out the initial public offering.

Continuing the services of the financial PR firm after the company has gone public is a natural next step, especially through the first year, with a focus on holding and gathering further support for company stock among shareholders.

Of course, an effective financial public relations program extends beyond simply maintaining positive relations with shareholders. Although an outside entity, the PR people will be working as part of the company's management team. Activities should be directed to include employees, potential shareholders, the financial press, analysts, and concerned members of the community, all with an eye on the goal of earning the company the favorable recognition it seeks.

Qualifying the Financial Public Relations Firm

Three basic areas should be evaluated before making a final selection of a financial PR firm.

1. Standard Public Relations Functions

Management should ask the financial PR firm to submit samples of its work as well as recommendations to show that it can perform the job required by management, including assisting and guiding the company in putting together and properly disseminating shareholder letters, press releases, quarterly and annual reports—all with professionalism. It should go without saying that management would expect the firm to familiarize itself with the company's philosophy, people, business, and industry. The public relations people should be expected to prepare an analysis of the market for the product or service. They should also have a keen understanding of the company's position and potential in its industry and know all about the competition and what it is doing.

It is also the responsibility of the financial PR firm to make certain that all written material submitted to management is free of errors in spelling, sentence structure, and punctuation. Management should expect the financial PR firm to be accomplished in article writing, company brochures, employee newsletters, financial news releases, investor relations, press relations, PR counseling, annual and quarterly reports, employee manuals, external publications, general publicity, press information kits, speech writing, and promotional literature.

Management may decide that some of these areas could be better accomplished in-house or by a regular PR firm. Even so, these are areas about which a financial public relations firm should have a working knowledge.

Management should also be able to call upon its financial PR firm for recommendations about ancillary services, such as market planning, special events, marketing research, finished art, media analysis, photography, catalogues, sales contests, dealer sales ads, industrial exhibits, press tours, marketing counseling, broadcast production, illustrations, media buying, print production, incentive programs, convention planning, direct mail, video presentations, logos and trademarks, packaging, sales meetings, technical literature, letterhead and sign graphics, premiums, slide presentations, and price and parts lists, to name a few. These are services usually handled in-house or by advertising agencies, art services, media companies, broadcast companies, and PR firms. However, a financial PR firm should be aware of the need for these services when they arise and should be able to counsel management and make suggestions.

2. Broker Contacts

The street contacts of a financial public relations firm can be of immeasurable benefit to an IPO. These could include personal introductions to individual brokers, broker/dealers, financial analysts, and market makers, as well as individual investors. If the choice between one financial PR firm versus another comes down to a toss of the coin, common sense says to choose the one that has the best contacts in the financial community.

It also pays to take the time to personally make contact with some of the clients of the financial PR firm to find out if the CEOs of these companies were satisfied with their broker contacts.

Other information worth seeking out:

- Verify the experience the financial PR firm professes to have in the industry.

- Determine if any of its clients might present a conflict with the company, or if the firms complement each other. If the company is in the computer business, for example, and the financial PR firm represents other companies in the computer business, it may have difficulty finding this IPO unique.

- Make sure the firm doesn't have more accounts than it can handle, leaving it without enough time to give the company the kind of service you expect to receive.

- Make certain that the broker contacts are right for the company.

- Look for assurances that the firm is capable of providing on-time service and meeting important deadlines.

3. Compatibility

It's extremely important that the financial public relations firm and management are philosophically compatible. Several meetings should give managers an indication whether there is mutual respect and they would enjoy having the firm on their team.

Summary

Establishing and maintaining a strong, positive financial public relations program can be most important for an IPO. The most exciting company in the world can turn into a disastrous IPO if investors are not attracted to the stock offering. It takes determined financial public relations to gain the needed investor attention.

Selecting the right financial public relations firm requires careful consideration. The firm must be professional in its approach, experienced in the industry, and capable of handling all the day-to-day public relations functions you expect.

The right firm will have good broker contacts, and be able to assist the company in its continuing search for qualified brokers and investors. Also important is the ability to plan an aggressive program, reaching out and convincing the greater financial community.

It has been proven many times over that those companies that take advantage of the art of financial public relations, even on a limited basis, are many times more successful than those companies that neglect this vital aspect of corporate life. When used properly, financial public relations can provide a synergism that will enhance total corporate growth and the achievement of the company's financial goals.

12

Transfer Agents

Transfer agents are the record keepers of all stock transactions and shareholder information for a public company. That includes all the pertinent information regarding a particular stock and its purchaser: the shareholder's name, address, social security number, and number of shares purchased.

A *registrar* serves as a cross-check on the transfer agent and has the responsibility of making sure that the company's stock is not overissued. Registrars keep track of all the certificates that have been lost, destroyed, or canceled, along with an accurate accounting of the exact number of shares and certificates outstanding at any time. The functions of the registrar and transfer agent are normally held by the same firm and referred to collectively as the transfer agent.

An OTC (over-the-counter) company may, if it chooses, keep records internally with a day-by-day transfer journal and shareholder's certificate ledger. However, the exchanges, NYSE and AMEX, require that the jobs of the transfer agent and registrar be handled by outside independent services.

That is really the best way to go. No matter how small the IPO, the company is ill advised to do the job itself. It can become an administrative nightmare, as well as a financial liability. Any inaccuracies can subject the company to claims for mishandling its stock. Some underwriters make it mandatory that all companies doing business with them retain independent registrars and transfer agents.

The services that transfer agents provide extend beyond simply transferring stock and recording the transaction. For example, a client instructs his or her broker, Paine Webber, to buy 100 shares of General Motors. The broker may have to buy them from another broker, Merrill Lynch, on the client's behalf. The shares are delivered to Paine Webber, who in turn delivers the certificates to the transfer agent with instructions to cancel the Merrill Lynch certificates and issue a like amount in the client's name. The transfer agent also becomes involved in the issuance of new shares. Let us say that a company works with an underwriter to raise capital by selling an additional 5 million shares. The transfer agent issues the shares to the buyers and makes sure the certificates issued are valid, fully paid for, and nonassessable.

The transfer agent must also report to the IRS when cash dividends are paid, a 1099 form for U.S. citizens or a 1042 form for foreigners. It's the transfer agent's responsibility to comply with relevant SEC regulations.

Other essential services provided by the transfer agent are:

- Preparing and mailing proxy cards and proxy material to shareholders of record and notifying shareholders of the annual shareholders' meetings

- Tabulating and certifying proxies

- Providing mailing lists of shareholders for quarterly, annual, and special reports, as well as newsletters and required SEC reports

- Determining and preparing stock dividends, as well as paying stock dividends, cash dividends, and issuing stock splits

- Providing a complete mailing service that includes stuffing, sorting, and postage application

- Corresponding with shareholders concerning lost or undelivered dividend checks and verifying payment of these

- Handling correspondence with shareholders, brokers, banks, and underwriters concerning shareholders' accounts and address changes

- Verifying signatures of assignors and guarantors

The position of a transfer agent is highly specialized. Independent transfer agents are regulated by the SEC and are subject to outside audits. As a further safeguard, the SEC reviews record-keeping procedures through occasional unannounced visits.

Transfer agents are hired by the public company. They can be found through word of mouth, through attorneys, underwriters, brokers, and bankers. There are also many small companies that specialize as transfer agents, including many banks.

The transfer agent plays a key support role for public companies. Therefore, the CEO of an IPO should take the necessary time to search for a qualified, independent firm that can handle the job, rather than try to do it internally. A reputable transfer agent will encourage investigation. It's worth looking for one that instills trust, confidence, and offers service at a competitive price. And it is always worthwhile to cross-check applicants' performance with other publicly held companies.

Summary

A transfer agent is the keeper of shareholder information, which covers the orderly transfer of securities and the maintenance of security holder's records for public companies. No stock transaction by an IPO, or for that matter by any public company, can be completed without the services of a transfer agent.

Although the SEC allows OTC companies to keep records of stock transactions internally, it is not advisable to do so, as it can be very complicated and can lead to claims against the company.

Selecting a transfer agent need not be a complicated procedure. Look for a firm that is thoroughly familiar with all federal and state rulings and statutes that affect securities transactions. Important also are trust, compatibility, and a reasonable price.

PART III

BEFORE THE OFFERING

13

Incorporating the Public Company

From a legal standpoint, a public corporation is different from a privately held corporation. Much of the difference arises in the wording of the charter, or articles of incorporation, and the corporation's bylaws. It is therefore imperative that legal counsel retained by the company be completely familiar with the specific terminology used to set up public corporations. The following explanation should help the entrepreneur to better understand the differences.

State Laws

Incorporation laws often vary from state to state, and they vary in complexity. Some state laws are more liberal and flexible than others. One of the most conducive to incorporating public companies is the state of Delaware. As a result it has more incorporations by public companies than any other state.

There are many subtleties to the Delaware incorporation laws. They are among the least strict and least confining, allowing a liberal interpretation by the Delaware courts. That's why public companies throughout the nation consider Delaware the most attractive location for incorporation. Many states are now changing their laws to be as inviting for incorporation as Delaware in an effort to keep companies from switching to Delaware when they grow larger.

Actually, it makes sense for a company to incorporate in the state where its primary business is located, because it must conform with other laws of that state regardless of where it is incorporated. So it's worth having legal counsel investigate the advantages and disadvantages of the resident state's incorporation laws. But management must also consider whether its lawyer's recommendation for the home state is based on familiarity with that state's laws and filing procedures and weigh the benefits of filing in another state.

Some specific points to consider in deciding about incorporation:

Fees

Public companies involve larger numbers of authorized and outstanding shares than private companies. Many states set their fees by the number of shares declared.

Directors

Some states have laws pertaining to the ratio of directors to shareholders. The more flexible the law, the more latitude for the company.

Indemnification

In the 1980s, there were an increasing number of shareholder lawsuits against principals of public companies—making the state's officer and director indemnification laws a very important consideration in deciding where to incorporate.

Doing Business

The Model Corporation Act lists activities that do not constitute doing business in a state. If the company's primary offices or facilities are located in a state other than the state of incorporation, it may not be considered to be doing business in that state. The company may be required to file as a foreign (out-of-state) company. Check this list carefully.

Articles of Incorporation

It is important to note that some portions of the articles of incorporation differ between public and private corporations. The numbering of articles can also vary, as not all articles apply to all corporations.

Article I: Corporate Name

Before finally deciding on a name, a search must be conducted through the state secretary of state's office to determine if the proposed company name is available. It is common practice to reserve specifying the corporate name until the actual incorporation filing.

Article II: Purpose

It's best to state the corporate purpose in broad, general terms to allow for changes in direction or for expansion. The more liberal states allow such statements as "to engage in any lawful business," or "to establish a retail shoe outlet and any lawful business." Some states require the purpose to be defined more specifically, such as "to operate a single location, retail only, children's shoe sales outlet." The broader, the better. Otherwise an amendment to the articles of incorporation may be required.

Article III: Duration

This article sets forth the length of time the corporation will exist. Generally, "perpetual existence" is the best way to handle it.

Article IV: Capital Stock

This article designates the classifications of stock to be issued (common, preferred) and par (face) value and number of each type of shares authorized. For later flexibility, these items should also be stated as broadly as possible. At a minimum, both preferred and common should be designated. Because of the complexities, this article is generally subdivided into four sections:

Section 1. Classes and Shares

This section simply states, "The authorized capital stock of the corporation shall be (number) shares of Common stock, _____ Par Value, and (number) shares of Preferred stock, _____ Par Value."

Playing the numbers game for an IPO can be costly, albeit necessary. Many states charge incorporation filing fees by the number of shares authorized. Consequently some companies purposely keep the number low. But that policy won't work with a low-priced IPO stock. For example, if a company expects to raise $2 million at 10 cents per share, 20 million shares are required. Further, if the 20 million shares offered to the public represent only 20 percent of the company, at a minimum, there must be 100 million shares outstanding—not counting shares that may have been issued in connection with pre-public financing.

Additionally, if the public company plans to do additional financings, or make acquisitions for stock, it will initially need to authorize, at a minimum, four times the expected number of shares to be outstanding at the initial public offering. This could bring the total number of the company's authorized shares to 400 million.

These decisions must be made before incorporation because increasing the number of authorized shares after incorporation requires changing the articles, for which shareholder approval must be obtained. The process can be very costly to a public company with hundreds or thousands of shareholders. For example, suppose the company wants to make an acquisition. Without those authorized shares, the company must first call a shareholder meeting. Then it must distribute proxies. Then it must hold the meeting to obtain authority to increase the number of shares. Then it can make the acquisition. The process could well take several months. Therefore, an adequate number of shares should be authorized initially to cover any contingency.

Section 2. Preferred Stock

Public companies may issue preferred stock. Private companies rarely do. That's because preferred stock is similar to a debt, in that it requires the paying of dividends (like interest), which are taxable to the company.

It's up to the board of directors to determine the dividend amounts, accumulation time, and voting and convertibility of preferred shares. (*Convertibility,* depending on the specific incorporation laws of the state, means the company may be allowed to issue preferred stock as a debt instrument that contains a voluntary or involuntary conversion to common stock at a predetermined time in the future.)

Section 3. Common Stock

The broad rights pertaining to common stock are at the discretion of the board of directors. Basically there are four designations of common stock:

1. *Authorized.* These are the total number of shares of stock the company is authorized to issue according to the laws of the state where the company is incorporated.

2. *Issued.* These are shares of authorized stock that are issued to stockholders for some consideration.

3. *Outstanding.* These are the issued shares that are actually held by stockholders.

4. *Treasury.* These are issued shares that the company has repurchased and replaced in the corporation's treasury to be resold, redistributed, or canceled.

Usually, an opening phrase on common stock certificates will state that it is second in line to preferred in case of liquidation and for dividends. There also can be a statement about the voting rights, usually one vote per share (preferred stock is generally nonvoting). However, particular classes of common stock can carry multiple votes. All of these are decisions made by the board of directors.

Section 4. Proxy Rules

This section simply authorizes the board of directors to adopt a resolution whereby shareholders may certify in writing to the corporation that their shares are held (controlled or voted) by one or more persons.

Article V: Voting

This article declares that "cumulative voting in the election for directors is *not* authorized." In essence, it bans an old practice whereby a few persons holding a distinctive class of common stock could rubber-stamp the decisions of the directors of the corporation. This practice is now prohibited by the stock exchanges.

Article VI: Preemptive Right

This article states that the shareholders do *not* have the right to acquire before others unissued or treasury shares of stock or warrants.

Article VII: Registered Office and Agent

Article VII gives the address of the registrar of stock for the company, and names some specific person acting as the registrar. This is primarily for the public's protection, so that anyone wishing to contact the secretary of state regarding the company will have a specific person to refer to. As a rule, it is the company attorney.

Article VIII: Board of Directors

This article discloses how the directors are compensated, the length of time they are elected to serve, and procedures for elections, and filling vacancies. The article is often divided into the following five sections:

Section 1. Number

This section establishes the number of initial directors.

Section 2. Classification

This section divides the directors into three classes, as equal in number as possible. Generally, the term of office of Class 1 directors expires at the first annual shareholders' meeting. Class 2 directors are elected for 2 years. Class 3 directors are elected for 3 years. At each annual meeting it is common procedure for all directors to be reelected. The chairperson and the president are almost always class 3 directors, which assures them of a 3-year tenure as board members. Classification of directors is one form of *hostile takeover defense* for public companies.

Section 3. Initial Directors

This section notes the names and addresses of the initial directors.

Section 4. Nominations

This section establishes the procedure for nominating and electing directors. It specifies shareholder nominations and time restrictions.

Section 5. Powers of the Board

This section sets forth the powers of the board within the confines of state statutes, including to manage and govern; to make, alter, or amend the bylaws; to fix the amount to be reserved as working capital; to authorize and cause to be executed mortgages and liens; to designate one or more committees; to sell, lease, exchange, or otherwise dispose of assets of the corporation; to merge, consolidate, or exchange all the issued shares of the corporation; to distribute to the shareholders, in partial liquidation, portions of the corporation's assets, in cash or in property.

Article IX: Conflicts of Interest

This article is usually comprised of two sections:

Section 1. Related Party Transactions

This section states that contracts between the corporation and companies that the corporation has an interest in are not affected or invalid because of those relationships. However, the SEC requires that directors with joint interest must disclose those facts and also must abstain from voting on issues that affect those companies.

Section 2. Corporate Opportunities

Section 2 says, in effect, that if the board has rejected taking specific action on a corporate opportunity, such as an acquisition, merger, new product, or employee, members of the board are free to pursue the opportunity personally.

Article X: Indemnification

Article X deals with the process of protecting or providing security against damages or loss as a result of actions taken by the company. This article has become one of great concern but the subject is too complex to fully cover in this book. There are many areas of concern for directors, officers, employees, and agents of a company regarding what may be considered their personal responsibility. Improperly written indemnification clauses can result in devastating financial loses to the company and those involved with the company.

The extent of "allowability" in indemnification allowability clauses depends on the law of the state of incorporation. Delaware offers the best protection. Unfortunately, few other states have followed suit. Many states' indemnification laws are simply not conducive to incorporating public companies. That is why it is so important to have a good lawyer who can make the proper determinations in this very important area.

Article XI: Shareholder Meetings and Votes

This article determines the time and place for shareholders' meetings according to the corporation's bylaws. State laws set specific minimums for a quorum for meetings, but generally one-third of the shares entitled to vote will constitute a quorum. The affirmative vote of a majority of shares represented at a shareholders' meeting is usually sufficient to pass a measure. Thus in actuality, it takes only 1 vote of more than one-sixth of the total shares (quorum = 1/3 plus 1 vote over a majority present = 16.6 percent).

Some state statues establish different quorum and voting standards. Also, some state laws require higher numbers than a quorum for dissolving a company, selling off assets, or approving acquisitions or mergers. Legal counsel should be cognizant of the specifics of these laws.

Article XII: Amendments

This final article addresses the amendment of articles of incorporation, usually requiring, at a minimum, the affirmative vote of a majority of the shares.

Bylaws

Bylaws are the rules governing a corporation. They are voted upon at the organizational meeting of the board of directors. They amplify the articles to cover in detail all areas of corporate responsibility, as outlined here:

1. *Offices.* Location of the principal offices and any additional offices, including those of subsidiaries.

2. *Meetings of shareholders.* Time and place for annual and special meetings; notices of meetings; fixing of record date; proxies; how meetings must be conducted; formal and informal; voting privileges; required quorum.

3. *Board of directors.* General powers; number of directors; terms of office; qualifications; notice of meetings; regular and special meetings; quorum; action by consent; conducting of meetings; compensation; filling of vacancies; resignation; removal.

4. *Officers.* Number; elections; terms; removal; vacancies; president; chairperson; vice presidents; secretary; treasurer; assistant secretaries and treasurers; salaries; method of selecting officers.

5. *Contracts, loans, checks, and deposits.* Contracts; loans; checks; drafts; deposits; authority to sign checks.

6. *Certificates for shares and their transfer.* What certificates look like; who can sign them; transfer of shares; limits on transfer; cancellation; lost, stolen, or destroyed certificates.

7. *Seal.* Form of corporate seal.

8. *Waver of notice.* Who has the authority.

9. *Amendments.* Who can make them.

Summary

The legal makeup of a public corporation is by necessity different from that of a privately held company. State laws for incorporation also vary. Some are more lenient, such as the state of Delaware, whose liberal laws are the reason many public companies incorporate there.

State the purpose of a public corporation in broad, general terms to allow for changes in direction. Plan ahead about the number of shares of authorized capital stock to be issued if the corporation has thoughts of additional financings or acquisitions.

Include protection for officers, directors, and management against lawsuits and other hazards.

It is extremely important in an incorporation to enlist the services of qualified, experienced SEC counsel—someone who is well aware of the significant differences between the articles and bylaws of public and private companies. State statutes vary, and must be carefully reviewed to determine the best situation for the company's operations.

The articles of incorporation for a public company need not be complicated, but if all necessary points are not properly addressed at the outset, *they can become complicated.*

14

Stock Control

When entrepreneurs anticipate going public, their fantasy is usually to own the lion's share of the company stock. As reality sets in, they grudgingly accept that 100 percent ownership of a public company is not only unrealistic, it's impossible. Nevertheless, they determine not to give up more than 49 percent stock ownership of the "baby."

It is highly unlikely that they will retain even a majority ownership in the stock itself, but all is not lost. The founders of a company that goes public, will almost always retain control of the company through voting stock, which for all practical purposes amounts to control of the company.

A 5-year study by Venture Associates Ltd. revealed that the founding members of companies that received public financing in the $.5 million to $5 million range retained, on average, from 20 percent to 40 percent voting stock control. The study also revealed that in many cases, according to various IPO advisors, founders of potentially viable public offerings that insisted upon retaining at least 51 percent voting stock control never realized their dreams of a successful public offering. There are, of course, many public companies that have been successful in their entrepreneurial pursuits without giving away very much of the store. Quantum and Apple are two such companies; they raised the capital they needed, but gave away only 15 percent to 20 percent to the public.

Quantum Computer, for example, raised $32 million in its public offering of only 15 percent of the company. At the time, the company's five top officers and founders owned only 10 percent of Quantum, but it had an IPO valuation of $21 million! However, it bears mentioning that prior to the public offering, private financing from individuals and outside investors gave the company crucial millions it needed for research and development. Quantum also had money for the building and testing of the prototypes, for establishing marketing and sales organizations, and for a vast distribution network. For that financing, the investors received a considerable piece of the action. But then the Quantums and Apples are exceptions to the rule.

Percentages Do Not Necessarily Mean Control

It is important to keep in mind that shrunken stock percentages do not necessarily mean loss of control. Management of a number of large, successful, old-line companies today hold as little as 2 percent to 8 percent voting stock, but retain firm control of the companies. An example is the Ford Motor Company, with annual sales exceeding $40 billion. It is unequivocally controlled by the Ford family (including various Ford foundations). Between them they vote less than 6½ percent of the total stock outstanding, but they hold the top management positions and they name the directors—evidence that it's not so much the actual physical ownership that's important, but the control of voting stock that influences the direction of a public company.

To further clarify the question of percentages and the effect on voting stock, here's a hypothetical case of a typical low-priced OTC stock offering:

The Horatio Alger Company is composed of four founding principals. Each has contributed several years of concentrated effort and labor, plus $100,000 of family and friends' money. Each owns or controls the stock ownership of 25 percent of the company.

They decide to go public. An offering is structured whereby 40 percent of the company will be offered to the public for $4 million. An additional 15 percent is offered and subscribed to by private placement investors for $500,000, a sum used to underwrite the cost of going public and for essential operation capital for the interim. At the time of public issue, the founders, including the board of directors and corporate management, directly control 45 percent of the outstanding stock.

Since the private investors became involved with the company because they liked its potential, they will put their voting power behind management all the way. They know their best interests will be served by going along with management's recommendations. Consequently management, including the board of directors, effectively controls not 45 percent, but 60 percent of the outstanding stock.

As far as the 40 percent purchased by the public is concerned, investigation has shown that the public shareholders normally vote, at minimum,

50 percent in favor of management's recommendations, even in circumstances where management may be doing an extremely ineffective job in running the company. This voter apathy gives management an additional 20 percent vote control, which, added to the above 60 percent, gives total control of 80 percent of the company's stock, as well as the votes of the board of directors and corporate management.

It can with reason be said that the odds of management retaining vote control of a public company are better than the odds of betting on a fixed horse race.

Summary

The control of a public company by its founders and management is rarely predicated upon the amount of stock they personally own. Rather, in almost all cases, it is dependent upon the amount of voting stock they control as a group that includes the founder, key management, officers, directors, inside shareholders, as well as the public shareholders.

As long as management is making the day-to-day operation decisions and recommendations on policy decisions to its board of directors, voting control is a foregone conclusion. With few exceptions, it will safely remain in the hands of the entrepreneur and the founding management team of a public company. Really.

15

Valuation and Pricing

A major bone of contention between the underwriter and the entrepreneur of an IPO is the *issue price* of the company stock. The entrepreneur just knows that the stock is worth much more than the offering price of the new issue. But the underwriter wants to create a demand for the new issue, and do it quickly. And the best way to do that is to offer the stock at a price low enough to encourage potential investors to flock to their brokers and buy it before the stock price begins to rise.

Eventually, of course, the entrepreneur grasps the gist of the psychological game and grudgingly accepts the expert advice of the underwriter. The two finally reach an agreement that neither is really quite happy with. On larger offerings, this process usually goes on until the day the issue is cleared for selling. For smaller offerings, where less money is at stake, both company and underwriter seem to agree on the stock price much sooner.

Preliminary Considerations

Prior to the wrangling about value and pricing, however, the type of security to be offered must be determined. The first one that usually comes up in discussions is *straight common stock.* It gives the holder voting rights of one vote per share. Dividends are paid after those on preferred stock. There are alternatives that management may want to consider, as common stock can take many forms.

If the company has a very strong balance sheet and a long-standing management team with a successful record, the company may want to consider offering a nonvoting common stock that is first in line for dividends, or a class of common stock that has less voting power, perhaps one vote for two shares held against voting common that is held by the company. An example of nonvoting stock comes from Coors Brewery. It's a publicly held company, but the public has no votes: The voting stock is all controlled by the Coors family.

Warrants are another form of security. Warrants offer the investor a right to buy a specified number of shares of common stock at a predetermined price and time. By way of example, an "A" warrant could be exercisable 12 months from the initial effective date of the registration statement for a 3-month period at a 50 percent premium over the initial offering price of the common stock.

That means, if the IPO price was $3 per share, the warrant would be priced at $4.50 per share when it was eventually purchased. The owner of the warrant would be able to exchange the warrant at whatever price the common stock was selling for at the time of the exchange. The stock may, at that time, be worth $6.00 a share. Or say the investor has the right to buy the warrant for $4.50, and the stock goes up to $6.00 per share. The owner of the warrant simply buys the warrant for $4.50 and exchanges it for a share of stock, making a $1.50 profit.

A "B" warrant could be available for 2 years' redemption at 100 percent premium. That would be $6 per share. The owner would not want to exercise it until the stock reached around $6.50.

The general attitude about warrants, and what makes them seem so attractive, is that offering warrants is the company's way of saying it is confident the company will succeed. That's why warrants are occasionally attached to a common stock offering as a unit. That means with each purchase of a share of stock, the company gives the buyer a warrant that can be exchanged for a share of stock at a specified time for a specified price—regardless of what the stock is selling for at the time. Some companies use the unit plan as a merchandising device to entice a potential investor to buy the stock.

Management should be aware that, when exercised, warrants will dilute all shareholders' positions. For example, if a completed IPO has 3 million shares outstanding, of which 1 million are held by the public (33 percent of the company), and if the shares are sold as a unit, one warrant for each share, warrant entitling the purchase of one additional share, after all the warrants are exercised the company will be 50 percent publicly held.

Another question is whether the warrants should be commissionable to the brokers. They often are. Warrants can be attached (not tradeable on their own), or detached (separately tradeable). If the warrant is separately tradeable, it has a market value of its own and it trades in the market.

Another possibility is the case of a new issue at, say, $1 per share of common stock with an "A" warrant exercisable at $1. The initial trading value of the detached warrant could be 1/32 bid (32 cents). Should the stock increase in value to $4.50, technically the warrant would be worth $1.50. The warrant purchase value would then probably go up to ⅛ (12 cents) or even 3/16 (18 cents). That's a ready-made profit of 38 cents, as the warrant can be purchased for 12 cents. There are investors who purchase warrants only under those circumstances.

Warrants can provide many benefits to companies and attractive commissions for brokers. But before going into warrants, which can be very complex, the company should look into every aspect carefully, and discuss the possibilities in detail with legal counsel, accounting, and the underwriter.

To repeat: A warrant is a *right to buy.* If the warrant is to be exercised, money must be put up.

Alternatives

Instead of common stock, the company can offer preferred stock with a dividend provision. Or the company could offer a *convertible debenture,* which converts preferred stocks or bonds into specified shares of common stock at a specified time and an advantageous ratio. Normally this type of offering is not feasible for start-up or early stage companies. Convertible debentures or preferred stock offerings require a consistent positive cash flow to meet regular interest payments or retire bonds. Furthermore, if there is no established market for the common stocks, convertible securities are unlikely to attract investors.

All types of unit offerings should be carefully scrutinized for investor market reception and current market trends. Even more important, they should be examined for their long-range implications. It may prove that the company gave away more of the store than it should have, and the entrepreneur may end up owning too little of the company.

Selling Shareholders

Selling shareholders are usually principals of the company who sell their personally held company stock with the proceeds going to their personal benefit. Assuming the stock has increased substantially in value, the venture capital firm that provided initial equity financing may sell some of their stock to regain their investment. This means of "turning" their investment, which can represent a sizeable sum, is seen mainly with large, mature, and successful companies.

Existing shareholders of small low-priced offerings seldom sell their stock positions, as it could result in a loss of control of the company. In the case of the more mature companies that are profit producers, these sales permit original insiders to take out a small percentage of their initial investment. This gives the original founders an opportunity to "cash-out" on sweat-equity.

Where the total proceeds needed by the company are too small to justify an IPO, existing shareholders can sell some of their holdings to increase the total offering size and make the offering meaningful.

Valuation versus Pricing

Value and price are two important factors in an IPO. *Value* refers to the estimated valuation of the company and the total dollar amount expected to be raised based on the capitalization of the company. The underwriter will generally conduct a survey of competitive or comparable public companies, which will help provide a preliminary valuation. Other points that enter into a valuation include:

- Efficiency ratios (sales per employee)
- Leverage ratios (debt to equity)
- Interest coverage
- Profit margins, gross and net
- Use of proceeds
- Earnings ratios (net as a percent of sales to net worth of assets)
- Operating history
- Operating base (regional, national, or international)
- Quantity and experience of management
- Product differentiation and innovation
- Single or multiple product company
- Patent/proprietary product position

Price refers to the price per share to be asked. It is primarily based on what the market will bear. Aiding in the decision-making process is information that is furnished in the company's business plan, which details the existing operations and projected future operations.

On offerings for large companies, underwriters prefer to come out with offerings of at least 500,000 shares. They will often go along with a minimum of 300,000 to 350,000 shares of public float—the stock owned by public stockholders. They want to obtain a broad distribution of the stock and provide for liquidity in the aftermarket. Another reason for the minimum is because institutional investors usually purchase blocks of 10,000 to 50,000 shares. Because SEC rules require owners of 5 percent or more of the outstanding shares of a company to disclose what they do with the stock, many major buyers of large blocks of stocks of a company will only buy up to 5 percent of the outstanding stock and avoid reporting requirements. They may also be concerned that substantial buy or sell orders can create large fluctuations in the market.

The average national offering falls between $20 and $30 million. Offerings totaling over $100 million are rare. Underwriters prefer offerings in the $10 to $30 million range, involving 10 percent to 40 percent of the company. Many offerings start at the $5 million figure, but most offerings in the $5 to $10 million range are underwritten by regional rather than national firms.

Price/Earnings Ratio

IPO entrepreneurs should be familiar with the P/E (price/earnings) ratio of companies in their industries. This standard measurement of the price of the stock versus the earnings of the company is figured by dividing the stock price by the earnings per share. For example, if a stock is selling for $15 per share, and the earnings per share are $1, the stock is selling at a ratio of 15 to 1.

The P/E ratio is the prime standard for performance comparison. It is used both for current/historical and future/projection analysis. After the market crash of 1929 and throughout the depression years of the 1930s, the United States had a major concern about debt. Consequently, the debt/equity ratio, which compares the liabilities of the company with shareholder equity, was considered an important analytical tool when valuing a prospective IPO. Today, while debt/equity is still considered, the most popular ratio is price/earnings, sometimes referred to as the P/E multiple.

P/Es that are based on the last 12 months' earnings are referred to as "trailing earnings." Earnings that are shown "as reported" are based on the total number of shares outstanding as of the date of issue of the financial statement. P/E ratios are also often shown as projected, reflecting the company's projections for the amount of earnings per share at some point in the future, usually the next quarter or year.

All popular stock guides, and many daily stock quotation services publish current P/E ratios. They are also published daily in *The Wall Street Journal*. There are also category and industry listings, such as for electronics or autos.

It's not unusual for companies in the same industry to show large discrepancies in their P/E ratios. A particular company may be the subject of a takeover attempt or may just have received a large long-term contract or announced a significant new product. On the downside, a company may have experienced negative earnings for several quarters or may be a defendant in a major lawsuit. It doesn't take much to affect the P/E ratio of a company.

Pricing

The pricing of an issue is as difficult as the valuation of a company. The financial industry itself has some psychological quirks that affect pricing. Many underwriters are conditioned to follow historical traditions in pricing a stock. The price shouldn't be too high or too low to appeal to their targets. For example, stocks under $5 a share might be considered too risky, and stocks over $20 may carry too much prestige for the issue. Whereas some brokerage houses feel that stocks under $10 a share appear too speculative, stocks above $20 a share keep too many investors away, since they can't make a large enough purchase. The purchase price of a round lot of 100 shares at $30 a share would be $3000, which may be just high enough for an individual investor to say No. There are fixed psychological points that influence the underwriter's pricing positioning.

One formula for pricing that underwriters like to use is "discounting." Underwriters often attempt to price a new stock issue at 15 percent to 30 percent below what they consider its true market value. This creates an incentive for investors to put their money into a new issue and offers the prospect of showing an immediate return, at least on paper.

Timing is also critical in price setting. Late-breaking bad news about the IPO's industry could prove disastrous. Underwriters will keep a close watch on the industry and competitive companies, and the final price may not be set until the day of an offering.

Valuation and pricing for larger underwritings are often based more on intuition than on facts. A general range may be agreed upon early in the IPO discussions and refined as the registration statement is prepared. When the preliminary prospectus is distributed, the managing underwriter solicits and receives indications of interest from the up to 40 brokerage firms that are involved in the selling syndicate.

The underwriter prepares an *indications of interest book,* which details the interest on the part of the selling syndicate. It shows how many shares each firm is willing to subscribe to and the price at which it believes it can sell the shares. This input is used in the final price determination. It gives the underwriter an indication of how many shares the market can bear and how much of the company will have to be given away for the least number of shares. All of the preceding information, plus whatever research has turned up on valuations and P/E ratios, go into the underwriter's final price determination. At that point the number of shares to be offered and the price at which they will be sold is printed in the final prospectus.

Low-priced Issues

Valuation and pricing for smaller IPOs with low-priced issues and total offerings of $5 million or less are much simpler. On smaller deals, the company basically informs the underwriter that it has put together a business plan and says how much money it will need. For example, a company may tell the underwriter it will need $2 million to implement the business plan and explains how it intends to use the money. If the company's presentation is based on a solid business plan that the underwriter can feel comfortable with, they proceed to determine a price for the stock. Issues priced below $1 are simply based on the proceeds desired. At $1 a share, 2 million shares are issued; at 10 cents a share, 20 million shares. The price of the share is often set by whatever is the "hot" price in the market at the time.

A recent survey tracked new issues priced below $1 from 1980 through 1987 on a quarterly basis. During this period, the IPO market went from the doldrums to unjustifiable heights, and again slowed.

Some surprising consistencies came to light on issues priced at 1 cent, 5 cents, 25 cents, 50 cents, and $1. Dollar offerings averaged 30 percent of all the offerings, dime offerings averaged 25 percent, quarter and fifty-cent offerings averaged 10 percent each, with the balance of IPOs offered in that range totaling 25 percent.

During the early eighties when the IPO market was hot, the number of dollar offerings rose as small underwriters attempted to upgrade their underwriting image. The mid eighties saw a significant rise in true penny (1 cent) offerings. The interesting thing about them was about 60 percent to 70 percent of the new issues priced below $1 were blind pools or blank check offerings (see chapter 38). These are essentially pools from which shares are purchased without any particular company or investment being identified. Blind pool offerings are unusually small, with totals of $200,000 to $400,000, priced at 1 cent per share. The intent of the company usually is to acquire operating company, but all details are left to the discretion of the founders (officers and directors) of the blind pool.

Repositioning

At some point in time, a company may exhaust its trading capability in low-priced stocks and may decide to reverse-split them. For example, a reverse split of 10 to 1 would leave holders with 1 share in place of 10 they had owned before the split; 10,000 shares would become 1000 shares. If 1 share was worth 40 cents before the reverse split the holder of 10 shares would now own 1 share worth $4. From the company's perspective, a public share float (number of shares held by the public) of 100 million would drop to then become 10 million and show a P/E ratio more acceptable to investors.

The reverse stock split can be attractive to regional brokerage firms whose house rules prevent dealing in low-priced stocks. Now they can become involved in the selling of the stock.

Successful small underwritings are often compelled to perform reverse splits, not only to reduce the number of shares outstanding, but to post attractive earnings per share and P/E ratios. Shares gotta show some value before they can pay off in dividends.

Summary

The first consideration in valuations and pricing is deciding what type of security (stock) to offer. The company and underwriter may decide on straight common stock, nonvoting stock, or—frequent in low-priced offerings—common stocks with warrants attached (units). Unit offerings should be carefully appraised for their long-range implications for the company.

Valuation and pricing for small stocks are a lot less complicated than for larger issues. The small company makes a determination of how much money it needs, convinces the underwriter, and together they choose a stock offering price that feels right for the issue and the market.

The P/E (price/earnings) ratio is a valuable indicator, but more of a factor for high- than low-priced issues. Nevertheless, it is carefully weighed by most investors.

Pricing an IPO issue is often a matter more of intuition than science. Too low a price keeps some buyers away, and too high a price keeps other buyers away. Suffice it to say that the valuing of a company and the pricing of its stock can sometimes seem to require the services of a magician.

16

The SEC

Every aspect of going public is regulated by the Securities and Exchange Commission (SEC). Although mentioned earlier in the book, this bears repeating. The SEC, a quasi-judicial administrative agency of the United States government, is responsible for the administration and enforcement of the securities laws. It was created by the Securities Act of 1934, which was passed to regulate the securities exchanges and the over-the-counter market. Pursuant to the Securities Act of 1933, SEC supervises the registration of securities issues and guards against fraudulent sales practices. The '33 act makes all pertinent information about securities available to the buyer.

The commission is composed of five members who are appointed by the President of the United States. Only three may belong to the same political party, and each is appointed for a 5-year term. The President designates the chairperson. The commission's staff includes lawyers, accountants, engineers, securities analysts, examiners, and administrative personnel.

There are nine regional offices, located in Boston; Washington, D.C.; Atlanta; Chicago; Fort Worth; Denver; Seattle; San Francisco; and New York, plus additional branches throughout the country.

Operations are organized in several divisions:

Division of Corporate Finance

This division reviews registration statements filed by companies under the '33 act. It furnishes interpretations and advisory services for issuers, underwriters, and their lawyers as to statutes, rules, and regulations. The initial reviewing of registration statements, the major task of this division, is the responsibility of regional branches. Each regional branch is staffed by attorneys, accountants, analysts, and examiners.

Office of Chief Accountant

This office has final authority regarding accounting matters. It makes policy determinations regarding form and content of financial statements and decides complicated accounting disputes, from consolidated financial statements to Fair Practice Procedures.

Division of Trading and Markets

This division assists the commission and NASD (National Association of Securities Dealers) in the regulation of brokers, dealers, and investment advisors and in securing the cooperation of management of the securities exchanges.

Division of Corporate Regulation

This division assists the commission in the administration of the Public Utility Holding Company Act of 1935, the Investment Company Act of 1940, and the Bankruptcy Act and in making sure that the parties involved comply with the regulations.

Office of General Counsel

This office handles litigation for the commission. It prepares legal opinions and dispenses legal advice on behalf of the commission and its various divisions. It resolves differences of interpretation. It has broad powers and can, for instance, offer immunity on insider trader charges. It serves as a watchdog on international trading.

Office of Policy Research

This office, headed by the chief economist, analyzes proposals for modification of rules and regulations and prepares statistical data for internal and public publications.

Investigation and Enforcement

The SEC has the power to investigate complaints about securities violations from the general public as well as from federal and state agencies and enforce penalties for violations of its rules and regulations. The first step after receiving a complaint is a preliminary investigation. Most investigations are performed by regional offices, with informal interrogation of witnesses. If indications are that a violation may have occurred, the matter is returned to the commission, which can order a formal investigation.

If a formal investigation upholds the charges, the commission considers further proceedings. If the charge is against broker/dealers, the commission may institute administrative proceedings, under the Administrative Procedures Act, aimed toward remedial sanctions against persons or companies involved in the securities industry. The firm may be expelled or have its license suspended or revoked. An individual may be censured and temporarily or permanently barred from employment in the industry. Alternatively, the commission can request sanctions against violators by court order from a U.S. district court. A third possibility, reserved for willful violations, is for the commission to refer the matter to the Department of Justice for criminal prosecution.

Information Availability

Since the SEC is the primary repository for all public company filings and information, it is obligated to maintain public reference facilities in its regional branches. The SEC is also obligated to provide members of the public with copies of all public company filings at a nominal cost, including opinions of the commission, statements of policy, and interpretations. By law, the commission's decisions, reports, orders, rules, and regulations are always published. A summary of the releases are available by subscription to the daily *SEC News Digest* (from the Superintendent of Documents, Washington, D.C.). The commission also publishes reports on insider stock transactions.

The SEC staff provides advisory and interpretative assistance to members of the public and prospective registrants. This includes information forms and a list of items available. The SEC staff will also arrange for informal discussions on subjects pertaining to securities.

Summary

The SEC is the administrative agency of the United States government that is responsible for the administration and enforcement of the securities laws. It is the primary regulatory body for IPOs. Its headquarters is in Washington, D.C., and it has nine regional offices and many branches throughout the United States. Normally, the IPO entrepreneur would not have direct contact with the SEC—that's usually handled by legal counsel. However, the SEC staff is available to all persons to answer any and all questions and provide ongoing information regarding going public and continuing public company operations. Who could ask for more?

17

The Acts

The Securities Act of 1933 and the Securities Exchange Act of 1934 were passed in response to misuse and abuse of the system. The '33 act brought about truth-in-securities disclosure, and the '34 act regulates the industry through the Securities and Exchange Commission.

History

During the 6 years of Theodore Roosevelt's presidency, from 1901 through 1907, he led the attack on business monopolies and trusts. In 1907, a financial panic erupted on Wall Street. Stocks plunged. Many small businesses and banks closed. The exchange came under fire. In 1909, the Hughes Committee investigation recommended that the exchange regulate itself. In 1912, Congress formed the Pujo Committee, whose investigations raised suspicions about many leading trust companies and provided the foundation for the regulatory laws written in the early thirties.

The U.S. economy prospered as a result of World War I. Except for a brief recession in 1921 when the securities and commodities markets saw heavy losses, investments flourished in the U.S. business community—the stock market in particular. The unbounded investment enthusiasm was further promoted by cheap 10 percent margin credit. Euphoria continued until Black Thursday, October 24, 1929. The Great Depression followed.

Three years after the crash, in November 1932, Franklin D. Roosevelt was elected President. By the following May, Congress had passed the Securities Act of 1933. The reasons for this fast action were twofold. First, Roosevelt had campaigned for financial reforms; and second, the Senate Committee on Banking and Currency Reforms had completed a 17-month study that uncovered many unethical practices—including fraud perpetrated by exchange officials, bank officials, and important Wall Street figures. As a result of the study, a draft National Securities Act, modeled after the British Companies Act, was submitted to the House on April 10, 1933. With a speed unheard of today, the Securities Act of 1933 ('33 act) was signed into law May 23, 1933—just 6 weeks after its introduction. Sometimes referred to as the Truth in Securities Act, it is the foundation for the many rules and regulations governing entrepreneurs today. It regulates documents with two main objectives:

1. The registration of securities prior to their sale to the general public

2. Civil and criminal penalties for fraud connected with the registration of securities

A year later, Congress passed the Securities Exchange Act of 1934 ('34 act), which brought all stock exchanges under government control for the first time. The '34 act regulates *people* with two main objectives:

1. The registration of security exchanges and of broker/dealers

2. The regulation of business practices in the securities industry

Additionally, the '34 act established the Securities and Exchange Commission (SEC) to administer both the '34 and '33 acts and protect the interests of investors and the public.

The '33 Act

The intention of the '33 act is to ensure disclosure of all the sources of information about a company in a carefully and uniformly prepared document called the prospectus. The disclosure philosophy was explained by President Roosevelt:

> There is, however, an obligation upon us to insist that every issue of new securities to be sold in interstate commerce shall be accompanied by full publicity and information, and that no essentially important element attending the issue shall be concealed from the buying public.
>   This proposal adds to the ancient rule of caveat emptor, the further doctrine, "let the seller also beware." It puts the burden of telling the whole truth on the seller. It should give impetus to honest dealing in securities and thereby bring back public confidence.

The '33 act requires disclosures by any company that intends to sell securities in interstate commerce or through the mail; these disclosures are made in a registration statement and prospectus filed with the SEC. The registration statement details business and financial information about the company as well as the securities being offered.

The intent is to assure full and fair disclosure of relevant information to allow an investor to make an informed decision regarding the purchase of securities. Securities cannot be sold until the registration is approved.

It is important to note that, contrary to popular belief, the SEC does *not* review the validity of an offering, but only compliance under the act. The *merits* of the securities themselves, or of the companies offering the securities, are judgments that must be made by the investor.

Additionally, the '33 act contains provisions about fraud. These provisions apply to officers, directors, controlling shareholders, underwriters, and all those who sign the registration statement. Also liable are the experts who assisted in the preparation of the registration statement or who are actually named in it. Civil and criminal penalties can be imposed for misrepresentations, misstatements, or omissions in the registration statement.

The act exempts government securities, common carriers' securities, and securities sold intrastate. Also exempt are banks, nonprofit organizations, and offerings under Reg A, which sets limits under which an offer of securities may be made publicly, and Rule 146, which deals with private placement offerings. (See chapter 19.)

The actual forms and the information required in a registration statement are discussed in depth in chapter 24.

The '34 Act

The Securities Exchange Act of 1934 was drafted by the Securities and Exchange Commission. The original purpose was to oversee the implementation of the '33 act. Today, the SEC has the authority to regulate public companies and personnel in the securities industry and to enforce federal securities laws.

For the public company, the '34 act is notable in the following areas:

Periodic Reporting

- *Form 10–K.* An annual report which includes audited financial statements as well as information about the company and its management (see chapter 32)

- *Form 10–Q.* A quarterly report with unaudited financial statements and management discussion of continuing operations (see chapter 32)

- *Form 8–K.* To be filed with the SEC whenever significant events occur within the company, its control, or management that could effect an investor's decision about the stock (see chapter 32)

Proxy Solicitations

Regulations cover events such as elections of members of the board of directors or approval of major divestitures or acquisitions that require shareholder approval. (See chapters 13 and 32.)

Foreign Corrupt Practices Act (FCPA)

This act contains statutory requirements regarding the establishment and maintenance of proper accounting records. (See chapter 32.)

Tender Offers

Under the '34 act, the SEC regulates both the manner in which tender offers are made and management tactics that can be employed to resist tender offers.

Insider Trading

Insiders such as directors, officers, and shareholders are required to report to the SEC changes in their holdings in the company via forms 3 and 4. There are stiff penalties against trading on inside information not available to the public. (See chapter 32.) (See sections on inside trading and forms 3 and 4 in chapter 31.)

Other portions of the '34 act set forth in detail rules pertaining to the securities industry itself. The act gave the SEC authority over net capital and margin requirements and restrictions on broker/dealers and members of the stock exchanges, including the OTC (over-the-counter) market.

Other Significant Legislation

- The Public Utility Holding Company Act of 1935 requires the registration of all public holding companies and utility companies.
- The Trust Indenture Act of 1939 requires relevant information on the issuance of corporate bonds and debt securities.

- The Investment Company Act of 1940 requires the registration and regulation of investment companies and mutual funds and protects investors.

- The Investment Advisors Act of 1940 provides for the registration and regulation of investment advisors.

- The Securities Acts Amendment of 1964 was the result of the SEC *Special Study of Securities Markets.* It broadened basic securities laws, such as disclosure requirements and the regulation of brokers and dealers.

- The Securities Investor Protection Act of 1970 established the Securities Investors Protection Corporation (SIPC), which supervises the liquidation of securities firms and the payment of claims brought by their customers.

Summary

The '33 and '34 acts brought about extensive government regulation of stock exchanges for the first time. These rules and the Securities and Exchange Commission are responsible for a formal system of undertaking equity/debt fund-raising and the supervision of the continuing trading of public company securities. The '33 act brought about truth-in-securities disclosure, and the '34 act brought about regulation of the securities industry.

Other significant securities acts such as the Public Utility Holding Company Act, the Trust Indenture Act, the Investment Company Act, the Securities Acts Amendment, and the Securities Investor Protection Act strengthened the SEC. Today's investors can expect a safer run for their money. And today's entrepreneurs can expect to fill out more statements and abide by more regulations than ever before—before they can go public. Nothing is a piece of cake anymore.

18

Regulation D

Simply stated, it's against the law to sell stock unless you are licensed to do so or can qualify for an exemption from the SEC rules. The very worst that can happen is that you will have to pay penalties or you can be put in jail. For instance, section 5 of the '33 act clearly states that "it is unlawful for any person, directly or indirectly to sell a security unless a registration statement has been filed, or to sell a security or deliver a security after the sale unless a registration statement is in *effect* (emphasis added)." The '33 act does, however, contain some exemptions, but they fall short of really helping the little guy.

That concern made clear by small businesses is the sum and substance of Regulation D, commonly referred to as Reg D, which became effective April 15, 1982. It is not just another exemption. It is *the* exemption for small businesses that want to raise money by selling some of their stock. It is also a form of taking a company public without the burden and expense of full registration with the SEC. Reg D may also serve as a welcome alternate for some entrepreneurs.

For decades, the principals of many small U.S. businesses have complained about the expense and trouble of complying with government regulation. It goes back 200 years, to Adam Smith's push for a new era in British economic policy. Smith sought to "strip away the shackles of government regulations and constraining ideology, and replace them with the freedom of individual initiative and economic enterprise." Well, some things can't be rushed. The same kind of utterance came from Ronald Reagan when he said in 1978, "For several decades, an ever-larger role of the federal government has sapped the economic vitality of the Nation." The result of this early Reaganomics movement was to remove some of the federal restraints on raising capital. In 1980, Congress enacted the Small Business Investment Incentive Act.

One of the agencies affected by this act was the Securities Exchange Commission, which promulgated Reg D, effective April 15, 1982. This regulation, along with revisions that were instituted in April 1988, broadened the exemptions from the SEC's regulations, thereby easing restrictions on equity fund-raising.

Reg D established a new set of guidelines that replaced older rules that had been adopted under the '33 act. Those rules required full disclosure on securities and the registration of securities prior to their being sold to the public. It was proposed that the new federal rules be uniformly adopted by all the states, thus following the Reaganomics trend toward deregulation. Reg D also returned many responsibilities of government to the states. Many states have been slow to adopt Reg D. Consequently, entrepreneurs who are contemplating this type of action had better check their own state's securities regulations before relying completely on Reg D for their purposes.

The Regulation

Reg D reduces the registration requirements and costs, and has opened the door to substantial exemptions to the '33 act. The technical provisions, which were always subject to varying interpretations, have also been eased. The process now is simpler, which, in turn, has lessened the chance that the offerer (the company) may be subject to recision (giving back monies raised) to the offeree (investor) if a technical provision happens to be mistakenly violated.

Some risks continue under Reg D, but compliance is significantly easier than before Reg D. It also provides the company, its officers, and its directors with an insurance policy against possible charges of securities fraud.

Reg D consists of six basic rules. The first three are concerned with definitions, conditions, and notification. Rule 501 covers the definitions of the various terms used in the rules. Rule 502 sets forth the conditions, limitations, and information requirements for the exemptions in rules 504, 505, and 506. Rule 503 contains the SEC notification requirements. The last three rules deal with the specifics of raising money. Rule 504 generally pertains to securities sales up to $1 million. Rule 505 applies to offerings from $1 million to $5 million. Rule 506 is for securities offerings exceeding $5 million. Here's how they work:

Rule 501

This first rule defines the terms used in the regulations that are applicable to the offering and sales under Reg D. The following are key definitions:

Accredited Investors

The SEC has long had a definition for *accredited investors*—investors "sophisticated or wealthy enough" to be able to assess an offer or stand the risk of the investment without further information about investment. Prior to Rule 501, it was up to an attorney, accountant, or stockbroker to decide whether a potential investor met the very vague SEC requirements. Now the rule spells it out. Accredited investors include:

- Banks
- Savings and loans
- Credit unions
- Corporations and partnerships with total assets in excess of $5 million
- Broker/dealers
- Insurance companies
- Registered investment companies
- Nonprofit organizations with over $5 million in assets
- Business Development Companies (as defined under the Investment Companies Act of 1940)
- Small Business Investment Companies (SBICs)
- Minority Enterprise Small Business Investment Companies (MESBICs)
- Employee benefit plans subject to Employee Retirement Income Security Act (ERISA) (with some restrictions)

And more applicable for most companies efforts to raise money privately:

- Directors and officers of the company
- Individuals whose net worth exceeds $1 million
- Individuals whose income exceeds $200,000 annually (during the last 2 years as well as expected in the current year)
- Individuals whose joint income with a spouse exceeds $300,000 for 2 years

The term accredited investors surfaces again in rules 504, 505, and 506. In conjunction with accredited investors, the term "reasonably believed" is often mentioned. These terms will be used extensively by a company's legal counsel or underwriter, as these persons and the company have a legal obligation to declare (reasonably believe) if an accredited investor meets the requirements of Rule 501. If the company actually believes, *and* can prove it had reason to believe, it would have no continuing liability as far as accredited investors are concerned. As an extra precaution, however, the company should have the investor attest to the accredited investor facts and qualification in writing. This accredited investor document should be part of every offering memorandum.

Purchaser Representative

A purchaser representative is a person who is not an affiliate, director, or other employee of the company, or an owner of 10 percent or more of the company, or an owner of any class of the equity securities of the company. Furthermore, such persons should possess sufficient knowledge and experience in financial and business matters to make them capable of evaluating, on their own or together with the purchaser, the merits and risks of the prospective investment. Additionally, they must acknowledge in writing that they are acting as a purchaser representative, and they must make certain written disclosures as to the identification of the ultimate purchaser. This particularly applies to syndicates, multiple syndicates, and partnership holdings.

Number of Purchasers

Rules 505 and 506 limit the number of purchasers, but accredited investors are not included in the total. The rules further state that the company may sell its securities to an unlimited number of accredited investors in addition to a specified number of other purchasers, such as officers and directors. This also applies to *loosely related parties,* which in some cases may be counted as a single purchaser.

Rule 502

This rule establishes the *general conditions* pertaining to the exemptions. Several areas are notable:

- Qualifying for an exemption under Reg D is not dependent on the size of the company.

- The exemptions are applicable only to the issuer and not its affiliates, such as subsidiaries, or to others, or for resale of the issuer's securities.

- Some offerings of the "same" securities may be considered as a single offering (that is, *integrated*) if they are made within 6 months of the start or termination of the Reg D offering. This can save legal and registration costs, but there are technicalities involved, so it's best for the entrepreneur to seek knowledgeable legal advice on how to best handle integration.

- To further clarify the somewhat confusing interpretation of Reg D: There can be no general solicitation or quasi-public advertising connected with the offering. However, to add to the confusion, Rule 504 explains how this type of situation can be circumvented.

- Another general condition is that certain procedures must be followed by the issuer to guarantee that the securities are not being purchased for resale. The issuer must make certain that the purchaser is not an underwriter or an agent for an underwriter. Further, the issuer must provide a written disclosure of this resale limitation. And the certificate itself must contain a legend specifying the resale restriction. This may seem like a no-win situation, but take heart, Rule 504 contains ways of avoiding this problem also.

Rule 503

This is the rule that sets forth the information that must be filed with the SEC. It also specifies the timing and the type of forms that must be used in the filing.

The company (issuer) must file five copies of the notice of sales of its securities with the SEC on the required Form D, one of which must be hand-signed. This filing must be made within 15 days after the first sale and thereafter every 6 months, with a final filing within 30 days of the last sale. Compliance in filing is extremely critical. Should the issuers not comply, they run a high risk of the SEC rescinding the entire offering and requiring that all monies received be returned to the stock purchasers if they so desire.

Also, the SEC has the right to request, in writing, that the issuer provide the SEC with copies of all the information provided to the purchasers of the securities. This makes the information public record. However, the SEC rarely takes this kind of action. Even so, don't bet on it.

Rule 504

This rule is considered by many as the perfect answer for the company just starting out that needs to raise less than $1 million but can't afford to go through the whole SEC registration process. Until they grow to a point where they can afford it, Rule 504 offers such companies an out:

- An exemption to raise up to $1 million
- No disclosure criteria

- Few general solicitation and resale restrictions
- No limit as to the number of investors

Actually, Congress's original intent for Rule 504 was to "set aside a clear and workable exemption for small issuers to be regulated by state blue sky requirements, but, by the same token, to be subject to federal anti-fraud provisions and civil liability provisions." Rule 504 exemption is provided for almost any type of organization, including corporations, partnerships, trusts, or other entities. However, it is not applicable to companies already reporting to the SEC (subject to the '34 act) or investment companies.

The total offering amount under Rule 504 can be up to $1 million in a 12-month period, less the aggregate offering of all securities sold within 12 months before the start of a 504 offering. So, if a company has raised $100,000 in pre-private money in the previous 12 months, it can still raise up to $900,000 without being accused of breaking the rules, or "integration." Generally speaking, there are *no* specific disclosure requirements under Rule 504 (disclosing what the company is about, what it intends to do, or who is connected with it). This means that, theoretically, an issuer can have a purchaser sign a subscription agreement and purchase stock without any information about the company being disclosed. However, the rule is dependent on the blue-sky laws of each state in which the securities are offered. This means that if a state's blue-sky rules require disclosure, it must be provided regardless of Rule 504.

Rule 504 also provides that at least $500,000 of securities must be sold pursuant to a registration under a state's securities law. Consequently, an offer must comply with the blue-sky laws of each individual state in which it is offered. In many states, this negates the effective simplicity of Rule 504 and the federal government's intent, because many states' blue-sky laws are more restrictive than Reg D.

A word of caution to the entrepreneur—regardless of the amount of disclosure the issuer is willing to provide, Rule 504 does not dismiss the issuer from the federal requirements, nor is there an exemption from the fraud provisions, including the areas of material omissions or misstatements. The penalties for noncompliance are severe, including monetary fines and mandatory jail sentences.

Commissionable

One interesting aspect of Rule 504 is the provision for payment of commission. It was reasoned that if broker/dealers got involved with the selling of 504s they would provide an extra safeguard for investors. Additionally, it was felt that removing the ban on commissions, which can be as high as the market would bear (generally 15 percent to 20 percent), would bring the expertise and sales organization of the brokerage firms and investment bankers to the aid of the small business persons. Unfortunately, the measure hasn't had the desired effect, except for a few smaller brokerage firms. It seems the medium-size and large Wall Street firms simply could not justify the expense required to merchandise offerings under $1 million.

The one area in which Rule 504 has helped is in allowing the issuer to "generally solicit," or advertise, for subscribers to an offering. Some states have been quite lenient in allowing it. However, in practice, very few issuers have advertised their offerings in newspapers or through other common media as was expected.

Number of Investors

With its limited disclosure requirements, Rule 504 also allows an issuer to sell securities to an unlimited number of investors. Theoretically, a company could raise $1 million by selling its stock at a penny a share to 100 million different investors. Obviously, the economics are not too attractive, but there's no rule that stops an issuer from selling $500 blocks of stock to 2000 investors. Rule 504 is the only rule under Reg D that permits an unlimited number of investors.

A final note on Rule 504 is that the exemption provides for sales of securities of either debt or equity. This opens the door for combinations of both via convertible debentures. By way of explanation, convertible debentures are a debt issue (debenture) that is convertible to a preferred or, most commonly, common stock at some future date, usually at a predetermined price.

Rule 505

Compared to Rule 504, Rule 505 is comparatively hassle-free.

- It exempts offers and sales of issuers other than investment companies.

- The offering in total cannot exceed $5 million during a 12-month period, less what has been raised by pre-private money, as mentioned in the discussion of Rule 504, plus inclusion of any future offerings contemplated in the 12 months following the last sale under Rule 505.

- The sales cannot be made to more than 35 nonaccredited investors and they must be accompanied by the same kind of disclosure information as is required in Part I of the filing for an S–18 registration. (See chapter 24)

- Sales can be to an unlimited number of accredited investors.

- No general solicitation (advertising) is allowed.

- Rule 505 carries the same filing notification requirements as Rule 504.

- Rule 505 carries a disqualification from using the exemption if the issuer, defined as just about anybody connected with the company, including its officers, directors, principals, or underwriters are "bad boys," as defined in Rule 252(c)–(f) of Regulation A. Loosely, a *bad boy* is a person who has incurred the wrath of the SEC for the potential (without necessarily having been convicted) of having committed a securities violation. However, the SEC can waive the misconduct disqualification. The issuer should seek advice of counsel if anyone connected with the company has had previous problems with the SEC.

- The same fraud, misstatement, and material omissions compliance apply as for Rule 504.

Obviously, the largest drawback to selling stock under Rule 505 is the limited number of nonaccredited investors allowed, which naturally means that the average investment per investor has to be considerably more than under Rule 504.

Rule 506

This is the last rule under Regulation D.

- It exempts offers and sales of issuers including sales by investment and reporting companies.

- The offering amount must be for offerings over $5 million, with no time restrictions.

- Sales cannot be made to more than 35 nonaccredited investors. The nonaccredited investors must be capable of evaluating the merits and risks of the investment, and it is up to the issuer to verify that the investors are knowledgeable enough to make that evaluation.

- Sales can be made to an unlimited number of accredited investors.

- No general solicitation (advertising) is allowed.

- Rule 506 carries the same notification requirements as rules 505 and 504, with the primary emphasis on filing every 6 months.

- Rule 506 does not contain "bad boy" disqualifications, but as in all Reg D rules, the SEC's antifraud provisions apply. This leads most issuers to voluntarily make relevant disclosures to safeguard against later charges by disgruntled investors that they were not informed of all material facts.

Uniform Limited Offering Exemption (ULOE)

At the time Reg D was adopted by the SEC, it was planned that the various state legislative bodies would adopt uniform parallel exemptions from blue-sky laws. This continues to be promoted by the North American Securities Administrators Association in the Uniform Limited Offering Exemption (ULOE). Progress is not as fast as was hoped. Some states have implemented the revisions or modifications of them, but a majority of states are still only considering ULOE in their securities commissions or legislative bodies. Legal counsel of a company should be able to advise on the current status in the state the company is concerned with.

Regulation D may be the answer to many an entrepreneur's dreams. But because of the contradictory nature of some of the rules, well-versed legal counsel should be considered a necessity.

Summary

The intent of Regulation D was and remains a very good one. It has made raising money for small businesses a lot less cumbersome, less expensive, less time consuming, and less restricted than previous regulations. However, it is still not law in all states.

In many states today, an issuer of securities still must register them with the Securities and Exchange Commission unless an applicable exemption from registration is available. Regulation D contains the kind of exemptions that many small business persons have been looking for. These exemptions can easily be used in private or limited offerings. But the final authority on the employment of Regulation D has been left to the individual states and their blue-sky laws.

When the various states' securities commissions and their respective legislatures rework their blue-sky laws to integrate the benefits inherent in Regulation D, it could prove to be a boon to small companies seeking investment financing. Meanwhile, it behooves entrepreneurs to investigate their states' blue-sky laws and consider them carefully prior to starting fund-raising under Reg D. They should also consider rereading this chapter.

19

Alternate Methods of Private Financing

The enactment of Regulation D in 1982 simplified and facilitated the registration process for selling securities. That's a good reason for entrepreneurs to strongly consider Rule 504 of Regulation D, or state equivalents, for fund-raising efforts as an alternate to an IPO—if they can qualify for the exemptions.

Actually, there are a number of rules and exemptions that are worth looking into for the same reason. They can be found under the headings of intrastate offerings, Regulation A offerings, offerings under Section 4 (2), and offerings under Section 4 (6).

As pointed out in the last chapter, the principal advantage of an exemption from registration is that the buy and sell transaction can take place as soon as the parties decide to proceed. It eliminates the necessity of preparing and filing a prospectus, and it saves legal costs, plus accounting and registration fees.

Exemptions under the '33 act are listed as exempted securities and exempted transactions. They can save both time and money. The only drawback is they take a legal genius to interpret them. They're full of loopholes, and the courts have shown no qualms about ruling *against* the entrepreneur in their interpretations. Regardless, the end results should make them worth pursuing. But since the whole area of exemptions is so complex, the entrepreneur should not proceed without first seeking the advice of qualified legal counsel to determine the best form of exemption to apply for. Here's what the exemptions do:

Exempted Securities

Section 3(a) of the '33 act exempts a number of securities because of the particulars of the issuer. For example, federal, state, and local governments are exempted so as not to hamper their ability to secure financing. Religious, charitable, educational, and nonprofit organizations are exempted. Also exempted are securities that do not present a substantial risk to the investor, such as short-term notes, drafts, bills of exchange, and insurance policies (except variable annuities).

Exempted Transactions

Section 4 exempts certain transactions from the provisions of Section 5, which says, in effect, that a registration with the SEC must take place every time a security is sold. Exempted are transactions by any person other than an issuer (company), underwriter, or dealer. This is aimed at ordinary daily stock stales by the shareholder. For example, if Mr. Jones owns 100 shares of IBM, he does not have to register the transaction of selling it to his broker.

Section 4 exempts transactions by an issuer not involving any public offering (the private sale exemption). This is an extremely complex area. It is meant to exempt the owner of a business who is selling his or her business to another person or a small number of persons (fewer than 25).

Section 4 permits broker/dealers to trade for their own account, or as brokers for others (retail customers) without registration.

Some transactions are allowable for brokers to make without going through the whole registration process, such as those covered in Rule 144, which allows a broker to sell privately held securities of a public company after they have been held for the required holding period. This covers the sale of restricted stock without the requirement of registration.

At the beginning of this chapter we mentioned other rules and exemptions that are worth looking into. They're also worth going into in more detail:

Intrastate Offerings

This exemption falls under Section 3(a) (11) and Rule 147. It exempts certain offerings from the registration requirements of the '33 act. It refers to "Any security which is a part of an issue offered and sold only to persons resident within a single State or Territory, where the issuer of such security is a person resident and doing business within, or if a corporation, incorporated by and doing business within, such State or territory."

The SEC makes clear that the intrastate exemption is "intended to apply only to issues genuinely local in character, which represent local financing by local industries, carried out through local investment." It puts complete responsibility on the company to ascertain the residency of each and every purchaser. It's specific in that the selling of a single share out of state during the distribution periods may result in the entire issue being considered a violation of the '33 act. Good faith on the issuer's part that the purchaser is a resident is no defense when it comes to the company's liability.

Briefly, the intrastate exemptions specify:

- The offerings are allowed in only one state.
- The issuer must be a resident of the state.
- The issuer do the majority of its business in the state.
- There are no dollar amount restrictions.
- Financial sophistication of investors is not required.
- There are no SEC filing requirements.

Lest there be any confusion, the issuer, if a person (sole proprietorship, partnership), or if a company (incorporated), must be resident in the state in which the securities are being offered. This means that the principal office *must* be located in the state.

To further clarify, *doing business* in the state is interpreted as deriving at least 80 percent of the company's consolidated gross revenues within the state, with at least 80 percent of its consolidated assets located within the state, and intending, and in fact using, 80 percent of the net proceeds derived from its offering in the state.

There are also *no* restrictions as to the total dollar amount of monies that can be raised or as to the individual amounts that can be subscribed for. And there are *no* restrictions as to the number of investors that can subscribe to the offering. However, it must be stressed, the rules are strict that every investor *must* be a resident of and maintain his or her principal residence in the state.

The original purchaser/resident investor must also be made aware that he or she may not resell the securities until the distribution is complete, and the securities, according to the SEC, "come to rest in the hands of the resident investors." What's more, a precedent has been established in the courts that all of the stock must stay in the original state for as long as 1 to 2 years—depending on the court. That means if Ms. Smith, the purchaser resident of the stock, decides to move out of the state before the waiting period has passed, she, legally, cannot take the stock out of the state, as that would be construed as an interstate purchase rather than an intrastate purchase.

It is the responsibility of the issuer to (1) obtain a written statement from each purchaser confirming the purchaser's residence, and (2) place a legend on the certificate or other document attesting that the securities have not been registered under the '33 act. The legend must also set forth the limitations on resale (as presented in the above paragraphs). If the issuer transfers its own securities, stop transfer instructions must be issued to the transfer agent, or the issuer must make proper notations to the effect in its own records.

It is most important that the issuer disclose in writing the limitations on resale and include the legend and notation requirements in connection with any offer (prospectus) or sales of the securities in question. Substitute certificates must carry the same information.

A word of assurance is in order. If the issuer can prove he or she acted with diligence on the above matters, it's unlikely that the '33 act would be interpreted harshly by the courts.

As far as financial sophistication is concerned, there is no requirement. The company (issuer) has *no* responsibility to ascertain that the purchaser of its securities is a savvy investor. There are *no* accredited or nonaccredited investor rules. Furthermore, the disclosure requirements are nonrestrictive, and the amount of disclosure is strictly left up to the individual issuer. Naturally, the standard provisions for fraud, misstatements, and the omission of material information *do* apply.

Referring to the above, an SEC filing is not required. The issuer must only comply with the individual state's securities rules and regulations.

Finally, because of the leniency for intrastate offerings, some financial promoters create intrastate "shells." They then sit on them for a year or two, after which they try to sell them to entrepreneurs as public company shells. That could spell trouble! These shells, although they are public, are only public in one state. If the purchaser (entrepreneur) intends to broaden the securities shareholder base to other states or intends to conduct business in other states, a registration will have to be made with the SEC, which is time consuming and can be very expensive. (See chapter 38.)

Regulation A Offerings

Regulation A is seldom used, mainly because in some instances, depending on the dollar amount of the issue, it requires registration with the SEC. Regulation A is available to all issuers except investment companies or issuers of fractional undivided oil and gas interests or other mineral rights.

It provides exemption from registration for up to $1 million in a 12-month period. Reg A also contains "bad boy" provisions, which prohibit "use of the exemption if the issuer, its underwriters, or any of the directors, officers, or principals have engaged in certain specified acts of misconduct."

Reg A has *no* restrictions on the qualifications of the investor (accredited or nonaccredited) or on the number of investors. Additionally, there are *no* restrictions on the resale of the securities, and an issuer can do some forms of advertising and general solicitation. An offering circular is required unless the total offering is less than $100,000, and the offering must be filed with the regional office of the SEC. This registration requires submission of 2 years of financial statements, but they do not need to be audited. However, under blue-sky laws, most states require audited financials.

Another reason Reg A is used infrequently is one of its sections that refers to "sterilized" stock. It deals primarily with the issuer (company) that has been in existence for less than 1 year prior to the offering, but has not realized a net income from the operations. It also concerns an issuer that was organized for more than 1 year, but has had no net income for at least 1 of the last 2 fiscal years. It says, in effect, that all securities issued to promoters, directors, officers, underwriters, dealers, and securities salespersons must be counted as part of the monies that constitute the offering. Otherwise the stocks must be placed in "captivity" (sterilized and not useable). It makes for too many unhappy people among the principal performers.

Section 4(2) (Soon to Be Replaced by Rule 506 in Reg D)

This is a subtle kind of exemption that has been used as an alternate for raising private capital. It has been used by the likes of IBM and General Motors. They use this kind of exemption for spin-offs to form subsidiaries or to make special investments, without having to go through a whole Regulation D process. With Section 4(2) they only are required to file a few sheets of paper. It's a very short form of filing for a highly sophisticated investment. As a rule, the investors who buy the stock are very sophisticated investors who understand the whole process. To further clarify Section 4(2):

- The exemption is only available on an offering made exclusively to persons able to fend for themselves, with access to the same kind of information available in a registration statement.

- It is the sophistication of each offeree (subscriber) that determines whether that condition of the exemption is met.

Section 4(6) (Now Replaced by Rule 505 in Reg D)

This is also a specialized kind of exemption, and it is used primarily for sophisticated investments. For the issuer it means:

- Sell only to accredited investors.
- Maximum sought is $5 million.
- No public solicitation is permitted.
- Filing is made on Form D.
- Requires no disclosure documents. By way of example, Company A goes to Company B, an automobile maker, and says it is working on a system that will computerize an entire car. The company needs $5 million to proceed. That is all it is willing to tell Company B. Company B knows Company A and accepts the explanation. It invests in Company A. Because Company B is considered a sophisticated investor, a disclosure document is not required.
- The $5 million cannot be a part of other offerings that took place in the previous 12 months. That would be considered "integrated" by the SEC, and is not allowed.
- Previous offenders of SEC regulations ("bad boys") can use this exemption. It is also available to investment companies as issuers who have been offenders.

Avoiding Integration

Entrepreneurs (issuers) using Regulation D or one of the alternate methods of private financing are exempted from many SEC rules, but they can't have their cake and eat it too. Some proposed public companies have attempted to use a private exemption *intrastate* and then made a public offering *interstate*. If the offerings are found to be a part of the same transaction, that's a definite no no. They must be completely separate transactions.

An offering may be considered exempt in isolation, but it becomes nonexempt if integration is determined due to its being connected with other offerings. The SEC knows all the tricks. If there is the remotest possibility that an exemption may be misconstrued because of an offering made at a later date, the transactions could be considered integrated. The best way to avoid this is to secure the advice of qualified legal counsel regarding integration and multistep financing plans. Or it could easily result in a lot of time, effort, and money down the drain.

Summary

There are alternate methods to Regulation D under the '33 act that offer exemptions from the rules and regulations of the SEC (see table 19.1). They fall in the categories of exempted securities and exempted transactions. Certain issuers of securities are exempted, and certain transactions are exempted. Also, under Rule 504 of Reg D, alternate methods of private offerings are exempted. They are intrastate and Regulation A. However, they are considered too restrictive for secondary or long-term financing.

TABLE 19.1

Comparative Table

Item	504	505	506	Intrast	Reg A	Sec 4.6
Dollar limit	1 million	5 million	None	None	1.5 million	5 million
Financial Statements	No	Varies	Varies	No	2 yrs unaud	No
Number of Purchasers	No	35 nonaccd	See 505	No	No	No
Qualification for Purchasers	No	No	For nonaccd	All resident	No	All accd
Resale Restrictions	Yes	Yes	Yes	Yes	No	Yes
Disclosure Requirements	None	Only accd	Only accd	None	Yes	None
Qualification for Issuer	No invstmt cos	No	No	Resident	No invstmt cos	No
Solicit & Advertise	Varies	No	No	No	No	No

NOTE: The above chart refers to the rules and regulations covered in chapter 18 (Regulation D) and chapter 19 (Alternate Methods of Private Financing).

When used for fund-raising as represented, these exemption provisions can save a great deal of time and a great deal of money for the issuer. However, they require extremely qualified legal counsel to interpret them and to guide the issuer through them. An offering can easily become nonexempt if integrated with other transactions. It could then be voided by the SEC.

The pitfalls are many . . . but so are the rewards.

20

Due Diligence

Due diligence refers to the process that must be complied with prior to an offering being made to the public. The purpose is to ensure that the company has complied with all the legal requirements established by the SEC. This includes examining and confirming that the corporate records, financial statements, and background information about the company preparing to go public are honest and correct.

Part of the due diligence process includes what has often been referred to as corporate cleanup. This could be likened to kicking the tires of a car you're thinking of buying. It amounts to the broker/dealer checking out the background of the entrepreneur, the company, and the people who will be running it. This is also the time when the broker makes sure that the company is ready to go public and is a good investment prospect for customers. Due diligence and corporate cleanup are interrelated, and as long as they are accomplished, it doesn't make much difference which comes first.

Legal Responsibility

Actually, the burden of complying with the due diligence process usually falls on SEC legal counsel. It is their responsibility to list, gather, and authenticate things such as articles of incorporation, bylaws, patents, the completeness and correctness of corporate minutes, and other information related to corporate documents. And strange as it may sound, they must also verify that the company exists. Read on:

In the early 1980s an IPO was handled by a major New York underwriter. It was backed by a major accounting firm and a prestigious Wall

Street law firm. The offering raised over $20 million through a series of private and public financings. But as it turned out, the company never existed. It seems that the small group of corporate officers of the "company" (primarily a husband-and-wife team) completely fabricated this nonexistent company, including a brief and illustrious historical and operating track record. For a year or so, they created a continuing operations record. They invented financials and sales from an office that was never visited by any of the underwriters, accountants, or attorneys. After the completion of the public offering, the company supposedly showed revenues in the millions of dollars, but, in fact, the company was strictly a paper company.

Naturally, the "experts" were very embarrassed, their insurance companies were quite disappointed, the public shareholders were outraged, and the operating principals were incarcerated.

Many stories abound of "black boxes" that were figments of the imagination of enterprising entrepreneurs. There are also hundreds of stories about precious mineral or oil and gas claims, and shopping center sites on swampland that were plain and simple scams.

Part of the due diligence activity of legal counsel must be to make a "familiarization visit" to the company's offices or plant site. And, of course, to charge travel time. More practically, competent legal counsel will assemble a due diligence file that will be maintained for review by the underwriter's counsel, audit accountants, and in some cases, the SEC. It should contain the following information:

1. Articles of incorporation (amendments) and those of subsidiaries

2. Bylaws and those of subsidiaries

3. Annual reports up to 5 years

4. Proxy statements and proxies up to 5 years

5. Letters from auditors up to 5 years

6. Legal counsel letters to auditors up to 5 years

7. Distributor and sales representative agreements

8. Listing of representatives by name and original contract date

9. Sales agreements and standard contracts

10. Stock option plans

11. Employment agreements

12. List of materials contracts, names, dates, terms

13. Officer and director questionnaires

14. Any other information management believes would be pertinent

Access must be provided to the following:

1. Minute books of company and subsidiaries

2. Terms of short-term financing agreements

3. Records of long-term debt

4. Copies of debentures and agreements

5. Leases

6. All materials contracts

7. Patents and licenses

8. Selling materials for last 5 years

9. Any other terms, agreements, contracts, or purchases that management may deem pertinent to their business

Legal counsel may also take it upon themselves to perform due diligence in other areas, such as notation of phone calls and written requests in an attempt to substantiate personal resumes and references of the management team. They may perform credit investigation and other background checks on management. They may contact key customers and suppliers and request copies of purchase orders sent to or received by the company.

Most of the above information sought by legal counsel may never be included in their findings. The main purpose for gathering it is to have the information available should it be requested by the SEC.

Corporate Cleanup

Corporate cleanup could actually be considered an extension of due diligence. Its purpose is to clarify, for the record, corporate transactions that are common in a privately held company. Another objective of corporate cleanup is to assure that the management team remains operative, that it will continue to be in control of the company and work together for its future success.

The process of cleaning up the corporate structure may necessitate the consolidation of several of the company's operations, partnerships, or various corporations that are under the company's ownership and control, which may mean merging them into one corporation. This could become a considerable undertaking—especially for an existing company with a lengthy operating history. Corporate cleanup could also encompass real estate purchases, mergers, acquisitions, liquidations, capital contributions, and stock exchanges.

Another area that commonly falls under corporate cleanup is employment agreements with employees, management, and company officers. This may require dissolving some existing agreements, entering into new or revised ones, changing some of the compensation terms, and even issuing replacement of stock or new stock options.

Cleanup might also involve restructuring loans to or from officers and directors. It could also amount to no more than executing formal promissory notes where none existed before or establishing interest payments that are more in line with present common market rates. If such existing loans were to show bias, they could be found in violation of state laws; hence they cannot be carried into a public company.

Occasionally it becomes appropriate to remove some personal assets that are deemed not legitimate enough to be carried on the company's books, such as resort properties, autos, planes, or the CEO's favorite yacht. Making this information public can pose unwanted tax problems to the principals involved and may require a reissuing of the financial statements. However, eliminating these items from the company books not only saves the company money, it prevents shareholders from charging corporate waste.

Other important areas that need cleaning up before the company becomes public are the adoption of defenses against hostile takeover attempts ("shark repellents") and the limiting of liability clauses ("golden parachutes"). They would more than likely require changes in the corporate charter (bylaws) or articles in order to comply with SEC rules. In a private company, a simple phone call, a letter, or a lunch meeting is usually all that's necessary to make a change in the bylaws. However, once the company is public these actions require shareholder approval, which could not only take months to accomplish, but mean considerable extra cost to comply with the stringent SEC public company proxy rules. Obviously, this process would be less expensively accomplished when there are only a few private shareholders as opposed to hundreds of public shareholders after the company has gone public.

Back to the ever-present concern about hostile takeovers. One way to deter or defeat unwelcome tender offers is to adopt staggered multiyear terms for directors. This assures that the *very key directors* are continued over extended periods by electing, for example, two directors for 3 years, two for 2 years, and three for 1 year at *each* annual election. This approach is considered a pretty safe shark repellent.

Instituting "golden parachutes" provisions can also serve to protect employment benefits. They can include favorable severance settlements for key management in case of unfriendly takeover or an abrupt change of control by merger or acquisition.

It should be noted that more and more states are approving or revising laws that limit officers' and directors' liabilities. And it is mandatory that the company adopt the most current state laws. A word of advice: A company incorporated in a very conservative state should entertain the idea of reincorporating in a state with a more liberal set of state laws.

Another thing that bears considering is the fact that too many defensive bylaws, such as golden parachutes, turn away some underwriters, especially on larger offerings. Their attitude is that these can make the issue more difficult to sell, as they create suspicion, and therefore make the issue unattractive to public investors. Also, there are a few states that may disqualify the offering as not in compliance with the blue-sky laws. Although smaller companies are not bothered as much by these issues as larger companies, management should be aware of them and should consider the pros and cons with the SEC legal counsel regarding their particular circumstances.

As a safeguard against possible litigation, legal counsel must also be expected to review all contracts for unusual provisions; inspect loan agreements for restrictive clauses; review IRS audits; and examine employee benefits and pension plans for compliance with ERISA (Employee Retirement Income Security Act), which sets standards for retirement and pension accounts. They should also be responsible for checking federal, state, and local compliance on anything from hazardous wastes to zoning.

Accounting Due Diligence

As mentioned in chapter 8, strict adherence to due diligence procedures is required on the part of the accountants for a public company. The accountant is responsible for reviewing all purchases, invoices, and canceled checks and must provide assurances that the company's financial statements are fair and correct. The audit accountants must follow the guidelines of Regulation S–X which deals with the form and content of financial statements and their ultimate certification. They must also comply with GAAP, the generally accepted accounting principles (see chapter 8 for details) for presenting audit information. The accountant must then make certain that the company complies with the Foreign Corrupt Practices Act (FCPA), which helped to strengthen accounting standards.

If the accountant concludes that management's internal accounting controls are noticeably weak, due diligence must be intensified or the *accountant* can be held accountable under the Securities Act of 1933.

The SEC must rely on the validity and authenticity of the accountant's audited financial statements that are included in the registration statement. This puts the responsibility on the accountant to perform a "reasonable" investigation, and ultimately to provide "comfort" letters (assuring letters) to the SEC and underwriters, which list very specific procedures they have performed . . . and then, all is well.

Dual Responsibilities

Since a number of areas of due diligence and corporate cleanup can be designated the responsibility of either legal counsel or accounting, a company's management usually has to make a decision as to who does what. For example, both legal and accounting can become involved in pension plans. Lawsuits, warranty disputes, and employee-union relations differences could also involve legal as well as accounting issues.

Summary

Due diligence and corporate cleanup are considered separate actions, but they are, in reality, part of the same process. Where due diligence investigates the correctness of legal records and the fairness of financial statements, corporate cleanup sets them right. They are, in essence, uncovered by due diligence and corrected through corporate cleanup. Due diligence points the gun, corporate cleanup pulls the trigger. You can't do one without the other.

It is the responsibility of both the legal counsel and accountants to give assurances to the SEC that all regulations have been complied with, that the company going public is a viable company, and that the registration statement and prospectus are correct. At that point, after satisfying the underwriter and the SEC, the selling of the offering can proceed.

21

Private Financing

Prior to a public offering, entrepreneurial financing of brand-new start-up companies has been known to come from any number of sources—from grandma's cookie jar to funds solicited from friends or rich relatives. Some came in for a piece of the action, some as a loan, and some as both. Start-ups are often financed in three stages: pre-private, private, and—the final stage—the initial public offering (IPO).

Pre-private

Pre-private financing usually takes place during a company's formation stage. First, the entrepreneur and the prospective management team formulate a business plan. They identify the key team players, design a prototype product or service, and, it is hoped, have substantial market research available. The next step would be to legally form the company and then devote the time and attention that must be given to the intended business and, more important, to the more formal fund-raising process.

Pre-private financing could take the form of debt, equity, or a combination of both. The amount to ask for depends on what is necessary to get the show on the road. It could be as small as $5 (for a Kool-Aid stand) to $10,000 to as much as $100,000. The use of the proceeds should be calculated to provide bare-bones financing for the initial incorporation and legal costs, and for limited company operations. Enough should be included to offset the necessities and cost of having to raise additional capitalization the first go-around.

Typically, the providers of this founders' financing are the members of the management team and close family and friends. In order for the company to be legally prepared to receive those funds, there should be a legal agreement between the parties. It need only be a simple preincorporation or presubscription agreement. As a hypothetical explanation: the entrepreneur tells the money source about this great idea for a company that's going to be started but needs money to get it going. For $5,000 (or whatever amount) the potential investor will be given an agreement that gives him or her an undiluted percentage of the company. Based on the investor's reliance on the entrepreneur's intentions, the investor agrees to give $5,000 for x *percent* of the company. This is called a preincorporation or presubscription agreement. Often, the founders, if other than the management team, are offered options to further their equity positions.

The risk/reward ratio at this level of financing is obviously very high. At the time, the company may not have completed its business plan or comprehensive market research; may not have completely developed, tested, or market-tested its product or service; and may not yet have a fully identified, much less working management team. All of these uncertainties make the company a high-risk investment, and the pricing of its stock or terms of its debt should reflect this. So, depending on the total amount invested, a 5 percent to 20 percent value of the intended public offering price would not be unreasonable.

For the entrepreneur, a brand-new, clean corporation makes an ideal IPO. From an accounting standpoint, there is nothing to audit, which means spending a minimum of time and expense. From a legal perspective, there is nothing to refer back to as the company is structured from scratch. Its articles and bylaws will reflect it is "to be" a public company. (Refer to chapter 13.)

If pre-private financing is necessary for a company already in existence, it would be best handled as a debt with options attached and with provisions to convert it to equity. That eliminates a lot of the complications involved in corporate cleanup.

Private

Private financing is the second step taken in a company's financial organization on its way to achieving an initial public offering.

The second-level private financing is undertaken after the formation (pre-private) stage is completed, both in the company's operations and its overall financing scheme. By the time the pre-private financing has been accomplished, a detailed business plan should be substantially completed. The company's product, if it is new, should have gone beyond its design stage and its first- or second-generation prototype. If the company is a service company, then a very limited beta test should have been performed (a survey that gives an indication of the volatility that can be expected from this type of issue compared to the movement of the market in general). Or, at a minimum, a number of interviews with potential users of the service will have taken place. Also, key management people should be in position to come on board full time. In all probability, the CEO is already devoting full time to the company.

At this juncture, the business will have been incorporated to fit a public company status, and an SEC-qualified legal counsel retained. At minimum, identification of, if not the retention of, an SEC-qualified accountant has been finalized and the firm involved in setting up the corporation's books to meet SEC accounting requirements.

The period between private fund-raising and an IPO is the time used by management to get everything in place in anticipation of the IPO. It is a tough time for key management. Although they may not be on board full time as yet, there always seems to be a myriad of things to be done. These are activities that might involve management team development, facilities identification, completion of a detailed business plan, preparing a comprehensive marketing plan, coordinating and supplying information to legal counsel, as well as compiling a list of investors from which to solicit private financing.

This is also a time of helplessness, because the company cannot pursue its primary reason for existence, namely, to produce a product or service and start operating. It's the lull before the storm. But it is a critical time, as all necessary documents must be assembled to complete the registration statement. And all areas of planning must be diligently pursued and reworked if necessary.

One of the major tasks and objectives of the company at this point is preparing for and obtaining the public underwriting. Consequently, the primary use of the monies will be to put together a prospectus, and also to supply bare-bones financing for the corporation.

On the corporate level, the proceeds will be used to pay key executive staff salaries; to obtain minimum office space (probably with small office equipment rentals); to provide for stationery, phones, and minimal daily operating expenses; and to initiate the hiring of administrative staff.

On the financing side, one of the most expedient ways to procure private financing would be to use Regulation D and follow the format for a public registration statement. In reality, the Reg D private placement document, which has probably been written as a 504 (considered to be one of the most workable exemptions for small offerings), contains 90 percent of the information required for a registration statement. The portions that will change between the private offering and a public registration are additions to the board, an accurate identification of the management team members, the inclusion of audited financial statements, the identification of permanent office or manufacturing facilities, and internal progress reports on the company's product or service development.

More than likely the pre-private financing was obtained in exchange for equity or as a debt, possibly as convertible debt. If that was the case, an effort should be made to pay some or all of the debt from the private financing proceeds. Here's how it could work: If the equity on the pre-private agreement amounted to 5 percent to 20 percent of the intended IPO valuation (that is, ½ to 20 cents per share on $1.00 IPO), the private financing will be offered at a 25 percent to 40 percent valuation of the IPO offering price (that is, 25 to 40 cents on a $1.00 IPO). This level of IPO discount acknowledges to the private investor the high-risk nature of the investment, while offering a higher than normal potential return for purchasing restricted securities.

Generally, $50,000 to $300,000 is raised in a private offering. Reg D allows up to $500,000, but consideration should be given to the amount of equity that was raised in any pre-private financing. These amounts may have to be deducted from the $500,000 cap to avoid integration, which is not allowed by the SEC. This is one area where money talks.

Summary

Before going through the expense of an IPO, the entrepreneur may find it necessary to defray some of the costs by first seeking private offerings. He or she would then use that money to offset the costs of going public and still have capital that would enable the company to continue at a minimal existence level until the IPO is completed. This can be accomplished through pre-private and private financing.

Pre-private is a "friendly" borrowing of money to take the company through its formation stage. Private financing, which is usually used to keep the company operating until it goes public, is state and government regulated. For entrepreneurs these can be considered survival kits to keep them in business until they become a business.

22

Underwriters

The primary goals when going public are to have a successful offering; to receive a fair price for the stock; and to have a stable, liquid aftermarket trading in the stock. The *underwriter's* responsibility is to assure that these goals are achieved.

There is nothing to prevent a company from acting as its own underwriter. There are no set rules or regulations. (See chapter 23.) However, the business of selling securities is so specialized, it is best left to the acknowledged specialists in the field.

Underwriters are sometimes referred to as investment bankers. In fact, on their calling cards, almost all are listed as investment bankers. But for our purposes, and from a practical point of view, they are underwriters. Their main function is to underwrite stock issues, whereas conventional investment bankers are known to perform a variety of services involving the raising of capital. Underwriters usually represent a firm, a broker/ dealer that specializes in underwriting securities. In simple terms, that means they buy a company's stock from the company, or take it and sell it to other dealers or the investing public.

Choosing an underwriter has occasionally been likened to choosing a spouse. Management is looking to establish a relationship of mutual confidence, respect, and trust. There is also a little bit of love/hate involved in it. Nonetheless, during the IPO process, the two teams invariably build a close personal relationship that, it is to be hoped, will flourish for years to come.

The underwriter who leads or heads an IPO is given the title of managing underwriter. It's the responsibility of the managing underwriter to form a selling syndicate or group of other investment bankers (broker/ dealers) that will participate in the distribution of the securities. Conse-

155

quently, the selection of the right managing underwriter is critical from the start. The company's reputation will ultimately ride on the managing underwriter. In turn, his or her reputation on the street, and successes and failures reflect on the company.

Types of Underwriters

The types and nature of underwriters have varied over the course of financial history. From the market's inception through the mid 1950s, underwriting represented the principle source of income for securities companies. Since then, because of the unsteadiness of the stock market, the majority of underwriters have come to operate as broker/dealers and enjoy a mix of income from underwriting fees and stock commissions. They no longer draw a distinction between wholesale, retail, or a combination of the two. The only distinction shows itself in larger firms that have departmentalized separate divisions for wholesale and retail. In either case, the game is the same.

Wholesale

Traditionally, the wholesale investment banking firm was a separate entity from retail investment banking. It did not cater to the general public or individual investor, but concentrated its efforts on distributing large blocks of stock to retail firms. Those wholesale investment bankers that exist today are specialized underwriters who make large financial commitments to place large blocks of stock with institutional investors. They also put together large selling syndicates among broker/dealers.

Retail

Retail broker/dealer firms traditionally relied on wholesalers to put together IPOs. They functioned primarily as participants in the selling syndicates. Their retail brokers sold and distributed stocks to their individual private retail investors.

In the past, the size of an underwriter's firm was thought to be related to the affiliation with the issuer. The larger the firm, the more committed the relationship. Because of that general feeling, the National Association of Securities Dealers (NASD) conducted a study that attempted to determine if being associated with a larger underwriter's firm was more beneficial to the new IPO. The study questioned whether a directorship or continuing advisory position was part of the underwriting agreement. The results follow:

Large-size Firms

These are national firms, often with hundreds of brokerage offices located across the country, with thousands of individual retail brokers with millions of individual personal accounts. Their IPO interests are exclusively underwritings totaling $15 million and over. Many of the underwriting clients are *Fortune* 1000 companies, with an emphasis on the top 500. Their main involvement is the issuing of secondary financings. These large firms usually have extensive investment banking departments that can supply help and expertise on anything from initial financing to large institutional private placements for both debt and equity, to mergers, acquisitions, leveraged buy-outs, and sophisticated merchant banking functions. They can operate on a local, national, or international level. The NASD survey found that 43 percent of these large firms had financial advisory relationships with their public offering clients and were on a retainer basis with many of them.

Medium-size Firms

For the most part, these are regional firms, serving a limited geographical area, often with a dozen or so branches and a few hundred brokers. Many operate in a single state, or in a group of states that are defined as a region. They are primarily interested in IPOs in the $5 million to $15 million range from established companies with a profitable operating history. Their investment banking departments usually offer full service, but with less depth in personnel and experience than the larger firms. The NASD study revealed that only 14 percent of the medium-size firms had a financial advisory relationship with their IPOs.

Small-size Firms

There are fewer small-size firms operating today than in the recent past. The economics of operating a small firm with a full back office to serve retail customer needs is simply not financially justifiable. Consequently, many have merged or been acquired and integrated into one of the medium-size firms. Those that remain are boutique-type firms that usually specialize in particular areas of business or low-priced OTC stocks. Most small firms do not have specific investment banking departments or personnel other than the multiple-skilled owners. Their IPOs are usually smaller in size (up to $5 million). The NASD survey showed that less than 8 percent of the small firms had any continuing financial advisory relationship with their IPOs.

Industrial Classification

There are many underwriting firms scattered throughout the country that specialize in industrial offerings, often for specific industries. They usually work with established selling syndicate groups that share their interest in a particular industry. Although they don't limit themselves to a particular size offering, most of them tend to concentrate on regional and smaller firms. They know the territory and they know the industries. For example, in the Midwest, agriculturally oriented IPOs receive the greatest interest. In California, high-tech industries are in favor. In the Northeast, there has been a long-standing love affair with medical issues.

For the entrepreneur, there are definite advantages in establishing a relationship with an underwriter who has a proven track record in a particular industry. For one thing, the company's management doesn't have to spend a lot of time educating the underwriters or brokers about its industry. In addition, the selling syndicates know how to reach the investors who are inclined to purchase stocks in a particular industry. There are, however, drawbacks to be considered. Since these underwriters specialize in particular industries, there is always a possibility of a conflict of interest. So entrepreneurs need to use their best business judgment in deciding who to go with. It pays to do a little research into the IPOs the underwriter has handled in the past 5 years. Nevertheless, the underwriter's base knowledge and understanding of the industry can save a great deal of time and educational effort.

Types of Underwritings

As we have mentioned earlier, there are two basic types of underwritings, *firm commitments* and *best efforts*. Both can have an option variable.

Firm Commitments

Firm commitments are the most desirable kind of underwriting. As the term implies, the underwriter agrees to make a firm commitment to purchase the entire amount of the company's stock issue regardless of its ability to resell the securities to the public. In actuality, the selling of the stock to the public by the syndicate members is a foregone conclusion. The stocks are usually presold before any signing takes place. However, if the underwriter or syndicate members misjudged and can't resell the securities, they simply buy them in their own account and sell them at a later date. This assures the issuing company that it will receive a set amount of dollars at a set date, usually 5 to 7 days after the effective date of registration. Of course, there is a high level of risk involved for the underwriter, but this type of underwriting is normal for most large and regional firms.

Often, underwriters issuing a firm commitment agreement will request an overallotment option, known as a *green shoe* (see chapter 31). This is the variable option for firm commitments. The green shoe allows the underwriter to purchase a specific number of additional shares of the company's stock, usually 10 percent to 15 percent of the total issue.

Best Efforts

This type of agreement states that the underwriter will extend its best efforts to sell the company's stock, but does not agree to purchase the unsold securities for its own account. In effect, the underwriter is acting as an agent of the issuer or company. Best efforts are not as desirable as a firm commitment, but it's the agreement most commonly used for low-priced IPO issues. Large underwriters don't do best efforts agreements, and they are seldom done by regional underwriters.

Options

Some best efforts agreements come with a variable option referred to as all or none. It specifies that the underwriter must sell the whole transaction or the entire amount of the issue will be canceled. There can be no partial sales. Today all or none is being replaced in many agreements with a mini/max, or minimum/maximum, clause. This allows the company to determine a medium dollar amount of an offering. Let's say the offering is for $2 million. The minimum is then set at $1.7 million, with a maximum set at $2.3 million. That means if the underwriter raises $1.9 million in a best effort, the company will accept it as it is above the minimum. Obviously, the goal is to achieve the full amount of $2.3 million. But accepting the medium amount prevents a lot of time and effort being wasted on an unsuccessful all or none underwriting.

Finders

Finders are individuals who serve as intermediaries in bringing together underwriters with companies who wish to go public. Most often they are lawyers, accountants, and management consultants. They play an important role for both sides in introducing clients to underwriters and investment bankers.

That doesn't mean the entrepreneur or prospective IPO management team can't seek out an underwriter directly. It's just that reputable finders can be a major time saver as they command the respect of underwriters. They usually are familiar with underwriters' calendars and schedules, as well as knowing how best to approach the investment banking community. Many underwriters will not even consider an IPO without a finder's recommendation.

The ideal finder not only knows how to present the prospective underwriting to the underwriter/investment banker, but is familiar with the form of corporate structure needed to make the project appealing. An underwriter also expects that the finder will have performed due diligence on the company by investigating its business history, the current condition of all aspects of the company, and the company's future projections and prospects, as well as the background of the management team.

The finder also serves as a bridge between the company and the underwriter. This may come as a surprise, but because of the nature of the financing, few of the smaller underwriters have highly qualified people who can really understand the technical aspects of a company and work closely with the company throughout the underwriting process. While all underwriters may understand the registration and selling process, they don't always comprehend the inner workings of the company. They depend on the finder to bridge the gap. What's more, seldom do they have a continuing interest in the success of the company after the public funding is completed. This is especially true of low-priced issues. For that reason alone, all low-priced issues should strongly consider the retention of a qualified management consultant to be a finder.

Finders' compensation depends on the deal that is cut. Some finders work exclusively for underwriters. They could receive a flat fee, a percentage, warrants, or all of these. If compensation comes from the issuer, it could also be in the form of stock, plus consulting fees. It depends on the role played by the finder and the involvement. But whether fee or percentage—which has been known to range from 1 percent to 15 percent—it should all be in writing, as full disclosure is required in the prospectus by the SEC and NASD.

Shopping

Shopping a deal can often do a company more harm than good. A company planning to go public may put out feelers to a number of prospective underwriters/investment bankers to see if there would be any interest in underwriting the offering. They would be shopping for the best deal. But there are advantages and disadvantages to this practice.

On the one hand, shopping can assist the company in gaining a better understanding of how much the market values the company. If a company shows merit, underwriters are willing to take the time and effort of a preliminary investigation, which will determine whether they would be interested in proceeding and proposing a deal.

If a company is determined to shop, it is best to select three to five prospective underwriters and hold simultaneous preliminary discussions. The company should deal openly with the underwriters and inform them, without revealing names, that it is also talking with other firms. It should be made very clear that the company is exploring the possibility of going public. Be forewarned that underwriters are competitive, but they don't care to get into a bidding war with each other. However, if underwriters feel positive about the company, they will advise the management of their interest and pursue the matter from there.

Now for the bad part. Underwriters hesitate to expend the time and effort required to investigate a proposed project if they don't feel they would be seriously in the running. They may require an exclusivity. Also, if the company shops over an extended period of time and is turned down or receives just moderate indications of interest, word can spread around the street, and could cause irreparable damage to the company's plans. Underwriters have a habit of talking to each other about their business, especially about syndication. When a company exposes itself to an underwriter, chances are the underwriter will test the waters with peers to see if there is any interest in syndication. If prospective selling syndication members have turned down participation in the offering previously, it is very difficult to regain their interest. Also, underwriters/investment bankers don't care to take on a project if they know it has been rejected by some of their peers. The fact that it has been shopped around may force the company to revalue the deal, most likely downward.

Generally speaking, simultaneous shopping should only be considered by major companies when pursuing larger underwriters. It should be very carefully considered when pursuing underwritings for smaller, lower-priced issues. Then again, there are times when entrepreneurs need to rely on their gut feelings.

Underwriter Selection

There are, essentially, four important areas to be considered when selecting an underwriter: performance, experience, distribution, and aftermarket (aftermarket is terminology used to show how the issue has performed following its going public). Each is important and each requires special attention. In the final analysis, however, *compatibility* may rank above them all. The company management team and the underwriting team have to get along if the process is to succeed. All through the underwriting/IPO relationship, each will be testing the other's patience. As mentioned earlier in the book, there are mounds of paperwork on both sides that must be cleaned up. They invariably result in creating one roadblock after another. What it really boils down to is the company wants its money, and the underwriter wants to sell stock. It takes a lot of doing on the part of the entrepreneur/CEO to make sure that the underwriter is completely comfortable with the IPO's progress and does not slack off on his or her end.

Performance

The entrepreneur has an obligation to self and company to select an underwriter that has a good reputation on the street and credibility for putting together strong-selling syndicates. It also pays to inquire about the firm's basic philosophy: Is it aggressive or conservative, and does that stand fit in with the company's goals.

Ask Questions

The process of qualifying and selecting an underwriter should include contacting principals of other IPOs and questioning them regarding their experience and feelings regarding the underwriters being considered. Here are some questions to ask:

1. Were there any last-minute surprises?
2. Were you satisfied with the interest they showed in your company and with their knowledge of your industry?
3. How do you feel about their syndication abilities?
4. Have they maintained an adequate aftermarket interest in your stock?
5. Are you satisfied with the aftermarket performance, and how much do you attribute the price movement to your underwriter's support?
6. Is your underwriter continuing to support your stock through research reports and by soliciting additional market makers?
7. In retrospect, would you use the firm again?
8. Would you recommend it?

Also to be considered in the underwriter selection process is the possibility that the company may, in the future, require additional rounds of financing in the form of debt, equity, or combinations. Management should be satisfied that the potential underwriter can provide this service, as well as offer continuing financial advice that might also encompass mergers and acquisitions.

Before a final decision is made on the choice of an underwriter, the management team should take the time to research the underwriter's performance on previous offerings. This information can be found in the publication *Going Public: The IPO Reporter.* It has information on all the new IPOs and tracks their performance in the aftermarket. Other publications that list recent underwritings in the OTC market, with special emphasis on smaller issues, are *The National OTC Stock Journal* and *The Penny Stock News.* They usually carry semiannual and annual listings of underwriters and underwritings.

Good underwriters are particular too. They must protect *their* reputations, which can be a significant factor in attracting new investors. A top firm very often has underwriting standards that exceed those set by the SEC, NASD, and state requirements.

Distribution

A broad distribution of an IPO's stock is the goal of any company, because it means the stock has been sold to many individual investors in smaller amounts. That usually results in a larger and more stable aftermarket for the securities. Fewer shareholders, holding large blocks of stock, can adversely effect a stock's selling price should they all decide, for whatever reason, to sell their holdings of the stock at the same time.

Most underwriters of larger issues traditionally attract institutional investors. But institutional investors are seldom attracted to low-priced issues. Also, some institutional investors, by policy, do not invest in certain industries. So the company should know in advance if the proposed underwriter's particular institutional investors have any interest in its type of company.

Some underwriters are more sophisticated in assembling selling syndicates than others. They know how to assess their investor makeup and then seek out selling syndicate members that will complement the issue.

If international exposure is important to the company, or if the company plans to sell its product or service to an international market in the future, the company should be sure to make the managing underwriter aware of its plans. Also, if the company has particularly strong geographical areas where its customers or clients are located, the managing underwriter should try to get selling syndicate members who are also located in these communities.

Throughout this process, the company ought to have an idea of the makeup of clients that are trading with the underwriter. Do they have the reputation of being quick turnovers—anxious to dump their stock and move on to the next hot deal—or are they interested in purchasing the stock for long-term investment?

Aftermarket

Once the initial securities are sold, stock movement is important. There needs to be a strong aftermarket performance and perceivable trading activity in the stock. This requires the managing underwriter and, it is to be hoped, all selling syndicate members to expend all their efforts toward making a market in the stock. It means they keep the trading activity going of buying and selling the stock by maintaining inventory in the stock and buying and selling from their own accounts as opposed to just functioning as agents. (See chapter 36.) In addition, the underwriter needs to continue to sell the company to new market makers.

A large part of the aftermarket activity is devoted to maintaining existing shareholders' interest and attracting new shareholders. This can be achieved through cooperation between the market makers and the lead underwriter, who is expected to be able to furnish syndicate members with analysts' research reports about the company. (See chapter 37.) It's the company's responsibility to provide a continuing flow of information to the market maker's analysts. If the underwriter has a reputation for supporting stocks in a particular industry, it's reasonable to assume that the firm's analysts also have a respected reputation on the street for their expertise in that industry.

The Underwriter's Dilemma

The underwriter must make critical judgments on the ability of a company to provide a product or service that profitably fills the needs of its own customers, the investment community. If its judgment is wrong, it can fail also. Testifying to that are the many defunct companies that were taken public by underwriters now defunct largely because of misjudgments in this crucial area. This is especially true regarding low-priced issues, where IPO money has often been referred to as venture capital.

In many cases, entrepreneurs have put together companies that they hoped would fill a product or service void in what was expected to be the next hot industry. The energy industry, especially solar, was a good example of this. The nation has an oil energy crisis, fueled by increasing demand and supposedly limited supply. In the panic, big and small businesses, including the government, jumped into the fray to produce solutions. The general public was primed to look to solar energy as a hot industry. That created a hot demand on the part of investors to get in on the ground floor of what were felt to be the IBMs of a whole new industry. Underwriters were quick to recognize the investor product demand and were very receptive to looking at prospective IPOs with the word *solar* attached. The outcome was predictable. Many of the new companies were not able to fill the customer need economically or efficiently, and, in reality, the customers' needs never truly materialized! Consequently companies failed, and underwriters were left with egg on their faces.

Solar energy is just one extreme example of the underwriter's dilemma. Next it could be steam-powered spacecraft. The industry trends generally stem from news stories about problems looking for solutions, specifically something that could solve a need in our society.

Underwriters are more comfortable when they are interested in a particular product or service for which they would like to do an IPO. An overriding factor is the enthusiasm an underwriter shows for the basic business of a company. The underwriter also wants to feel philosophically in tune with the company. If these factors are met, the underwriter will proceed to qualify the company in four essential areas: management, product or service, finances, and business plan.

Management

This is probably the most important factor in qualifying a company. An assessment is made on the capability, integrity, intelligence, and desire to achieve. The management team members' past performance will be checked, individually and jointly, if they have worked together before. Their successes as well as their failures will be taken into consideration. The underwriter will want answers to such questions as: Does management have personal capital at risk? Are the key management positions filled, that is, chief operation officer, marketing director, financial officer, technical and production personnel? Can they inspire and lead the company's employees? Do they have good management capability?

Product or Service

The underwriter must assess the industry in general. Is it in a fast-growth posture? What is the quality of the product or service and its relationship to the competition? Are the competitors larger or smaller, and is there a defined market niche? How long is the life of the product or service and has a second generation been identified and determined feasible? Can a corporate identity be established? Are there copyright, trademark, patent, or proprietary issues involved? What type of research and development is planned? Has a market plan been developed? Has the product or service been test-marketed?

Finances

The underwriter will conduct a financial review to ascertain how effectively capital has been spent to date. Is the company using financial resources and alternatives to best advantage? What is the current asset, equity, and debt structure? Are there past earnings, and how do they compare to the industry norm? Is the projected growth reasonable? At what level of sales will the break-even point be reached? When will additional capital be needed? Is the financial valuation supported by net earnings projections?

Business Plan

The underwriter will review the business plan to gain insight into the company's business history, products or services, manufacturing or production operations, market analysis, competition, and management. Of course, of primary interest in the business plan is the use of proceeds. A heads-up underwriter will try to make sure the funds received from the proposed IPO will be sufficient to accomplish the company's growth goals and will not be used to fill the pockets of the management team or to bail out key stockholders.

The main purpose for these reviews are to give the issue the best possible chance for success by eliminating all the negative factors. The entrepreneur and the management team should look upon this interrelating and investigative process by the prospective underwriter as a positive approach toward building the confidence and trust so necessary for both sides.

Indirect Costs

Underwriters' warrants come under the heading of indirect costs. They are often issued to the underwriter by the company for little or no cost. It frequently amounts to about 10 percent of the total of the new issue of securities being sold to the public. For example, the underwriter will be given 1 million warrants which carry the rights to purchase 1 million shares of stock if the public issue is for 10 million shares. The underwriter is usually given the rights to purchase these additional shares at a 20 percent premium over the initial offering price. On a $5 new issue, the underwriter would agree to pay $6.00. The warrants are normally exercisable 12 months after the initial effective date. But the exercise period has been known to be extended to as much as 5 years.

Another form of indirect compensation is to agree to give the underwriter a continuing input into the company's operations. This can be by way of a board of director's seat or as a member of the board of advisors. It could be a salaried position or as a consultant under a continuing agreement.

Negotiations

For the edification of the entrepreneur, the terms of an underwriting agreement are always negotiable. This includes the fees, the type and price of the securities being offered, the total size of the offering, the timing, rights for future financings, the states in which the issue will be offered, the composition of the selling syndicates—even the corporate structure of the company and the makeup of the board of directors.

It is not unusual for the actual negotiation process to begin the moment the IPO is presented to the underwriter, and it could continue until the final agreement is signed. That could be the same day, or the day before, the issue is declared effective.

Although there are no set rules or even official guidelines regarding the underwriter's compensation, each individual offering is reviewed by NASD and state securities authorities for fairness to all sides, including the investor. NASD in particular will scrutinize the total amount of compensation and expenses received by the underwriter. It reviews commissions, accountable and nonaccountable expenses, warrants, advisory fees, finders fees, consulting agreements, as well as stocks or securities received. As a rule, it will question compensation that equals or exceeds a value of 15 percent of the total amount of the offering. If it concludes, for whatever reason, that the compensation is excessive, it has the power to bring the proposed underwriting to a complete halt.

NASD is especially cautious of the purchase of the company's securities by officers, partners, managers, and brokers who are affiliated with the underwriting firm. Although these purchases are *not* illegal, NASD may require the owners to agree to restrictions on the resale of their stock. If there is any difference between the amount paid by these individuals and the price set for issuance to the public, NASD may declare the difference as additional underwriting compensation. This could become another negotiating point in reaching an agreement with the underwriter.

Letter of Intent

At some point in the discussions with the underwriter, the company and the underwriter must come to some form of agreement that justifies proceeding further. This comes about in the form of a letter of intent. It is simply an agreement to agree. In practice, it attempts to eliminate as much ground for misunderstanding as possible, especially as to what the parties will eventually agree upon.

With a few exceptions, the letter of intent is a nonbinding agreement. As soon as an underwriter agrees to enter a firm commitment deal, it must set aside a certain amount of its capital to assure that it is financially capable of completing the project. This does not apply to best efforts underwritings. Despite the rules, a final agreement is seldom signed until the day before (after close of market) or the day of the offering.

The binding part of the letter of intent is that the entrepreneur is responsible for the payment of certain costs regardless of whether the underwriting is ultimately completed. This refers to any expenses incurred by the underwriter in preparation of the underwriting.

The contents of the letter of intent are extensive. It covers many points that are agreed upon in the final definitive agreement. What follows is a sample outline for a letter of intent.

Letter of Intent Outline

Introduction. This attests to the fact that preliminary discussions have been held between the company and the underwriter. Based on these discussions, the underwriter agrees in principle to underwrite the proposed public offering in accordance with the terms set forth in the letter of intent.

1. *Representing Counsel.* Identifies the legal counsel for both the underwriter and the company.

2. *Registration Statement.* Specifies the particular form of the statement to be submitted (S–1, S–18, and so forth) along with covering information; establishes the time frame for each aspect of submission, and responsibilities of each party (company and underwriter).

3. *Underwriter's Counsel.* Sets forth areas of responsibility of counsel, such as NASD or state blue-sky filings, the number of registration statements that are required, and the filing fees.

4. *Public Offering.* Affirms decisions reached in the preliminary agreement as to a minimum/maximum amount or range of shares, type of secu-

rity to be offered, as well as the price range. This section also discloses the type of offering—best efforts or firm commitment and indicates the date the offering is expected to be released, extension clauses, escrow agent, and transfer agent designation.

5. *Percentage of Ownership.* Specifies the number of shares to be offered to the public and what the minimum/maximum ranges of percentage of stock ownership will be.

6. *Commencement of Offering.* Usually declares that a bona fide public offering will be made by the underwriter within 3 business days of the effective date of the registration.

7. *Future Sales.* The company pledges not to make any additional sales of its securities without the underwriter's permission for a certain period of time, usually 12 months from the effective date. This clause will also contain certain restrictive covenants regarding the sale of stock by existing shareholders.

8. *Reciprocal Indemnification.* States that the final agreement will provide for reciprocal indemnification by both the underwriter and the company regarding liabilities under the '33 act.

9. *Questionnaire/Information.* Notes specific information that must be supplied by the company to the underwriter.

10. *Litigation.* Declares that either party will inform the other of any litigation or suspension actions by regulatory agencies.

11. *Blue-sky Laws.* Discloses states in which the proposed offering will be registered and who is to handle the registration.

12. *Adverse Change.* This is the underwriter's backing-out clause, which says in effect that it can pull out of the deal, "solely on its own judgment." This is usually invoked in cases where there are material adverse changes in the company's financial or business conditions, or adverse stock market conditions.

13. *Underwriter's Commission.* Sets forth the commission percentage/range the underwriter is to receive.

14. *Expense Allowance.* Determines the nonaccountable and accountable expense reimbursement from the company to the underwriter, including the nonrefundable amounts from deposit.

15. *Underwriter Warrants.* Specifies the intended warrants to be issued to the underwriter and the terms of exercise.

16. *Rights of Refusal.* Affirms the terms regarding the rights of refusal, on the part of the underwriter, for representing the company in future financings.

17. *'34 Act Registration.* Declares that the company will file the required Form 10, which specifies that it must become fully reporting after the completion of the initial offering. (This may not be applicable, depending on the company's or the underwriter's wishes.)

18. *Additional Points.* These can cover any agreed-upon understandings, such as conflict with law; agreements to consolidate, merge, or sell certain subsidiaries or divisions or assets; board of directors positions; on-going consulting agreements; exemptions in certain states; net worth; debt reduction or limitation; and sales figures to be met before or maintained until the underwriting is effective.

19. *Formal Agreement Contemplated.* A statement to the effect that this is a letter of intent and that a definitive agreement will be executed immediately prior to the effective date of the proposed offering.

Note that this generalized outline for the letter of intent is intended for the purposes of assisting the reader in gaining a fuller understanding of the process and should not be considered all-inclusive.

Underwriting Agreement

The definitive underwriting agreement is almost redundant, except for the final stock pricing and the amount of stock to be issued. All of the points have already been thoroughly discussed and agreed upon. The document is usually a formality, signing of which takes place after the market has closed on the day prior to the effective date of the offering. At this last moment, the company still has a legal right to back out of the deal. If it does, however, it becomes responsible for all of the accrued expenses of the offering.

The managing underwriter will also have met previously with all the selling syndicate members, and they will have concluded an *agreement among underwriters.* This document designates the number of shares each has committed to and authorizes the managing underwriter to sign the underwriting agreement with the company on behalf of the syndicate members. Among other items, the agreement among underwriters sets forth the terms of the agreement between the managing underwriter and the selling syndicate members regarding commissions, expenses, and any warrant distributions.

The underwriting agreement itself is an extremely involved document which can number as much as 15 to 20 pages. While these agreements may vary in details, they generally follow a pattern containing numerous warranties, conditions, and covenants that establish the rights and obligations of all the parties. A model outline with brief explanatory notes follows:

Introductions and Definitions

This section introduces and identifies the parties to the underwriter's agreement, and also acknowledges the selling syndicate. The security to be offered is defined as either debt or equity, common or preferred, and the number of shares to be sold are clearly specified.

Representations and Warranties

This provision covers the guarantee by the company that the representations and warranties made by the company regarding the underwriting are true, correct, and complete as of the date the agreement is put into effect. Additionally, the company warrants that it is properly incorporated and accredited. More specifically, the company avows:

- That all outstanding stock is duly authorized, validly issued, fully paid, and nonassessable.
- That it has conformed with the requirements of the '33 act, including the registration statement (with names of the accountants and proof of their independence).
- That the company has the power to issue the new stock.
- That *no* material changes have taken place in the company's capital structure.
- That there are *no* violations in the articles of incorporation, bylaws, or other documents of the company or its subsidiaries.
- That the financial statements present a fair and truthful picture of the company.
- That there are no legal actions pending (unless noted).
- That the company has not attempted and will not attempt to manipulate the stock in any way.
- That the company has not been involved in bribery or made any unlawful political contributions.
- That all trademarks, patents, and so forth are legitimate.

Terms of the Offering

This portion of the underwriter's agreement will not include the offering price of the stock until the actual signing. But it will include the underwriter's pledge to buy and pay for the securities (firm commitment or best efforts). It will also verify the timing involved, and any minimum/maximum or green shoe provisions (mentioned earlier in this chapter).

Covenants

In this section the underwriter spells out the company's responsibilities:

- The company is responsible for paying all fees, including stock transfer and registration.

- The company is responsible for keeping the registration statement up to date. This is most critical. If changes are necessitated in the registration statement, the company is required to inform the underwriter and then make the appropriate filings with the SEC, NASD, and the states. Those changes will necessitate *stickering* the prospectus (pasting in changes), which is time consuming and expensive. For that reason alone, the entrepreneur and company should be cautioned not to enter into any new negotiations, bring out new products, lose major customers, make any significant management changes, or *any* consequential changes while the registration is in effect.

- The company agrees to file for registration in the necessary states.

- The company agrees to furnish quarterly and annual reports.

- The company agrees to abide by the uses of proceeds set forth in the prospectus.

- The company promises not to buy or sell any other securities without the underwriter's written permission (with qualifiers for the selling shareholders).

Conditions

There are three basic conditions that must be complied with: one that seems to work for the benefit of the company, one that seems to benefit the underwriter, and one that benefits both the company and the underwriter:

1. The underwriter relies upon the accuracy of the company's representations and warranties.

2. The company must furnish the underwriter with letters from the company's legal counsel that assure the accuracy, truthfulness, and completeness of the company's representations and warranties.

3. Neither party can sell stock until the offering has been declared effective by the SEC.

The above are usually attested to by an accountant's comfort letter.

Indemnification

Under the '33 act, an investor can file suit against officers of the company, principal shareholders (10 percent or more ownership), directors, underwriters, or any person or organization voluntarily named in the registration statement. The indemnification provisions excuse liability for material misstatements or omissions by the company in the registration statement. These indemnification provisions are applicable to both the underwriter and the company—indemnifying one from the other. What they imply, in essence, is that if all parties concerned perform their individual due diligence activities adequately and can prove that they have done so, the courts *may not* hold them liable.

Cancellation

This section contains a clause that allows the underwriter to cancel the offering after the effective date but prior to the closing, providing the underwriter can show cause and justification. Examples of justification are natural catastrophes affecting the company (flood, fire, and so forth); declaration of war; a national banking moratorium; and national or international general economic, political, or financial problems.

The balance of the agreement contains the normal boilerplate provisions that are part of most agreements.

To repeat, the definitive agreement is very lengthy and involved. In an effort to be thorough, no stone is left unturned. Pro forma copies are furnished to all parties prior to the signing meeting so that relevant details can be reworked before the actual signing takes place. Actually, as a rule, the agreement has been thoroughly gone over and approved long before the signing. The signing is the culmination of what seems like months of blood, sweat, and occasionally, a few tears.

Summary

The choice of an underwriter is probably the most important decision for a successful IPO. The relationship is more than just a business arrangement: It must be based on mutual confidence, respect, and trust. There are many determining points, including the type of underwriting to undertake.

The selection process requires assessing a prospective underwriter's capabilities in experience, performance, and aftermarket support. Underwriters are also concerned about the companies they work with. They're concerned about the company's management, product or service, financial condition, business plan, and integrity.

Consideration should also be given to engaging a finder in pursuit of the right underwriter. Finders are often the vital link in bringing the company and the underwriter together, and in creating a good working relationship between the two. They play an important role for both sides during the negotiations that lead to the signing of the letter of intent.

Above all, the company and the underwriter must be compatible. They must believe in each other, and each must do its respective part in assuring a successful offering. After all, it takes two to tango.

23

Self-Underwriting

Can a company go public without an underwriter? There are no rules or regulations that prohibit this, but the chances are slim of a company going public *successfully* without an underwriter. This does not mean it has not, or is not being done. Hundreds of small companies have done it. But few have ever gotten beyond "small."

The fact is that a self-underwriting IPO over $5 million is as rare as finding a gooney bird perched atop a telephone pole in Kansas City. Small offerings under $1, and under $.5 million, however, are not uncommon. Traditionally, self-underwritings are more popular when a "hot new issue" market exists. Investors tend to get caught up in that speculative new issue fever and throw normal IPO caution to the wind. It happened in the mid 1980s when hundreds of self-underwritings popped out from under the woodwork.

The Big Fallacy

Supposedly, the big benefit of doing a self-underwriting is saving the underwriter's fee. The entrepreneur should look at these figures: Discount or selling commission savings amount to approximately 10 percent of the total underwriting, plus the possible savings of unaccountable expense allowances of 3 percent to 7 percent. Most companies however provide for underwriter's commissions in their registration statements. They do that because if they intend to do any kind of selling, they will be coming to underwriters to participate in a selling syndicate. This means that the company will be paying the underwriter commissions on part of the issue.

The problem is that underwriters, as a rule, will not subscribe for more

175

than 10 percent of a deal without having their name on the cover of the prospectus. If they do the work, they want to share in the credit. That leaves the company desperately seeking participation for the other 90 percent of the offering. Another problem is that underwriters want warrants. If the market is tough, the company will have to make deals with underwriters to entice them to sell their new issue. Expense allowances and warrants are part of the cost of doing business with underwriters.

There's more to consider. Even if a company finds a broker who expresses interest in soliciting sales for the company, the brokerage firm must first approve the broker's participation (unless the broker is working individually). Also, unless the particular broker carries a great deal of clout, his firm will likely deny participation. The reason for this is that creditable brokerage firms are reluctant to expose themselves to liability connected with selling stock in a new IPO unless they have conducted "due diligence," or unless another firm is leading the IPO. What's more, selling small amounts of stock can't justify the cost of conducting the due diligence, especially without reimbursement or warrants. Considering that the broker/dealer commission of 10 percent is split, usually 3 percent to the firm and 7 percent to the broker, and considering the deals and aggravation the entrepreneur/company must go through as a self-underwriter, one has to ask—*where's the savings?*

The Carrot

Directed stock will perk up the ears of any broker. It's a lists of names, addresses, and phone numbers of friends, family, and business associates of the company. These are persons who are likely to purchase stock in the IPO because they know the entrepreneur and management team and want to participate. What makes this list so desirable is that it gives the underwriters and brokers an opportunity to open new accounts and sell additional products. Naturally, the company that attempts a self-underwriting wants to keep this list to themselves, thus saving the commission. However, the list may be impressive enough to make the individual broker or broker/dealer want to work out a compromise in this area.

Market Makers

In order to trade the stock in the aftermarket, after the offering has been completed, the company needs market makers. They are the specialists who help to create the aftermarket interest. Unless there is a broad distribution of the stock, and there appears to be a lot of interest in its trading, plus continuing efforts to keep up that interest, it is difficult to achieve broker/dealer trading participation. That requires additional time, effort, and expertise in that area on the part of the company. Whereas, if an underwriter is used—it is their responsibility to line up other market makers and assist the company in expanding the aftermarket interest.

Blue-Skying

Every state has rules and regulations regarding the selling of securities, particularly new issues, which is another roadblock the self-underwriter must be prepared to face. They were enacted to protect gullible investors from purchasing stock from unscrupulous promoters. Getting these stocks approved by a state's securities agency is called *blue-skying.* Blue-sky laws also require the registration of broker/dealers. Since self-underwriting requires the "blue-skying" of their issue, they must wait till the market makers tell them in which states they plan to trade. Unfortunately this can cause delays in trading. Applications must be submitted and approved before trading can commence; and if the company arbitrarily does its own blue-skying without foreknowledge as to which state it will trade in, it can cause unnecessary expenditures of legal and filing fees.

Pros and Cons

The fact is—self-underwriting does not carry the prestige of a project that receives the acceptance of the brokerage community. Underwriters tend to look at self-underwritings as issues that are substandard, or where the issuing company is *too cheap* to retain a real underwriter. It also has a tendency to turn off new issue investors.

The tragedy is that if the company fails to complete the offering it becomes almost impossible to raise funds from other sources, and highly improbable that an underwriter would consider taking on the issue.

Another thing that should be considered by the entrepreneur is that the SEC approval process always seems to take longer with self-underwritings. The general impression is that the SEC doesn't seem to attach as much urgency to self-underwriting as to those handled by "legitimate" underwriters. In addition there are many stories about a greater number of amendments being required by the SEC on self-underwritings.

So much for the cons. We're still trying to come up with something for the pros.

Whether justified or not—the financial community has placed a stigma on self-underwriting. The general reaction is, "This deal must not be good enough to attract an underwriter." Another concern of the financial community is that the efforts expended by the company to do a self-underwriting can become a large distraction to the management team's real business of running the company. Not only in dealing with the SEC and state rules and regulations, but working with broker/dealers and market makers in order to keep the issue in the public eye.

True, it is very difficult to operate any kind of company and also devote time to making individual sales of stock. Unless there is a real bona fide reason, such as the management team having the whole issue resold, it is advisable to consider leaving security selling to the pros.

PART IV

THE PUBLIC OFFERING PROCESS

24

The Registration Statement

The Securities Act of 1933 requires the registration of any form of securities sold to the general public (see chapter 17).

Anyone who purchases unregistered securities has the absolute, unequivocal right to rescind that purchase. This means getting the purchase money back *in full*. If the stock is sold at a loss, the purchaser can sue for damages and the amount of the loss. This assurance is effective for 1 year from the date of the original purchase.

To avoid breaching the securities laws, the entrepreneur *must* prepare and file a registration statement with the Securities and Exchange Commission (SEC) disclosing all the information pertaining to the stock offering. In the following pages, we will attempt to bring to light the full process of assembling these documents, including the different types of forms that are used, the various regulations that affect the registration, and a detailed explanation of each part of the document.

The registration statement is composed of two parts. The first part is the prospectus. The second part is the registration statement itself. The prospectus is printed in booklet form. The first printing is the preliminary prospectus, also called a *red herring* because it contains certain caveats (warnings) printed in red ink to inform the reader that the prospectus is not in its final form. The purpose of the prospectus is to gain interest from prospective investors in the underwriting and to solicit "indications of interest" from the selling syndicate. Participating broker/dealers commonly distribute the red herring to their retail customers and then report to the lead underwriter the amount of stock they feel they can sell based on the indications of interest. The final prospectus includes the offering date, the price of the stock, and other pertinent information. Copies of the final version are sent to all the people who received the red herring. They contain the effective date of the registration statement from the SEC.

181

The following are headings that require disclosures in Part I of the registration statement:

1. Covers
2. Summary
3. The Company
4. Use of Proceeds
5. Dividend Policy
6. Dilution
7. Capitalization
8. Select Financial Data
9. Management's Discussion
10. The Business
11. Management and Certain Shareholders
12. Legal Proceedings
13. Description of the Securities
14. Financial Statements

The following subjects are addressed in Part II of the registration statement:

1. Expenses of Distribution
2. Indemnification of Directors and Officers
3. Recent Sales of Unregistered Securities
4. Exhibits and Financial Statement Schedules

The Regulations

Information concerning SEC regulations that require specific forms and formats must be included in the company's disclosures. Of particular concern in this regard are regulations S–K, S–X, and C. (The government seems to be continually changing the filing details, but accounting and legal counsel can keep up to date through releases and bulletins that are available.)

Regulation S–K

The full name of this regulation is S–K Standard Instructions for Filing Forms under Securities Act of 1933, Securities Exchange Act of 1934, and

Energy Policy and Conservation Act of 1975. This regulation specifies the requirements for the nonfinancial portions of the registration statement. All areas of the S–K will be addressed later in this chapter.

Regulation S–X

The full title of this regulation is Form and Content of and Requirements for Financial Statements, Securities Act of 1933, Securities Exchange Act of 1934, Public Utility Holding Company Act of 1935, Investment Company Act of 1940, and Energy Policy and Conservation Act of 1975. This regulation specifies the financial statement requirements and denotes the form, content, and time periods for submissions. It is primarily the responsibility of the audit accountants to follow through on the requirements of the articles of this regulation, listed below. It should be noted that not all articles are relevant to IPOs

Article 1	Application of Regulation S–X
Article 2	Qualifications and Reports of Accountants
Article 3	General Instructions as to Financial Statements
Article 3–A	Consolidated and Combined Financial Statements
Article 4	Rules of General Application
Article 5	Commercial and Industrial Companies
Article 6	Registered Investment
Article 6–A	Employee Stock Purchase, Savings, and Similar
Article 7	Insurance Companies
Article 8	Bank Holding Companies
Article 9	Interim Financial Statements
Article 10	Pro Forma Financial Information
Article 11	Form and Content of Schedules

Note that the information requirements are lengthy and complex. More complete information can be found in a booklet available from the SEC titled "Small Business Informational Package."

Regulation C

This regulation denotes the proper procedures to be followed in the actual preparation and filing of the registration statement itself. It deals with the mechanics of paper size, number of copies, size of type, and other detailed filing requirements. Regulation C also addresses the following areas:

1. Definition of terms
2. Confidentiality of information

3. Incorporation by reference

4. Delayed and continuous offering and sale of securities

5. Written consents

6. Acceleration of effective date

7. Amendments and withdrawals

Financial Reporting Releases (FRRs)

Financial reporting releases (FRRs) expand on the financial statement disclosure requirements of Regulation S–X. They also report on current accounting practices and changes that have been instituted. FRRs have the status of a regulation.

Staff Accounting Bulletins (SABs)

Staff accounting bulletins (SABs) are additional information sources that are published; they include interpretations and practices that are currently being followed by the SEC staff. The information pertains to financial statement disclosures.

Filing Process

The filing process begins with the submission of the registration statement to the SEC. The registration statement requirements are detailed in SEC forms that are designated S–1 through S–18. Actually, some of the S–numbers between 1 and 18 don't exist. That's simply the way the government numbered them. S–1 is the most complete form and most generally used. However, almost all small IPOs (under $7.5 million) use the simplified form, which is S–18. (For the differences between S–1 and S–18 see table 24.1.)

Filing Types and Descriptions

We will concentrate on the requirements mentioned in forms S–1 and S–18. The other forms contain information requirements for specific businesses (oil and gas, real estate companies, investment trusts, and so forth) and special situations. For example, forms S–2 and S–3 are commonly used for secondary offerings. They are used for a company that has already completed an initial public offering, is now an existing public company under the '34 act, and has been fully reporting to the SEC for 3 or more years.

TABLE 24.1

Differences Between Forms S–1 and S–18
Summary Chart

	S–1	S–18
Dollar Amount	Unlimited	$7.5 million
Existing Reporting	Yes	No
Filing Location	Wash DC only	Regional offices
Balance Sheet	2 years	1 year
Income Statement	3 years	2 years
Changes in Condition	3 years	2 years
Shareholders' Equity	3 years	2 years
Statement Preparation	Reg S–X	Generally Accepted
5-year Selected	Yes	No
Management's Discussion	Yes	No
Financial Analysis	Yes	No
Support Schedules	Yes	Limited

Form S–4 is used for a registration statement with the SEC for a company that is involved in a merger or acquisition.

Form S–6 is used for registering unit investment trusts.

Form S–8 is primarily directed to securities that are used for employee stock option plans or other employee benefit plans and trusts.

Form S–11 is the form used when registering securities for real estate companies and investment trusts.

Since 1933, Form S–1 has been the securities registration statement for all issuers. No other form had been authorized or prescribed. However, in April 1979, the SEC adopted a simplified form, S–18. S–18 has now become the more frequently used form for small companies registering less than $7.5 million in securities.

S–18, the option form, cannot be used by existing companies reporting under the '34 act, investment companies, or insurance companies. Filings of S–18s can be made at either the SEC's principal office in Washington, D.C., or at a regional office which has jurisdiction in the geographical area in which the company's principal office is located.

There is a definite advantage in filing at a regional office. For one thing, regional offices almost always respond more quickly than the Washington, D.C., office. A recent study showed that it took 52 days, from the date of the initial filing, to the effective date in a regional office, compared to 89 days for filings in Washington. Another advantage of dealing with a regional office is that the company's attorney, accountant, and underwriter usually enjoy a prior working relationship with the regional SEC personnel assigned to the underwriting.

Other advantages of S–18 over S–1 are: S–18 requires a balance sheet only for the last fiscal year, whereas S–1 requires one covering the last 2 years. S–18 requires statements of income, changes in financial condition, and shareholders' equity positions to cover the last 2 years; S–1 requires 3 years' coverage. S–18 does not require that financials be prepared in compliance with the SEC's accounting rules of Reg S–X as required by S–1, but according to generally accepted accounting standards (GAAP). S–18 does not require the company to produce 5 years of selected financial data, reports on management's discussions, analysis on individual managers' financial condition, or the support schedules and backup documents required by S–1. Finally, S–18 does not require the company to produce as detailed a description of the business, its properties, and management remuneration and transactions as S–1 requires. (See table 24.1 and chapter 20.)

The Registration Statement Part I (The Prospectus)

Although no special sequence is required for the contents of the prospectus and registration statement, over time an order has evolved as follows:

Outside Front Cover

The traditionally accepted size format for a prospectus has been 7½ by 9 inches. Today the trend is moving toward 8½ by 11 inches. Many underwriters are still using the 7½-by-9-inch size, but they are slowly moving towards the new size. The cover paper ranges from high gloss, two- to four-color, to conventional prospectus paper stock, which is almost tissue thin. The final decision in this area usually depends on the underwriter's preference and particular marketing format.

The cover page highlights key points about the underwriting. These include:

- Name of issuer (company)
- Company logo (optional)
- Title of offering
- Dollar amount of securities offered
- Number of securities offered
- A distribution table showing price to the public
- Underwriter's discount and commissions

- Proceeds to the issuer
- Net proceeds to selling shareholders
- Date of prospectus
- Name of underwriter (may also include logo)

Regularly required statements are normally printed in boldface roman 10-point type. The distribution table will include the maximum and minimum shares, and also dollars offered in a mini/max offering. A preliminary prospectus will show statements that are subject to change printed in red ink (red herring).

The following statement, customarily set in 10-point caps, must also appear:

THESE SECURITIES HAVE NOT BEEN APPROVED OR DISAPPROVED BY THE SECURITIES AND EXCHANGE COMMISSION NOR HAS THE COMMISSION PASSED UPON THE ACCURACY OF THIS PROSPECTUS. ANY REPRESENTATION TO THE CONTRARY IS A CRIMINAL OFFENSE.

Inside Front and Outside Back Cover Pages

Commonly, the outside back cover will contain the table of contents, notices pertaining to information about price stabilization, and details about distributing of the prospectus. The front and back inside covers are commonly used to display illustrations or photos of the company's products. The purpose is to improve the marketing of the issue. There are, however, negatives to showing pictures or illustrations that should be considered. They result in increased costs for reproduction and printing, and more important, there is a possibility of legal risk, as the illustrations can imply more than the intent of the product. Today this is becoming less of a problem, as the average prospectus reader's visual interpretations are more sophisticated. Nevertheless, attention still should be paid to what the illustrations depict and to the captions that accompany them.

Prospectus Summary

The first page usually contains a brief description of the company's business and products or service. It may include use of proceeds, risk factors, select financial data, and a description of the securities being offered. *This summary sheet is often what stock analysts and financial publications quote when describing the company and its offering. Consequently, great care should be exercised to write a succinct and favorable summary.*

The Company

This section is intended to provide more detailed information about the company, including the company's name, address, phone numbers, and locations of branches or subsidiaries. The section will note historical information, such as when the company was incorporated, and, if appropriate, a brief history and brief description of its business, products, or services.

Risk Factors

The more speculative the company, the greater the number of risk factors. By laying its cards on the table and disclosing the potential risks for the investor, the company protects itself against nondisclosure accusations. Examples of risks could include dependence on a single supplier or a large customer (such as the U.S. government or a major department store chain); uncertainty in the size of the market; lack of experience on the part of the management team; lack of, or a deficit in, operations or earnings history; operating losses; and any number of other things that could possibly point to a potential risk. It is not unusual to find a list of 15 to 25 risk factors on a new small start-up or early stage company.

Use of Proceeds

A great deal of thought needs to be given to the drafting of this section. The reason is that after the completion of the offering, the company must file continuing reports with the SEC explaining and substantiating that the money was spent as described (see Form SR, p. 254).

This section essentially explains the purpose of the offering, and more explicitly, discloses what the money will be used for. Uses must be listed in order of priority. Contingencies for any possible change in use must be explained. If, for example, the proceeds were to be used primarily to pay off an existing debt, this proposal would be easy to describe or explain to the SEC, underwriters, analysts, and prospective shareholders. However, if there are specific areas where the money is to be spent—which is usually the case—a detailed listing of each use and amount to be spent must be noted and justified. Should the amount seem unjustified in the eyes of the SEC and investors, it is likely to raise eyebrows—and questions.

Dividend Policy

This section reports on the company's dividend record and plans for future dividends. Most often, new companies' plans call for holding on to future earnings in order to enhance growth. So the decision is not to pay dividends in the immediate future. If that's the case, that decision must be disclosed. This section also contains restrictions that may exist on dividend payments, such as existing restrictive loans or provisions having to do with preferred stock.

Dilution

This section discloses the difference between what the existing shareholders paid for their stock and the price the prospective new shareholders will have to pay. It is generally exhibited in chart or tabular form. Also disclosed in this section are the prices paid for the stock by the officers, directors, and major original inside shareholders. The purpose for presenting the figures graphically is to show:

- The new intangible book value per share before and after the offering
- The book value increase per share as a result of purchases from new shareholders
- The amount of immediate dilution per share to new purchasers

Most commonly, the existing shareholders, especially the original founders, paid a significantly lower price for their stock, and there is often also a substantial dilution as far as new purchasers are concerned. Dilution ranging from 70 to 90 percent is not uncommon in small public company offerings. Apple Computer's dilution, for example, was 80 percent.

Capitalization

This section, which is usually presented in a table format, sets forth the capital structure (showing both debt and equity) of the company's financial position prior to the offering and pro forma after the offering.

Selected Financial Data

Note that this section applies only to S–1. It is *not* applicable for S–18 registrations. All S–1 registrations are required to supply financial data that take in the 5 years prior to registration. The data must cover net sales or operating revenue, income (or loss) from continuing operations, total assets, long-term debt, redeemable preferred stock, and cash dividends. Additionally, if the fiscal annual financial statement is more than 135 days old on the date the registration becomes effective, an interim statement, called an unaudited stub report, must be included. This report must cover the additional quarters. It should also compare the equivalent periods for the previous year of operation. All of this data is noted in gross amounts per share and adjusted to reflect the designated number of outstanding shares.

While stub periods are unaudited, the information should be presented with the same close scrutiny administered by audit accountants. Companies are usually allowed to include additional data that they feel will enhance the picture of their financial progress—as long as they don't go overboard in their assessment.

Management's Discussion and Analysis

Note that this section also applies only to S–1 registrations. It is customarily written for or by the company's management team and covers information and an analysis of the financial condition and the effectiveness of the company's operations. Its purpose is to promote investors' understanding of the company from a financial point of view. The report is required to cover the past 3 fiscal/annual years or go back 5 years if that can improve the company's financial picture. Any stub period should also be included. The report should cover specific information on the following points:

1. The company's liquidity and capital resources, including both short- and long-term commitments

2. Expected sources of capital and plans for future capital needs or commitments, as well as pro forma cash flows

3. Discussion about significant facts resulting in unusual or infrequent things or situations affecting prior years or anticipated in the future, such as capital gains due to the sale of real estate, a patent, subsidiary, a onetime sale, or whatever seems pertinent

4. Discussion of anything that could possibly affect the future cash flow of the company's operations, for example, a potential lawsuit, a product "going bad" and requiring recall, machines breaking down

The Business

This section is included in order to give the potential investor information to evaluate the strengths and weaknesses of the company, its products or services, and industry. The following are subjects that are applicable to most companies and require thoughtful explanations and responses:

1. Historical development of the company (5 years for S–1).

2. If the company has not had any operating revenue during the last 3 years, an anticipated operating plan for the next year must be proposed.

3. Financial information should be presented along with comparisons for the industry.

4. A description of the company's primary product or service.

5. A description of the principal markets and methods of distribution being used. If possible, this should also be broken down by the type of industry, geographical areas, and foreign markets.

6. A complete listing and description of any patents, trademarks, licenses, franchises, or concessions held by the company. Included should be an evaluation of their importance and the effort taken to secure them.

7. A status report on any new products (publicly announced), product development, and industry areas that are being entered or contemplated.

8. A report on the sources and availability of raw materials, whether from a sole source or multisource suppliers.

9. Disclosure of the seasonality of the business, if applicable.

10. Disclosure of working capital practices, such as the need to maintain a significant inventory to satisfy rapid delivery requirements, or procedures for allowing for extensions of customer payments and terms.

11. Disclosure as to the extent of reliance on one or a few major customers.

12. A listing of contract backlogs by dollar amount.

13. A statement on government contracts, if any, that are subject to renegotiation or termination.

14. An analysis of the competitive conditions in the company's industry.

15. The number of company employees.

16. The effects and costs associated with the company's compliance with environmental protection laws (if that is a consideration).

Properties

This section requires a disclosure of the location, and description of the physical properties owned or leased by the company. This includes all major plants, mines, branch offices, and so forth.

Legal Proceedings

This section requires a description of any ongoing or pending legal actions involving the company, either as plaintiff or defendant. It does not apply to routine litigation having to do with the company's ongoing business, such as routine collection matters.

Management

The management section is of paramount importance. Therefore it has been broken down into these specific headings: Directors and Executive Officers, Resumes, Significant Employees, Advisory Boards, Consultants, Remuneration, Principal Shareholders, Special Transactions.

Directors and Executive Officers

This part lists the name, age, and position of each director and officer of the company. Wherever relevant, their names are to be footnoted to point out their relationship to the company, such as founders or promoters. Also to be included are the terms of office for the directors, and which annual meetings their respective terms expire. An explanation of how the bylaws handle vacancies on the board also belongs under this heading.

Resumes

The full name of the person, executive position and/or directorship, and the date of involvement with the company must be declared. Prior employment for a minimum of 5 years, including dates, should be covered. Also to be included are family interrelationships, including spouse, parents, relatives through first cousins and by marriage, and any past negative encounters with governmental regulating bodies.

There is no special style or procedure that must be adhered to in the presentation of a resume. Some prospectuses show resumes of only 4 or 5 lines, while others are a full page or more.

Significant Employees

This section is devoted to employees who are not officers or directors, but whose expertise makes a significant contribution to the company and its operation. Formal resumes or disclosures about their backgrounds are not necessary.

Advisory Boards

As a general rule, resumes of advisory board members are not required, nor are there any formal disclosure requirements. However, since they are selected because of their special expertise, including their resumes could be a definite advantage and should be considered.

Consultants

This is not a mandatory requirement. It is strictly the entrepreneur's or the company's decision to include the consultants who are involved with the company. If their names are impressive, they are often included. Advertising agencies and marketing, financial public relations, or public relations people or business consultants can lend a special prestige to the company because of their technical expertise.

Remuneration

This section discloses pertinent information about all the officers and directors of the company, such as:

- Compensation, including salaries, stock options, royalty agreements, direct fees, incentive fees, and incentive options.
- Benefit compensation, such as auto allowances or autos furnished, insurance benefits or payments, housing, country club fees, major entertainment benefits, and other perks.
- Loans to officers, directors, or their families.
- Remuneration to principal shareholders. This part is often presented in chart form, listing the name, address, shares owned (direct, beneficially, and owner of record) by all officers and directors. Also listed are persons who hold 5 percent or more of the company's stock. This chart usually contains a heading that shows the percentages held by those listed prior to and after the offering.

Special Transactions

This section identifies special transactions with the management, officers, directors, and major shareholders (5 percent or more). If the company is less than 5 years old, it also includes promoters associated with the company. It will declare future transactions, such as golden parachutes (mentioned previously) covering compensatory arrangements with officers or directors that are contingent on their resignation or termination, or as a result of change in control of the company due to leveraged buy-outs, mergers, or acquisitions.

Description of Securities to Be Registered

This section, also referred to as "Description of Capital Stock," describes the particular securities being offered. It spells out all the particulars on the total authorized capital stock in both common and preferred shares, including par or stated values, dividend rights, conversion or redemption provisions, voting rights, liquidation, and preemption rights. It explains the transferability of each class of stock and any restrictions that apply to the various classes of securities. It also discloses pertinent information on all outstanding warrants, options, and incentive stock option plans and describes the rights they carry, as well as revealing plans for the stock. Special voting requirements are also noted in this section, and information is usually given regarding the company's transfer agent.

Underwriting

In some prospectuses, this section has been called "Plan of Distribution." It contains information about the principal underwriter(s), the selling syndicate members, the underwriter's method (firm commitment or best efforts), and the number of shares subscribed to by each underwriter or selling group member. It further describes the agreement between the company and the underwriter, the terms agreed upon—including commissions, warrants, commissions reallowed to syndicate members, and unaccountable expense allowances—as set forth by NASD under its Rules of Fair Practice.

This section should also include the name of the escrow agent and a brief description of the terms of the escrow agreement. It will note which exchanges the company's stock will be listed or traded on. Additionally, any material relationship between the company and the underwriters will be disclosed, such as the underwriter's right to arrange for a designee to the company's board of directors. It will also reaffirm the indemnification of the underwriter from any liability under the securities acts.

Legal Matters

This part identifies the company's legal counsel and its opinion as to the validity of the securities being offered. If legal counsel owns any of the company's stock, mention should be made of it. Commonly, the counsel to the underwriter is also identified in this section.

Experts

This area recognizes any experts whose counsel and help have been sought in the preparation of the registration statement, generally the audit accountant. It includes an indemnification statement that refers to the audit report regarding the company's financial statements.

Additional Information

This section is just what the heading implies. It is only included if there is additional information that must be dealt with according to Part II of the registration statement or that has been called for by the SEC.

Financial Statements

This section discloses all the company's financial statements and includes a confirming report from the auditing accountants. There is a difference between the requirements of an S–1 and an S–18 filing. Note the following:

	S–18	S–1
Audited balance sheets	1 year	2 years
Income statements	2 years	3 years
Changes in financial condition, stock equity	2 years	3 years
Management discussion	No	Yes

Remember, unaudited stub period reports are needed if the audited statements are over 135 days old. And they must be accompanied with a comparison to the preceding year's report.

The first page of this section should be the accountant's report or audit opinion. It generally runs 2 paragraphs in length. Sophisticated investors would simply glance at this page. But if it is longer than the expected 2 pages, they usually suspect that the company's financial health is not normal. If they are still interested, they will review the opinion to find out what the problem is. (See chapter 8.)

The accountant's report is followed by the actual financial statements, which include:

- Balance sheet
- Income statement
- Changes in financial position
- Shareholders' equity
- Notes to the financial statements

Generally speaking, financial statements need to be consolidated (combined) within subsidiary or multiple operations. Subsidiaries can be excluded from consolidation only if the consolidation does not result in a meaningful disclosure.

According to the rules, separate financial statements are required for unconsolidated subsidiaries that represent more than 20 percent of the consolidated assets or accounts (company and subsidiary) or greater than 20 percent of the consolidated income. Additionally, if there is more than one unconsolidated subsidiary, and the aggregate total of the assets *or* income exceeds 10 percent, then summary or separate financial statements must be included.

The rules are also specific regarding disclosure on businesses recently acquired or to be acquired. For example, Company A is going public. It has agreed to buy Company B for $1 million with monies derived from the offering. However, that will leave the principals with two companies—each having its own financial statement. The rules state they must have only *one* financial statement, even if the purchase is made after the offering has been completed. That requires the pro forma financial information (projected) to be recast to assume, on paper, that the transaction has taken place prior to the offering.

Pro forma financial information is generally required for significant business acquisitions and dispositions as well as for reorganizations, unusual assets exchanges, and debt restructurings.

Bear in mind, disclosure is required for any information considered material. Materiality can be determined by asking the question "Would a reasonable investor consider it important in deciding whether to buy the security at the price offered?"

The Registration Statement Part II

Part II of the registration statement contains information that is not included in the prospectus. However, because it is filed with the SEC, it is available for public scrutiny. It is prepared in an item-and-answer format. The following subjects and information are typically included:

- Miscellaneous expenses of issuance and distribution.

- Insurance documents or indemnification for liability of officers and directors.

- Listing of the sales of unregistered securities for the last 3 years. We mentioned earlier that the sale of unregistered stock was illegal, but this specific type of transaction is not necessarily illegal. It could concern money raised privately and prior to any thought of pursuing an IPO. In such a case, the entrepreneur or company did not use Regulation 504 (mentioned earlier). Or it could concern a combination of 504 that was ultimately ruled integration, and therefore disallowed, by the SEC. There could be serious consequences if it is discovered that the past issuance of stock violated the '33 act, so the company is advised to make a recision on the money by going back to the original investor and redoing the investment according to SEC rules.

- Various subjects, including a list of all subsidiaries, the underwriting agreement, corporate charter (articles of incorporation), bylaws, financial statement schedules, and copies of material contracts.

Misstatements

Everything in the registration statement must be true. There cannot be any omissions that could result in half-truths. The ultimate liability for misstatements lies with the issuer, or more directly, the officers and directors of the company.

If this truth standard is not met by the effective date of the offering, the security buyer has a right to sue the issuer up to the statute of limitations period of 3 years from the effective date. Please note: This holds true for all purchasers of the securities, including those purchased in the aftermarket, whether the buyer ever saw the prospectus or not. That's 3 years! Obviously, officers and directors are especially careful not to allow misstatements to occur.

Officers' and Directors' Questionnaire

All directors and officers of a public company are required by the SEC to give what seems to be an overwhelming amount of personal data for possible inclusion in a registration statement, prospectus, or proxy statement. This information is usually obtained by the company's counsel through a questionnaire. It is time consuming, extensive in its request for detailed factual data, and frequently requires an affidavit as to its veracity and correctness. The document has been known to be 20 to 30 pages in length, covering 30 to 50 specific bits of information. It covers the following points, not necessarily in this order:

- History of employment (past 10 years with contact names for verification)
- Statements regarding any family relationships within the company
- Listing of offices or directorships in other companies (especially public companies)
- Complete education history with dates and degrees
- Listing of all business and professional memberships, past and present
- Listing of all lawyers or accountants engaged in the past 5 years
- Extensive inquiry into all litigation or regulatory actions in the past 10 years
- Listing of all associations with security offerings during the past 10 years
- Listing of present and past fiduciary relationships
- Complete disclosure of compensation by the company, including salaries, options, incentives, royalties, insurance, and any special benefits accrued or contemplated
- Complete disclosure of the company's securities owned, including those controlled directly and those controlled by a beneficiary, plus disclaimers
- Disclosure of all past and contemplated transactions with the company

Periodic Reporting

The SEC requires all public companies to make periodic (annual) accountings of their companies. One of the forms used is Form 8–A, which is a general form for registration, and requires everything to be reported. Companies that have filed on the simpler Form S–18 (for offerings that do not exceed $7.5 million) can use Form 10–K (a form for companies with assets over $2 million). Reporting on Form 10–K has these advantages:

- The first annual 10–K report requires only 2 years of audited financial statements, as opposed to 3 years for companies that filed an S–1 (registration statement for securities for all users). Also, filing can be made under generally accepted accounting principles instead of the complicated Reg S–X procedures, which require more complete disclosures.

- The second annual 10–K report requires 2 years of audited financial statements also. However, the latest year is now subject to Reg S–X, and for comparative purposes, the first year's statement needs to be adjusted to bring it in line with the figures for the second year.
- The third year still only requires statements covering just 2 years; however, both statements must now comply with Reg S–X.
- The fourth year must now report fully, and requires 3 years of audited financial statements to comply with Reg S–X.

An Overview of the Process

The process of preparing a prospectus and registration statement for a proposed public offering often requires the skill of a magician and an adeptness at walking a tightrope. The prospectus is the selling tool used by the company, the underwriter, and the individual brokers to influence investors. The underwriter expects the company to come up with a clean, beautiful, saleable picture of the offering and still disclose all the material facts, without hype, without the hindrance of negatives, but complying with the SEC's strict rules and regulations.

The burden for carrying this off usually falls on the shoulders of the company's lawyers. They carry the principal responsibility for the assembly and preparation of all the nonfinancial parts of the registration statement. They have to make them look good—and legal. It requires complete cooperation and coordination between the company, underwriters, accountants, printers, public relations, advertising firms, and on occasion, postal and delivery services. The lawyers tread a thin line, covering all points of possible contention in order to provide the company with a registration statement that becomes an insurance policy against potential shareholders' lawsuits. This is not to imply that legal counsel would, or is expected to do anything that is not aboveboard. It's just that at times they must use all the intricate legal language at their disposal to make the company look good.

The Association of the Bar of the City of New York issued a report titled, "Report by the Special Committee on Lawyers' Role in Securities Transactions." It spells out guidelines that can help lawyers do the job that is expected of them. Some points are worth noting:

Guideline 4 states,

The lawyer should assist the issuer, on the basis of information furnished to the lawyer, in reaching its decision as to what information should be included in the registration statement, how it should be included, and to what extent its omission would raise questions under the '33 Act—i.e., he should assist the issuer in making judgements as to materiality and compliance with the requirements of the registration form and instructions.

The guideline further notes:

Within the confines of the agreed assignment of responsibilities and of a realistic evaluation of the extent to which a lawyer's consideration of essentially non-legal matters is useful to the client and warranted by circumstances, the lawyer should study documents or otherwise inquire into other matters, not primarily legal in nature and not within counsel's expertise as such, in order to provide himself with a background from which to assist the issuer in making its decision.

And in comment, it states:

The lawyer should not allow the impression to be created that he will normally "investigate" factual matters covered in a registration statement, personally examining into primary sources or data, or that he can verify the reliability of other persons providing this information.

Guideline 5 states:

The lawyer should assist in the drafting of the registration statement or portions thereof with the goal that, to the extent feasible, the registration statement says what the lawyer understands the issuer intends it to say, is unambiguous, and is written in a way that is designed to protect the issuer from later claims of overstatement, misleading implications, omissions or other deficiencies due to the manner in which the statements in question have been written.

And in comment, it states:

The lawyer's drafting services are significant since the manner in which the document is organized and written is of considerable importance; but the lawyer should not delude himself or the client into regarding the lawyer's drafting or organizing abilities as also giving the lawyer the ability to determine the substantive content of the document.

And finally, Guideline 6 takes the lawyer off the hook: "The lawyer should avoid statements in the prospectus which could give a mistaken impression that he has passed upon matters which he has not, or that he takes responsibility for the accuracy and completeness of the prospectus."

Without hedging, the report says in effect that legal counsel assists the company and its management in preparing the registration statement and in performing due diligence. Legal counsel, as the principal draftsperson, solicits information both orally and in writing, and exercises judgment as to accuracy and consistency of the information supplied.

However, in the final analysis, legal counsel only volunteers an opinion that the securities being offered are legally issued, fully paid, and nonassessable. The company and its management must assume the final responsibility. Management must make sure that the information presented is accurate, complete, and verified and the registration statement prepared properly. It's a dirty job, but somebody's got to take the responsibility.

Summary

The registration statement is considered a disclosure document. But it is really more than that. It is a selling document that contains information about the company that it is hoped will influence the prospective investor to purchase the issuing company's stock. It also serves as an insurance policy for the company. Full disclosure in the prospectus will help to insure the company from incurring lawsuits because of misstatements and inadequate disclosure.

Above all, it is a complex document that requires a great deal of preparation, as well as consideration of the literally dozens of rules and regulations handed down by the SEC.

Depending on the size of the offering, the simplified Form S–18 can be used for the registration statement in place of S–1, which is more involved and therefore more costly to do.

The task is by no means insurmountable. But it challenges the entrepreneur to assemble a team of professionals to assist in putting this document together and to make it come off like a simple letter home to mom and dad. However, management can't just leave it to the other guy. Management can't take a passive role in the preparation of the company's registration statement. To do the job right, management must become involved all the way. Especially, if it expects Ali Baba's magic doors to slide open smoothly.

25

Filing and Review

The process and procedures for a filing often require prefiling conferences. These are simply meetings with the SEC staff to discuss the proposed offering and to make certain that the relevant forms and regulations are complied with and that adequate disclosures are made.

The SEC reviewers do not pass judgment on or evaluate the quality of a proposed public company or offering. They merely try to keep the offering on the right track and to offer information on how to handle any technicalities that may crop up. They will advise an entrepreneur on the timing involved, on the initial filing procedures, and where it is best to file. For example, due to the complexities encountered in large offerings, it is best to file them with the SEC in Washington, D.C., where there are the people and facilities to handle them. Smaller regional offerings are most often filed at regional branches of the SEC. That's because small offerings are usually not as complex. The response to them is also faster at the regional level.

We will elaborate on all of these topics in the following pages. We will also discuss the actual filing as well as preliminary prospectuses, filing stickers, and the filings with other regulatory offices. We will explain the different types of reviews and amendments. And we will comment on SEC comment letters—letters from the SEC on how to properly complete the prospectus and registration statement.

A reminder to the reader—this book concentrates on small-company

S–18 filings. However, the subtleties of the larger S–1 filings will be pointed out where appropriate.

Prefiling Conferences

Some companies, especially those with newly developed or highly technical products, would be well advised to schedule a prefiling conference with the staff at their regional branch of the SEC. It is there to help—not hinder.

The SEC staff is adept at pinpointing problem areas that may arise during the process of assembling information for the registration statement. For example, a company may want to know how it can justify setting aside 25 percent of the offering for research and development; how to identify a broker who is also a shareholder; how to handle a legal or accounting problem in a filing, such as a partnership litigation; or how to deal with a questionable regulation compliance.

Any question about the prospectus or registration statement is open for discussion. Many questions about the filing can be handled on the phone. If the matter is more complicated, the SEC staff may wish to arrange a meeting in its offices with the appropriate specialty advisors to assist the company in determining appropriate actions or disclosures. More difficult questions could even be referred to Washington. If a response is urgent, a phone call instead of a letter is not out of order.

If a phone call determines that a prefiling conference is necessary, it's usually the responsibility of legal counsel to verify the appointment by letter, stating all the facts.

The company's legal counsel as well as the company's management team should come fully prepared, with their bag full of questions, for SEC staff conferences. If the questions are of a specialized nature, the appropriate company experts, such as the accountant, production chief, or whoever, should also be present. Generally, the SEC replies in writing. But bear in mind, the SEC does not suggest language for, or put into words, any of the specifics of a registration statement. Remember, the primary reason for prefiling calls or conferences is to assist in clarifying details that could effect a registration and to avoid costly time delays once a registration has been submitted.

The SEC, by the way, will accept limited questions without the company's name being discussed or revealed during the inquiry. For example, a lawyer could tell the SEC that his or her client is contemplating a takeover of General Motors and wants to know what the SEC's response would be to something like that. The client's name need not be mentioned. A term that describes that kind of questioning is no-name basis.

Filing Technicalities

After a thorough review by all involved parties, the completed registration statement must be signed by those who are a party to it. That could include the principal executive officers, the principal financial officer, and members of the board of directors. Each signature must be accompanied by the name typed or printed beneath the signature. If the person signing holds more than one executive position, the position being signed for must be indicated.

To avoid any inconvenient delays, it is possible to use a power of attorney for absent signers. The powers of attorney must be attached as exhibits along with a certified copy of a resolution by the board of directors authorizing such signatures.

Those experts (attorneys, accountants, and so forth) involved in preparing the registration statement must attest to the validity of the statement and furnish consents for the use of their names on the statement. The consents, which must be hand-signed, are filed with the registration statement. Also, three copies of the complete registration statement must be filed with the SEC in Washington, D.C., or at a regional office. One copy must be hand-signed (original signatures, not copies). Additionally, ten copies must be available for public inspection.

Unless all documents are complete, the SEC will not review the filing. Therefore, it is necessary to attach a cover letter stating that all filings under the statute have been filed and the submission is complete.

At the time of the filing, the registrant is required to pay the SEC a fee of one-fifth of 1 percent of the maximum price of the proposed offering, but in any case, not less than $100.

Initial Filing

When a registration statement is received by the Washington, D.C., office of the SEC or a branch office, it is assigned to an examiner. The examiner is backed up by an attorney, an accountant, an analyst, and when necessary, an expert in the company's particular field. For example, the SEC maintains oil, gas, and mining experts on staff, who review all filings in their respective domains. The examiners, in turn, are overseen by a chief examiner.

Examiners are responsible for reviewing the statement. They check for any inconsistencies. They make sure that it complies with all the SEC requirements. But the SEC seldom makes an independent investigation on the specifics of a particular type of business, although they have the right to do so. However, if the company will be doing business with branches of the government, especially the military, everything referring to those declarations will be thoroughly checked out.

Also, if the company is involved in a new industry, or one that is highly technical or complicated, the SEC will usually perform an extended review of the registration statement to give its staff an opportunity to familiarize itself with the product. Generally speaking, the easier a document is to read and comprehend, the less the scrutiny.

To emphasize its vigilance, the SEC will also occasionally release statements to interested parties that are ever watchful about things such as the insider trading scandals of 1987 and the proliferation of interconnected parties in blind pools in the state of Utah.

Timing

By statute, a registration automatically becomes effective 20 days after it is filed. However, with the ever-present backlog of filings, the rules have a clause in which the 20-day automatic effectiveness provision is voluntarily suspended. For the most part, a registrant can expect to receive an initial comment letter from the SEC 4 to 6 weeks after initial submission.

Comment/Deficiency Letter

The SEC reviews the registration statement that has been filed and then sends out a deficiency letter or a letter of comment. This comment letter represents the staff's views about what steps should be taken to make the prospectus complete and accurate.

It should be understood that "complete and accurate" is a subjective opinion by the SEC staff. Unfortunately, a proposed IPO has to be very careful in its review of the SEC's comments and should temper initial reaction. Justified or not, it's hard to find a filing that does not receive at least one comment letter. The comment on one submission requested that the company review the use and spelling of "principal" versus "principle." The SEC request, in this situation, was justified. The company corrected the spelling, as well as several other small items, and the offering was successfully undertaken with no more comments from either side.

One frequent subject of comment letter discussion is accounting. The SEC habitually requests additional information or requires further accounting footnotes to clarify such matters as policies and practices, related-party transactions, unusual compensation agreements (with both management and outside consultants), methods of off-balance-sheet financing, relationships between divisions or subsidiaries, and other components of the financial statements. Accounting comments are routinely clarified, as the rules and regulations for SEC accounting are fairly well defined.

Other areas of comments regarding the registration statement may not be as clearly defined. The staff's suggestions or notes to problems can be limited to such items as failure to comply with instructions on the registration form or a request to more fully stress a risk factor.

If the company believes that the commission staff's suggestions are inappropriate or that the criticisms are not well founded, the better part of valor is to cool it. It's best to simply comply with the request if the problem is minor. This will save a lot of valuable underwriting time in spite of a small loss of ego.

However, if the staff objections are major, or you do not clearly understand them, an attempt should be made to discuss them with the SEC staff. It is possible that the staff missed a point or asked for some information the company considers privileged and does not want to disclose. Many times, the problem can best be handled by complying. If the company does not wish to comply, it can request informal conferences. You will always find the SEC staff to be most generous with its time. Remember, the SEC's livelihood does not depend on getting the issue completed. But management will have the opportunity to convince it. If the SEC staff decides to be obstinate, the company can argue the point until the IPO window closes. In other words, the SEC has the ability to delay an offering for as long as it likes. If it is obvious that the company is acting in good faith, it will get full cooperation from the SEC. It may take some modification and compliance on the company's part, but it should eventually succeed in having the registration become effective.

Commission staff members can be unyielding when something does not smell right to them. They have a way of delaying the offering by issuing additional comment letters, often for obscure reasons, but with the end result of delaying the offering. Eventually someone has to give, and it usually is the company, by modifying or withdrawing the offering. Those are the choices.

Common Comments

Noted below are the most frequent comment letter questions and observations from SEC staff:

- What is the current status of the company, its business and the products or services?

- Are all known problems of a new product disclosed regarding development, production, marketing, and customer satisfaction?

- Is management's background and experience misstated or not fully disclosed, and were there any prior business failures?

- Are there any company-related transactions that are not fully disclosed?

- Note additional detailed financial statement disclosures, primarily by footnotes or added risk factors.

- The management's discussion and analysis is insufficient, primarily in its description of the business.

Types of Review

The following are four basic types of review by the SEC. All are aimed at determining the adequacies of the disclosure. All are usually followed through with a letter and phone calls. The staff's job is to find deficiencies. It almost always does, but not with any malicious intent.

Deferred Review

In the event that an initial review by the staff shows that a registration is so poorly put together that it is not even worth the time to comment on it, it will write what is called a bedbug letter, advising the registrant to withdraw the registration statement—under threat of a stop order.

Cursory Review

Cursory review is not often used. The comment letter will indicate that the staff has performed a cursory review and has not found any glowing deficiencies and that no written or oral comments will be forthcoming. It usually requests that all persons connected with the underwriting—company counsel, accountants, and underwriters, write letters to the SEC indicating that they are aware of the statutory responsibilities under the '33 act.

Summary Review

Almost identical to the cursory review, summary review also is not often used. The staff simply furnishes a few comments based upon limited review.

Customary Review

This preferred review includes a full review by the branch examiner with input by the accountants, attorneys, analysts, and all needed experts and a detailed comment letter signed by the branch chief.

Amendments

A company's replies to the SEC's comment letters are called amendments (to the registration statement). Several different types are used. They are:

Delaying Amendment

This amendment is designed to delay the 20-day effective date of a registration. If a company has received a comment letter, the registration technically becomes effective 20 days later. If the company has not had enough time to reply or to make up the deficiencies listed in the comment letter, it replies to the SEC with a delaying amendment requesting a new effective date. Failure to do so can result in a defective registration and/or the possibility that the SEC may feel compelled to issue a stop order against the company. Such action can result in civil liabilities against the company and its principals, as well as the underwriter. As a rule, each time the company replies to the SEC with further amendments, in whole or part, its action automatically restarts the 20-day period.

Substantive Amendment

This amendment is commonly filed to correct the deficiencies in a registration statement. Usually it is in reply to the SEC comment letter. But it can also be instigated by the company to update events in the company that took place since the original filing. The registration statement must be correct and current when it becomes effective. If a company allows a registration to lapse without it becoming effective or by not filing any amendments, the SEC will allow a time period of 9 months to expire be giving the company 30 days' notice and declaring the registration abandoned.

Price Amendment

This amendment is commonly used on larger registrations where the actual offering price and the total amount of stock to be offered are not determined until the day of the offering or the day prior to the offering. The purpose of the amendment is to insert this last-minute information. The SEC will then declare the offering effective immediately. This is usually done by phone, followed by a confirming telegram.

Filing the Substantive Amendment

The substantive amendment can be employed for all amendments filed after the initial comment letter. It is not unusual to follow the comment letter with as many as three or four substantive amendments. Each must comply with certain formal requirements, however. They must be filed with a facing cover sheet. They must also be consecutively numbered in the order in which they are filed.

On first registration, the SEC will issue a filing number that has to be used on all further correspondence and filings. Each amendment must be filed in triplicate, with one copy being hand-signed, plus eight additional copies to be made available to the public. If any of the amendments contain revised financial statements, a new hand-signed certificate is also required from the accountants.

Each amendment's cover letter must clearly indicate the SEC's reference number and the particular SEC comment number from the respective comment letters. The company comments have to reflect the action taken by the company regarding each SEC comment, such as withdrawal of a section, word change, or the changing of parts (any part or word), or the addition of new parts or language. Occasionally new parts or additional information is included, which must be noted in cover letters.

It is not uncommon, as a registration proceeds through the SEC bureaucracy, that at each review step, someone at a higher level on the SEC staff reviews the statement. This can become disconcerting for those in the company involved in the process. New comments or questions often come from the final reviewers. Also, a final reviewer will very often reverse a subordinate on a point that had been thought resolved.

The SEC, in its usual ambiguous manner, has been known to issue statements such as the following quote from a comment letter:

> As certain comments include requests for additional information, the staff may have further comments upon receipt of such additional information. Therefore, an appropriate period of time should be allowed for staff review of the amendment prior to any requested date of effectiveness.

The registrant company had better take care not to do what it would normally do with a response of this type, which would be to go over the head of the assigned reviewer. Diplomacy is the best policy. If a significant issue is involved, counsel should respectfully request a further review at the next higher level. The better part of valor is to allow the SEC staff to have the final word as to whether the company has adequately responded to their comments. Also, remember that the goal is to obtain the registration's effectiveness, not to prove who has the better legal mind.

Finally, because of the large number of filings and the constant heavy work load of SEC staff members, the company should copy all amendments and all correspondence to all staff members involved in the filings as a protection.

Preliminary Prospectus (Red Herring)

As mentioned in an earlier chapter, the preliminary prospectus comes by its nickname *red herring* because portions that are subject to change are printed in red ink. A preliminary prospectus is distributed by the company, its underwriters, and the selling syndicate members to prospective investors. The purpose is to gather an indication of interest from the investor. As a means of informing the reader that it is not the final prospectus, the following statement is printed in red ink on the cover:

> A registration statement relating to these securities has been filed with the Securities and Exchange Commission but has not become effective. Information contained herein is subject to completion or amendment. These securities may not be sold nor may offers to buy be accepted prior to the time the registration statement becomes effective. This prospectus shall not constitute an offer to sell or the solicitation of an offer to buy nor shall there be any sale of these securities in any State in which such offer, solicitation, or sale would be unlawful prior to registration or qualification under the securities laws of any such State.

On larger offerings, the red herring is distributed at the time the initial registration statement is filed. For smaller offerings it may be wise to hold off on the printing and distribution of this document until after the initial comment letter has been received from the SEC and reviewed and the first amendment filed. The main reason is the expense involved in the printing. When changes are required, a new printing must be done. According to the SEC, each person considering purchase of the company's stock is supposed to receive a copy of the final prospectus. They should also receive copies of amendments as they are filed. It becomes pretty obvious that this can involve a tremendous amount of time and money. That is why, in practice, it is better not to distribute the red herring until the initial comment letter is replied to and the company has a sense of the extent of the SEC's comments and how many more changes may be needed.

Current red herring printing costs and expenses for distribution can easily come to $3 each ($2 printing and $1 for mailing). Consequently, it is desirable to only have to distribute a red herring and a final prospectus to prospective investors just once. Unfortunately, this intention often falls by the wayside along with the best-laid plans.

The registrant should also make a point of keeping track of the name of each person who receives information on a new issue, including the red herring. Although the primary responsibility for this lies with the under-writer and by extension, the members of the selling syndicate, it's good to have a record of where the interest is coming from.

Stop Orders

Mentioned earlier in this chapter under the heading "Deferred Review," the SEC maintains an ultimate hammer called a *stop order*. This is an order from the commission suspending the effectiveness of a registration state-ment. Once the order is issued, it is unlawful to mail or commence to offer, sell, or deliver a prospectus *or* securities having to do with the offering. The effect of a stop order is to give warning to the public that the SEC has found the registration untrue, misleading, unreliable, or lacking material facts. The stop order can only be issued after a notice has been sent to the registrant granting a 14-day period to request a hearing. If the company corrects the deficiencies, a declaration will be issued by the SEC and the stop order will cease to be effective.

Obviously, a company wants to prevent this action from ever taking place. A stop order has an ugly way of tainting an offering and making the chances of it ever being sold very slim. After all this, you should know a stop order is rarely, if ever, employed.

Stickers

Section 10 of the '33 act states that a prospectus must contain all the pertinent information on the previous history of the company up to the effective date of the registration. It also requires that information about the company be noted in the prospectus *after* the effective date of the registra-tion (when the prospectus is already in the hands of the investor), and it must be kept current. It is possible to do this without having to do a post-effective amendment. It can be done by adding a prospectus supple-ment known as a sticker. The information is printed on a sheet of paper and glued to the cover page of the prospectus. This is referred to as stickering a prospectus.

Stickering is usually done for a period of 90 days after the effective date of registration. But in reality, it goes on for longer than 90 days. Stickering is often done until the offering is sold out and continued until it is very clear that a post-effective amendment is not called for.

These stickers (prospectus supplements) do not require SEC review. They are used to add information such as the company receiving a sizeable contract, especially if the contract was noted as pending in the prospectus, or to inform the investor of the hiring of a key officer or director that was noted as a possibility in the prospectus.

It's worth mentioning that the cost and follow-up of using stickers can be expensive. The underwriter and members of the selling syndicate must all be supplied with stickers to be attached to the prospectuses. The stickers must also be sent to individual prospectus holders. Therefore, it may be advisable for the company to delay the announcement of any important information until the *quiet period* is over. The quiet period is the 90 days after the effective date of registration, during which the company cannot make any additional comments beyond those referred to in the registration statement. The reason is that the new information could be considered a hype, which is not looked upon favorably by the SEC. For example, this information might refer to the signing of a contract or the completion of an acquisition or merger, which could push up the stock's selling price.

Acceleration Letter

An acceleration letter is a request to waive the normal 20-day waiting period prior to an offering being declared effective by the SEC. It is a letter from the company's legal counsel to the SEC to the effect that the company has completed its amendment filings and has complied with all the points in the SEC's comment letter.

The request to accelerate the effective date is very common with larger underwritings and is filed simultaneously with the pricing amendment. This amendment discloses the offering price of the security, the total number of securities to be offered, the underwriter's commission, and the net proceeds to the company.

This final, pricing amendment, along with the acceleration letter, is important because it requests that the stock be placed *now* with the investment public. The reason is that most larger offerings are firm commitment underwritings. The underwriter has its money at risk and does not want to risk a change in the market conditions, which may seem right at the moment. The SEC knows the importance and makes every effort to oblige.

State Filings

Even though a registration is filed with the SEC, the company's securities must also qualify under the various states' blue-sky laws—the state laws governing the sale of securities.

It is usually the responsibility of the managing underwriter, after determining in which states it will offer the securities, to file with those states at the time the initial filing with the SEC takes place. Many states will not allow a security to be sold or permit the distribution of a preliminary prospectus until that is done.

NASD Review

The National Association of Securities Dealers (NASD) must also put its stamp of approval on the offering. It is mainly concerned with Regulation S–K, which deals with the contents of the registration statement, and the underwriter's compensation. It reviews the selling commission of the underwriter, the reselling commission, or pass-through, to the selling syndicate members, and other items which come under the umbrella of the underwriter's compensation. These include such items as the amount and uses of the accountable and unaccountable expenses and the number, type, cost, and exercise price of warrants or options granted to the underwriter. NASD also reviews finders' fees and the possible association of any of the persons involved in the underwriting with a NASD member.

For what they may be worth, the following are some typical comments that have been culled from various NASD comments following its opening statement, "On the basis of our review, we have decided to defer an opinion with the respect to the fairness and reasonableness of the proposed terms and arrangements until we have received and reviewed the following":

- A statement as to the NASD association, affiliation, or relation of all officers, directors, and principal (5 percent or greater) shareholders of the registrant.

- Details as to the acquisition of the registrant's unregistered securities by any NASD-affiliated person including security holder's name, date of acquisition, amount acquired, consideration rendered, and whether such NASD affiliate will participate in any capacity in the offering.

- A statement as to whether the issuer intends to register as a broker/dealer or otherwise become a member of the NASD.

- Confirmation that the proceeds of the offering will not be comingled with the proceeds of any other public distribution.

To reiterate, NASD's concern is to determine whether the underwriter arrangements are fair and reasonable as pertains to protecting the public investor. The interesting part of this process is that the NASD does not have published rules as to what it considers fair and reasonable. It has issued some guidelines, but there are numerous cases where NASD has caused considerable delay in the effectiveness of a proposed underwriting while everyone concerned tries to figure out what it considers fair and reasonable. (See chapter 22.)

Therefore, it behooves the underwriter's counsel to apply for a NASD review as soon as possible after the registration statement is filed with the SEC. The review may require a renegotiation of the underwriter's agreement. Of course, looking at it from counsel's fatalistic point of view, the review *will* require a renegotiation of the underwriter's agreement.

Summary

The process for larger filings is more complex than for small filings. Large filings are best accomplished with the SEC in Washington, D.C. Smaller filings usually do better and are completed faster at regional branch offices. In both cases, it's best to start with a prefiling conference between the company, its securities counsel, and the SEC staff. The conference could take place on the phone or in person. The main purpose would be to clarify disclosure questions pertaining to general requirements or legal and accounting points.

All filings must be signed by the members of the company who are parties to the registration statement. The filing is then assigned to an examiner by the securities commissioner. The examiner reviews it with other staff people and writes a comment letter to the company.

The comment letter represents the staff's views regarding the completeness and accuracy of the registration statement. The depth and number of comments may vary, but they will certainly require the company to reply with as many amendments as necessary. At that juncture, the company usually issues a preliminary prospectus (red herring), which is partially printed in red ink to denote that it is not final. This is used to obtain indications of interest from the investment community for the company's stock issue. If there are changes in the company, its personnel, or its operations after the registration has been approved or during the 90-day quiet period (when no changes can be made), the company must announce any change by issuing a prospectus supplement (sticker).

The company must also file its registration statement with the securities commissions in the states in which it intends to offer its stock. The same procedure must be followed with the National Association of Securities Dealers (NASD).

The filing process takes a patient, nonconfrontational attitude on the part of management to get through the ordeal. If management chooses to confront the SEC, it can do so. If it's lucky it'll probably get two choices from the SEC—Do it our way, or don't do it.

26

Blue-sky Laws

The '33 and '34 securities acts and the Securities and Exchange Commission regulate the issuance of securities. But each state also has its own securities laws. And *each* state has the *final* authority as to which securities can be sold in its jurisdiction. These laws are referred to as *blue-sky laws*. Getting new issues approved by a state's securities agency is called *blue-skying*. As mentioned in the previous chapter, the underwriters must file in the individual states in which they intend to sell securities. The laws also require the registration of broker/dealers and investment companies doing business in the state.

These laws were first drawn up to protect "gullible" investors from purchasing stock from "unscrupulous" promoters trying to sell them the blue sky. That's how the law got its name.

Background

In 1911, Kansas was the first state to adopt the first omnibus securities law. By 1929, about half the states adopted similar laws, but each state had its own variations, which caused nationwide registration problems. Because of that, in 1929, a Uniform State Securities Act was approved by the Conference of Commissioners on Uniform State Laws and the American Bar Association. In 1948, the Investment Bankers Association began working on versions of blue-sky laws modeled after the federal law. Finally, in 1956, a new Uniform State Securities Act was approved by many of the states. Since then, there has been a continuing effort to adopt a nationwide standard that would be tied into the federal law. Most of the states have gone along with it, but some states are still doing it their own way. Interestingly, the state of Delaware and the District of Columbia are the only jurisdictions that do not have a local securities law as yet.

Some states have extremely tough blue-sky laws, while others are content to rely on an effective federal SEC registration statement. They also conduct their own style of reviews, as there is no set pattern for state review.

Types of State Review

Merit Review

Some of the "tough" states employ the Merit Review. Simply stated, if the state's securities commission or review board does not like the offering on its merits, it can deny it. Period! No questions asked! No appeal! Merit review states have an approval statute as apposed to the federal SEC disclosure rules.

Most of the states with merit review want satisfactory answers to questions such as the following:

- What percentage of the company is offered to the public?
- Are the promoters reaping all the benefits while the new investors are putting up all the money?
- Is the company an operating company with a product or service?
- Are the underwriter's fees, that is, commissions, warrants, unaccountable expenses, too high?
- Is there a holding period for insiders' stock (similar to Rule 144)?
- Have there been any criminal convictions of officers, directors, or insiders?

If the answers they receive are satisfactory, they can be quite reasonable.

Qualification Review

The statutes are basically the same as for merit reviews. The securities must qualify according to the state's standards or the registration can be denied or suspended. No sales can take place until the securities are approved.

Coordination Review

This review is a form of qualification. But most of the states that use it simply have a rule that no sales are allowed until the issue is declared effective by the SEC.

Notification Review

This procedure requires the filing of a Notice of Intention to sell. After the filing is reviewed, sales of the stock can take place immediately unless the administrator/reviewer takes action to hold up the offering. In this type of review, the underwriter must be careful not to assume that approval is automatic.

Violations

Violation of state statutes on the sale of securities can result in civil liability, and in some states criminal action is taken. All states have provisions prohibiting fraud that include penalties. These provisions enable the state agency to investigate principals, give public notice and warning, and obtain injunctions. This is often coupled with the power to subpoena and to examine witnesses as well as business records. Violations, at minimum, will cause sales to be rescinded and may also call for investor restitution.

Filing

Filing of the actual registration statement is up to the company's counsel or underwriter's counsel. The state's filing fees are usually paid by the company. The filing should be coordinated with the underwriters, as they are the ones who decide in which states to file. Their decision is usually predicated on which states their brokers are registered in, the location of their client investors, and the preference of the members of the selling syndicate. Some states require that the company retain local legal counsel to handle the filing, especially if there are proceedings before the state's securities commission.

Blue-sky List

The company's SEC counsel should furnish a preliminary blue-sky memorandum for distribution to various brokers that includes a list of the intended blue-sky states. It should also make note of any restrictions or other limitations, such as the number of securities that can be sold in a particular state. When all the blue-sky paperwork is completed and the offering is effective with the SEC, a final memorandum must be submitted.

Blue-skying can be a complicated process that requires a lot of coordination between the company, the underwriter, and state authorities in order to meet all the deadlines and keep the timing in place for an effective offering.

The good news is that after a stock is publicly traded, most states automatically allow it to be traded in their jurisdiction, especially if the company is listed in Moody's or Standard & Poor's. Stocks that are NASDAQ listed and traded (National Association of Securities Dealers Automated Quotations System) are also looked upon with favor by most states.

It is to be hoped that in the near future all the states will abide by the same set of blue-sky laws. Until then, it's a matter of taking them as they come.

Summary

Blue-sky laws were instituted to protect the investor from purchasing stock from promoters who offered what amounted to nothing more than blue sky, or lacked real substance. Each state now has its own blue-sky law, which essentially governs the sale of securities within the state. Some of the laws are similar to those of other states. There is a continuing effort to adopt a nationwide standard for states that would be tied into the federal law.

Some states have extremely tough blue-sky laws. However, all filings by companies and underwriters to sell stocks must be reviewed by each state's securities commission. Violations of state statutes on the sale of securities can result in severe penalties.

Those involved in the sales of securities within a state must also be registered in the state, including the company, the underwriter, broker/dealers, and the selling syndicate.

Complying with blue-sky laws can be almost as complicated as complying with the requirements of the SEC. It's almost like doing the same thing twice—only different.

27

Selling the Issue

The difference between selling large and small IPOs is the way the selling is handled. These dealings also depend on whether the issue is a firm commitment or a best efforts offering. As always, timing plays a critical role.

For example, on larger offerings (almost always firm commitments), where the underwriter has guaranteed the entire offering, the selling is usually done behind the scenes, prior to the effective date. That is, commitments have already been solicited on the stock before the issue comes out. It's a foregone conclusion that the underwriter has put out feelers about the issue and is reasonably certain that it will be sold out.

On best efforts offerings, the underwriters do not have to put their money where their mouth is. They makes no guarantees. However, the underwriters and their selling syndicates will be pushing the issue before and after the effective date. Remember, they don't make money on it unless they sell it.

While the underwriters are doing their thing, management will be doing *its* thing, which is complying with the SEC regulations. This includes the preparation of presentation materials and the presentation itself, completing the required materials (red herrings and final prospectuses), and of critical importance, scheduling its efforts. It must also be keenly aware of the SEC requirements (restrictions) that directly effect the selling process.

Management also must work within the framework of the quiet period we mentioned briefly in chapters 25 and 26. Loosely defined, the quiet period is that time from the moment the company's management entertains its first thoughts of going public until 90 days after the effective date of the registration statement. During those 90 days, according to the SEC, the company can only discuss or distribute information about itself and its activities that was disclosed in the prospectus.

There is a great difference of opinion, in both legal and financial public relations circles, as to what is legal and what is appropriate to communicate, and to whom, during this preregistration and registration period called the quiet period.

Despite SEC efforts to clarify the rules, the question remains a gray area, where legal counsel is usually consulted. The rules governing various segments of the registration process can be confusing to the well informed as well as those studying them for the first time. Let us try and shed some light on the subject.

As to preregistration, it is always difficult to know exactly when a company has entered its quiet period. Generally, it is some time prior to when the company submits materials to the SEC. One common rule of thumb is to assume that the SEC's registration publicity limitation begins about 60 days prior to any anticipated SEC filing date. This entire 60-day period prior to actual filing with the SEC is considered the preregistration period. The filing date is the date on which the company submits a registration statement to the SEC.

No Publicity During Registration

The registration period is generally assumed to extend from the date a tentative agreement or letter of intent regarding an offering has been reached with an underwriter until the conclusion of the post-offering period. It definitely includes the time period from entering registration until the effective date and 90 days thereafter. The effective date is the date on which the registration statement becomes effective upon SEC approval and shares are available for the first time to be sold to the public. In most cases, the effective date will be the date on which the final documents in connection with the registration procedure have been filed. The SEC rules limiting publicity usually apply throughout this period.

During the registration period, any release, speech, or publication not normally produced by the corporation should be carefully scrutinized by public relations and legal counsel for possible violations of the rules. In case of doubt, the SEC recommends consultation by companies and their legal counsel with the staff of the SEC.

Under the '33 act, it is unlawful to offer to sell a security during registration. Therefore, any type of extraordinary corporate publicity during registration may well be judged by the SEC as a selling effort on behalf of the security. In the eyes of the SEC, this holds true for any form of publicity which might tend to project an optimistic future for the issuing corporation in the minds of the investing public.

The rules specifically state that after the filing date and prior to the effective date of the registration statement, no written communication offering to sell a security may be made except the preliminary prospectus (red herring).

To further emphasize its concern about publicity as a selling effort, the SEC has said, "The release of publicity and the publication of information between the filing date and the effective date of the registration statement may . . . raise a question whether the publicity is not in fact a selling effort by an illegal means [other than the prospectus]." The SEC also is concerned that similar problems will arise "from publicity and the release of information after the effective date, but before a distribution is completed [before the stock is trading]."

Allowed Publicity

The SEC does encourage normal corporate publicity during registration. In a policy statement, the SEC made clear that companies in registration may:

1. Continue to advertise products and services. Materials such as sales promotion leaflets, displays, and general product or service publications may also be issued.

2. Continue to send out customary quarterly, annual, and other periodic reports to stockholders. News releases disclosing financial results for these periods may also be issued. However, these must not include short- or long-term growth estimates (other than a properly prepared forecast that conforms to current SEC forecasting guidelines).

3. Continue to make announcements to the press with respect to factual business and financial developments, such as receipt of a contract, the settlement of a strike, the opening of a plant, or similar events of interest to the community in which the business operates. News releases on personnel appointments and new products or research developments also fall within this category. However, such announcements must contain no estimates of how the new developments will affect earnings or sales, either in broad or specific terms, unless they conform with specific SEC forecasting guidelines which are outlined in the rules and regulations.

4. Answer unsolicited telephone inquiries from stockholders, financial analysts, the press, and other sources that concern financial information and business operations published in the registration statement.

5. Respond to unsolicited inquiries concerning factual matters from securities analysts, securities holders, and participants in the communications field who have a legitimate interest in the corporation's affairs.

6. Continue to hold stockholders' meetings as scheduled and to answer stockholders' inquiries at stockholders' meetings relating to factual matters. This includes giving speeches before trade and professional groups that were scheduled before the decision to register, providing the speeches do not contain projections other that those mentioned in the registration statement.

However, the SEC wants to make it clear that the prohibition of publicity, which might serve as a selling effort for a security in registration, still applies to corporate disclosure during registration:

Disclosure of factual information in response to inquiries or resulting from a duty to make prompt disclosure under the anti-fraud provisions of the securities acts or the timely disclosure policies of self-regulatory organizations, at a time when a registered offering of securities is contemplated or in process, can and should be effected in a manner which will not unduly influence the proposed offering.

The SEC further stresses, regarding publicity during registration: "Neither a company in registration nor its representatives should instigate publicity for the purpose of facilitating the sale of securities in a proposed offering."

The best guideline in the delicate area of publicity during registration is to refrain entirely from publishing any material during the pre-effective (quiet) period that is not a part of the registration statement. That includes any release, speech, or publication not normally produced by the company.

Again, the SEC recommends consultation by companies and their PR and legal counsel with the SEC staff in case of doubt or possible violation.

Brokers' Due Diligence Meetings

When first conceived, due diligence meetings were held within a few days of a company's stock effectiveness or trading date. The purpose was to assure all participating parties in an underwriting that the issue was about to be launched. These meetings were originally held in the company's office, and the invited participants were the management and directors of the company, the company's legal counsel, the audit accountants, the underwriter, key syndicate members and their respective legal counsel, the escrow agent, and representatives from the transfer agent.

Part of the ritual included the reading, word by word, sentence by sentence, and page by page of the entire prospectus. The idea was to make sure that nothing was printed incorrectly and that there were no last-minute changes, especially financial, and to acquaint the selling parties with the details of the company and its offering.

Eventually, these boardroom rituals became shows, and moved to grand ballrooms of hotels. The meetings were complete with dancing girls, theatrical spotlights, hors d'oeuvres fit for royalty, hundreds of guests, and elaborate presentations by the company's management team.

It got to the point that each subsequent meeting outdid the last meeting. Finally, in the early 1980s, the SEC stepped in and put a halt to these fabulous festivities, implying they had lost their purpose.

So back the meetings went to small rooms. Invited brokers had to be registered to get in. The hors d'oeuvres were not as tempting, and the atmosphere was strictly business.

Today, when the underwriter decides it's time to introduce the company and the offering to the brokerage community it does a road show or a brokers' due diligence meeting. These are formal and still somewhat elaborate meetings to which the selling group of individual brokers are invited. They are complete with such things as video tapes, charts, and products—everything it takes to tell the company's story. The complete dog-and-pony show. All the important people are invited. The company usually covers the cost, with occasional help from the underwriter. The reading of the prospectus takes place as before, and questions are answered.

Attendance can range from one to hundreds. The average number of attendees is usually 20 to 50. The turnout depends on the selling job before the show. The company can spend a lot of time, trouble, and money to put on one of these affairs. But it must be done, and more important, done well, because today's due diligence meetings are politically very important. And it is important that the IPO entrepreneur/CEO understand the politics involved. He or she will be dealing with brokers who come to these meetings because they are interested in deals. So management must impress upon them that this is the deal they've been waiting for. Remember, brokers need product to sell, and management and the company is the product. Management's job is to get the brokers on its side.

These are figures management hears: The average broker of a small-company new issue is good for selling about $5,000 worth of new stock. Some can do as much as $100,000. A good average is $25,000. The $100,000 brokers can often be counted on to do $200,000, because they are big producers, and they usually have four or five smaller brokers who like to tag along on a big producer's deals. Often two or three brokers will combine their efforts. The company needs these brokers, and these due diligence meetings are where it can make points with them by turning them on and cementing their commitment. It's a game of politics.

To make the most of it, the company needs to involve its financial public relations firm. The company's part of the meeting should be rehearsed over and over and over again. And the players should listen to all the constructive criticism that is given. Consider what is at stake. The end result can be very rewarding, and the deal will get done!

Timing

Due diligence meetings are best held within a week of the effective date, depending on the number of cities in which they will be held. However, plenty of time should be allowed for planning. It's not unusual to start working on them months ahead of the actual meeting dates. These meetings are team efforts, and call for the services of the underwriter and financial public relations firm to help coordinate them.

Actually, the meetings can be scheduled from as early as the printing of the red herring to as late as after the effectiveness of the issue. There are no set rules.

If the company is holding meetings in a number of cities, it should allow at least one day on either side of the meeting date. Figure a total of 3 days in each city. It will take that much time to make personal calls on individual firms, brokers, and potential investors. Breakfasts, lunches, coffees, drinks, dinners, and more drinks are the norm. Allowing enough time can save the company people and underwriters from frantically trying to accomplish last-minute arrangements as the actual date draws near.

Location

Choose a hotel that has catered due diligence meetings in the past, one that brokers are familiar with.

Scheduling

Again, there are no set days. Experience shows brokers seem to prefer Tuesdays, Wednesdays, and Thursdays. If possible, avoid conflicts with socially significant events like the world series, NBA play-offs, the Olympics and the day before or after a brokers' holiday.

The Presentation

The whole purpose of the presentation is to sell the company to the people who will, it is hoped, sell the company to the investing public. Every effort should be made to impress upon the invited guests the ability and depth of the management team. It's important also to set aside time for questions and answers about the offering.

Although those in attendance know why they are there, the presentation should be paced to hold their attention. And it should be formatted in an orderly fashion. The following is an example of what could be included in the format of a presentation and the sequence in which it could be presented:

1. Introduction by underwriter or designee.

2. Introduction of the cast: Underwriter's name, company name, number of shares being offered, blue-sky states, effective date, billing date, closing date, trading date, and other things that will be covered.

3. Brief description of the company.

4. Introduction of the president/CEO of the company preceded by a brief bio.

5. President/CEO thanks presenter and shares information about the company—details and history.

6. Presenter or designated person presents audiovisual aids (if they are part of the program).

   Note that there are many ways to go in the audiovisual area. Video can be very exciting for a formal meeting presentation, but it can be very expensive, depending on the budget. A 15-minute video can easily cost $5,000 to $10,000 for taping and editing; $20,-000 is not out of the question, as far as costs go. But amortized over all the cities in which it will be shown, it may be a bargain in time and effort that would otherwise be expended. Also to be considered is the need for a large room and the expensive rental equipment such as projection screens and sound systems.

   Slide presentations can also be very effective. Production and presentation costs would not be as high, and slides offer the advantage of flexibility. They can be stopped at any time to encourage discussion. Many firms already have slide material about themselves that can be easily updated. Script changes can also be easily accomplished.

   Stand-up charts and transparencies are another way to go, but they can be awkward because of the size needed for an effective presentation.

   Handouts of executive portfolios, including product brochures, offering circulars, broker fact sheets, and samples are also always appropriate. (This can be part of the presentation even when an audiovisual presentation is used.)

7. Presentation of management team speakers (as appropriate). If the management team is not asked to speak, each team member should be introduced and a brief bio given.

8. President/CEO or chairman of the board introduces the board of directors with brief bios.

9. President/CEO introduces board of advisors with brief bios.

10. Appropriate participant conducts question-and-answer session.

11. Closing remarks by the underwriter.

Remember, whoever is a presenter during the presentation must make frequent caveats regarding what is being discussed. Nothing can be presented that hasn't been printed in the prospectus. If something should happen to come up during the question-and-answer period about the competition a product would face, unless it is stated in the prospectus, the presenter should say no more than, "It is management's opinion that the competition is limited," or something can be "anticipated." To be completely safe, technically, one can only discuss what is in the prospectus.

Post Meeting

Much of the company's work begins after the due diligence meetings have been completed. Management should make it a point to keep in contact with the brokers who attended the meetings and keep them appraised of the progress being made by the company. By establishing communication lines with the brokers, the company will be keeping the pressure on, and the brokers will be more inclined to talk up the offering.

Tombstones

The company can help to create public familiarity with the offering and also give a hand to the brokers who will become involved by preconditioning the investing public with *tombstone* ads.

Tombstone ads are more in the nature of announcements rather than advertisements. A tombstone is a "boxed-in" ad (that's why it is called a tombstone) that appears in financial papers and the financial and business sections of newspapers and magazines that announces the particulars of a new issue. It mentions the name of the company going public, the underwriter, and the total dollar amount of the offering and makes reference to the prospectus. Most important, it includes the brokers from whom a prospectus may be obtained. It can run during and after the registration period and is not considered an improper selling effort by the SEC. A disclaimer also appears at the top of the ad, which says in effect:

> This announcement is neither an offer to sell nor a solicitation of an offer to buy these securities. The offer is made only by prospectus.

The company will place tombstones upon the advice or encouragement from the underwriter and its financial public relations group. Some companies run them at the time the red herring is printed, upon the effectiveness of the offering, and on completion and trading of the issue. They can be run once or on multiple occasions. The amount usually depends on the current stock market trends and the demand for a particular type of issue.

Tombstones should be considered an essential ingredient in selling an issue. The benefits easily outweigh the costs. Not running a tombstone can prove to be a grave error.

Summary

Selling a new issue is the final step toward a successful IPO. The entrepreneur/CEO must become involved and keep everyone else who is involved charged up in order to bring it to a successful conclusion.

Effective selling requires a knowledge of, and being able to work within, the framework of the quiet period, and knowing what can and what cannot be said by and about the company. The allowed publicity, when used properly, can be most effective.

Tombstone ads are a good means for introducing the company to the public and piquing the public's interest. But management must make every effort to put together effective due diligent meetings, using all the help it can get from its PR firm and the underwriter. These meetings will be presented to a largely critical audience of brokers who need convincing. The outcome of these shows can often spell the difference between the success and failure of an IPO. To make it work—everybody has got to get into the act.

28

Escrow

Generally, from the effective date of an offering to the day the offering is completed (when all the monies have been received), the money goes into an *escrow* account. At that time it is turned over to the underwriter, who then turns the funds over to the company.

If, as happens in many instances, the offering is not completed, all the money must be returned to the individual investors.

Technically, the underwriter escrows all the monies received from the selling syndicate or individual investors. Escrows are also used for private offerings.

The process of selecting and establishing an escrow agent is often a decision made by the company and the underwriter. The selection also depends on the type of offering. A firm commitment offering doesn't really need an escrow agent, at least not for more than a few days. The escrow agent simply holds funds from the syndicate members payable to the lead underwriter who is responsible to the company for the full amount of the underwriting, regardless of the sales of the syndicate.

However, in a best efforts offering there can be, and usually is, a time period of several weeks to more than a month when money is being held on the part of investors pending completion of the underwriting. In some cases, it is possible that several months could go by during which an underwriting is started but not completed. The escrow company, meanwhile, is holding the money, essentially retaining the use of the funds without paying interest on it.

It is not uncommon that the escrow amount could build to hundreds of thousands even millions of dollars during the month or more that it is being held. These are opportunities for the escrow company to make a great deal on interest by investing in short-term investments. It's done every day.

The benefit to the company and the underwriter is the leverage it offers them. This is very much on their minds when they select an escrow agent. Is there a particular financial institution they want to favor with their account—or a particular financial institution they want a favor from? Of course, escrowing for a public company offering is more complicated than, for example, a real estate escrow. Money and checks come in from many different investment firms; they must all be registered and social security numbers noted; the checks must be deposited and followed through for clearance. Incoming stock subscriptions must be tracked on a daily basis. Also, most financial institutions require a holding period on funds, and there are costs involved. Taking everything into consideration, the choice must also be made on experience as well as the best deal that can be secured.

Banks are often favored for this kind of escrow. Most banks will perform this service at no cost or for a very nominal setup charge (remember, they have the use of the money). But although banks are the industry's primary escrow agents, quite a few transfer agents also offer this service. If the company's normal bank is capable of handling large, complicated escrows, such as an offering, it should be used. If the company is looking to establish a new or second banking relationship, the escrow offers an opportunity to talk with other prospective banks and further the company's financial affiliations. And that's something the company can really bank on.

Summary

The selection process of choosing a bank or an escrow company to escrow the funds of an offering is a decision made by the IPO company and/or the underwriter. There are distinct advantages to be gained as well as some leverages that can be played out in deciding which financial institution should be chosen to handle an IPO escrow. The financial institution stands to make a good deal on interest from investing the money held in the escrow account in short-term investments. This offers the company an opportunity to improve its relationship with the financial institution it designates as its escrow agent.

Experience counts too. Whoever is chosen must be able to perform all the complicated escrowing requirements for a public company offering. There are many banks and escrow companies out there that can do the job. The question is—which one will offer the company the best fringe benefits? Nothing wrong with that.

29

Closing

The *closing* of an offering is that time when all the transactions pertaining to the offering have been completed and all the monies, stocks, and commissions have been received and are dispensed. It is possible to have more than one closing on an offering. Let us say, for example, that we have a $4 million offering. We can designate the first closing at $3 million minimum, and the second closing will be for $1 million.

Closings differ considerably between small offerings on a best efforts basis and the larger offerings that are firm commitments. The one thing they hold in common is that they mark the conclusion of a combined effort on the part of a lot of dedicated people, culminating in the payoff.

Closing Meeting

The attendance at a closing meeting can be rather large. It will include all the key players involved in the underwriting. The meetings are usually held in the conference room of the escrow company or bank that handled the escrow. Those in attendance will include:

For the company

- Usually the president (CEO)
- The secretary and treasurer (CFO)
- The company's legal counsel
- The company's accountants—with a final comfort letter in hand

For the underwriter

- A managing executive
- A syndicate broker representative
- The underwriter's legal counsel
- The back room office manager—the person who supervised the office responsible for stock transfers, securities going out, the tracking of stock confirmations, stock certificates coming in, money going out, and all the people who work in the office

Also in attendance are the transfer agent representatives, with stock certificates in hand, and the escrow company representatives, with checks in hand.

Best Efforts Closing

For the small, best efforts offering, the closing takes place after the selling period has been completed. The selling period is usually 60 to 120 days from the effective date, with an extension allowance of 60 to 90 days by mutual consent of the company and the underwriter. It's that time period between the effective date and the date the actual trading of the stock begins. To make certain there is no confusion, the closing period for a best efforts underwriting is noted in the prospectus, usually on the cover, and further noted in the section on underwriting. By that time also, the selling syndicate members will have collected their money from the individual investors, and all the monies will have been deposited in and cleared the escrow account.

On the closing date, the *big* meeting takes place, coordinated by the company's legal counsel, who brings along a closing memorandum. The memorandum simply states the actual closing process, informing those present who the recipients are of specific original documents and who will receive copies of the documents. All the necessary documents are signed by the various parties, including an incumbency certificate which states that the officers listed in the registration statement are still with the company. Also, a second comfort letter from the auditing accounts is normally presented, assuring that everything is financially correct.

The final order of business consists of an exchange of stock certificates or evidence of their transfer to the underwriter by the company via its transfer agent. (The underwriter will transfer the stock to the individual purchasers of the stock.) This order is occasionally reversed, with the underwriter giving the transfer agent a distribution list of the stockholders. Lastly, checks are passed out by the escrow agent, usually to the underwriter for its commissions and unaccountable expenses, and then the company is given its money. Receipts are common practice for all the transactions, with the end result being writer's cramp. If there are selling shareholders present, they will receive separate checks made out to them. And, with no more business to conduct—the closing celebration party begins.

Firm Commitment Closing

A firm commitment closing is more complicated and hectic than that for a best efforts offering. The principal reason is that the actual selling price of the stock and the total number of shares being offered are not determined (committed) until the day prior to, or sometimes the actual day that the stock starts trading. Naturally, this creates a great deal of anxiety among all involved. However, the paperwork and documentation for both are similar.

Since the selling price and the shares offered in a firm commitment offering are not determined until the day of effectiveness, the preparation for the closing starts prior to the effective date, with an actual closing usually scheduled a week or two later. Because of that, a grace period is granted to gather both funds and the needed closing documentation. The documents, which by the way also apply to best efforts offerings, include:

- A letter to the transfer agent from the underwriters specifying shareholders' names and stock denominations
- Verified certificates of incorporation and good standing of the company and its subsidiaries
- An assertion by the company that it has complied with all legal requirements and has received approval of all actions leading to the closing, and that no publicity or events occurred that materially effected the offering
- Certification by selling shareholders (if any)
- A stock disposition letter to the transfer agent from the company
- A final opinion to the underwriter from the company's counsel
- A stock issue validity letter to the transfer agent from the company's counsel
- A final opinion letter by the underwriter's counsel to the underwriter
- Exchange of receipts list
- Disbursement of official bank checks to the respective parties

The Difference

It is important to recognize the principal difference between a best efforts and a firm commitment underwriting. Under best efforts, when the registration is declared effective, the underwriter proceeds to sell the stock. The monies received are escrowed until the underwriters have given their best efforts and at least a minimum amount of stock has been sold to investors. As mentioned earlier, this could take 60 to 90 days, and a closing cannot take place until the money is in hand.

Under a firm commitment underwriting, the underwriter is committing the money to the company, saying in essence that it commits its dollars to the company prior to selling the stock to the public. In actuality, the underwriter has lined up buyers of the stock through syndicate members and broker/dealers. The underwriter's money is usually at risk only briefly—maybe a week or two. However, this risk is really only a book-keeping function, since the company does not receive the committed funds until the actual closing. In any event, the closing celebration usually makes up for all the stress and anxiety both sides have been put through.

Summary

The closing phase of an offering differs greatly between the best efforts for a small offering and the firm commitment for a larger offering.

In a best efforts offering, the price of the stock has been determined, and the closing takes place after the selling period is completed and all the money has been collected. In a firm commitment offering, the selling price of the stock and the total number of shares being offered are not determined until just prior to or the same day the stock actually starts trading. At that time, the total amount of the offering is committed by the underwriter.

The closing meetings and the business to be conducted at the meetings are much the same, however, and the closing celebration parties, after everyone has been paid off, are just as much fun!

30

Listings

The primary securities trading markets, where a majority of the stocks sold in the United States are listed, are:

The New York Stock Exchange

The American Stock Exchange

The regional markets

The Forth Market

The over-the-counter markets

We will be addressing all of these markets; however, in this book we are concentrating on the over-the-counter (OTC) market in particular, since almost all initial public offerings (IPOs) are traded OTC.

Since the early 1980s, the OTC market has gained overwhelming investor acceptance as a bona fide, legitimate marketplace. In fact, many members of the financial community consider the OTC market as a leader in trading innovations that will go well into the twenty-first century. It's the exchange where many of the nation's newest and most exciting issues got their start, among them, Microsoft, Apple, Genentech, Intel, and L.A. Gear.

What follows is a look at the markets, their methods of operating, and their listing requirements, which we hope will promote a better understanding of all the trading markets.

The New York Stock Exchange

In the past, the listing dream and final destination for all public companies was the NYSE. It carried the prestige of being the world's largest and oldest trading place. There are over 1300 members of the exchange, represented by over 500 member firms, and over 150 specialists. This august body is self-ruled by a 20-person board made up of members who own a seat on the exchange. Owners may be corporations, partnerships, or individuals. Membership is obtained by purchasing a seat on the exchange. These seats are limited in number, and in recent years, depending on the profitability of the market (based on investor interest and market volume), the seat prices have fluctuated from $750,000 to $1.8 million.

The exchanges (NYSE, AMEX, regionals) use an auction method of trading (as opposed to the OTC method of telecommunications). This means that an individual, known as a specialist, physically conducts trading activities at a trading post in one particular floor location (exchange). These specialists, or their firms, make a market in one or a group of assigned stocks. Their primary function is to bring buyers and sellers together, and their responsibility is to maintain a fair and orderly market. Specialists match buy and sell orders in their trading books. Only if there is an imbalance in the buys and sells do they trade out of their own account—this is done to preserve the orderly market in a particular stock and to make certain there is continued supervision of this process by the exchanges. During times of large or extreme market fluctuations, such as happened on Black Monday 1987, the specialists' trading system is put to the test. That is also when the value of the auction method of market trading is often questioned.

The NYSE currently lists over 1600 companies trading over 3500 securities. The reason there are more securities than companies is because there are various types of securities. Some companies have more than one of their securities listed and traded, common or preferred stocks, warrants, rights, and options.

Listing Requirements

The listing requirements for a company on the NYSE are extensive, as is the process. First, an application is made to the Department of Stock List. After the application is approved, it is sent to the SEC for final approval. The listing normally becomes effective within 30 days. The company is then assigned a post on the floor of the exchange. It has no choice or say as to who the specialists will be.

The form for listing is very similar to, and as involved as, a full S–1 registration statement. The company is required to keep all its information updated to the exchange on a timely basis. This includes disclosure of information that is of "substantial" character, that is, information that could have impact on the trading of the company's stock. This type of information must be phoned to the Stock List department at the same time it is released to the media so the exchange can consult with the specialists to determine if trading of the stock should be halted. In particular, this pertains to information on:

- Annual earnings
- Quarterly earnings
- Dividend declarations
- Merger and acquisition announcements
- Acquisitions for stock that increase the total amount outstanding by more than 20 percent
- Acquisitions where the stock/cash value paid is more than 20 percent of the fair market value of the company's stock
- Adoption of stock option plans
- Plans for golden parachutes for management or directors
- Shareholders' voting rights
- Tender offers
- Stock splits
- Changes in top management
- Significant new product developments
- Changes in, or new major contracts

The minimum listing requirements for the NYSE are:

- 2000 shareholders
- Publicly held shares with a market value of $16 million
- 1 million publicly held shares
- Income before taxes of $2.5 million
- Net assets of $18 million

Additionally, the NYSE requires "substantial representation" of outside members on the board of directors and, usually, an audit committee on the board that is made up entirely of independent, outside directors in order to maintain financial integrity.

Delisting

The delisting requirements are almost as ponderous as for listing on the NYSE. At the top of the list is the failure to meet reporting requirements. Next is the failure to maintain minimum listing requirements, although exceptions are made during the probationary period. A seldom-used reason for delisting is inactive trading of the stock. Also, the exchange can deny listing if there are questionable transactions between officers, directors, or major shareholders of the company. This could pertain to things such as direct or indirect ownership of property or equipment leased to the company, sales or service to the company with interlocking ownership, and ownership of subsidiaries.

If the company requests delisting, it must get the approval of two-thirds of its shareholders, with less than 10 percent objecting.

The American Stock Exchange

The American Stock Exchange (AMEX) is the United States's second largest exchange, listing about 1000 securities. It is the world's largest trader of foreign stocks, and the companies listed on the AMEX are generally smaller in size than those on the NYSE. The AMEX is also considered a specialist trading market, very much like the NYSE. However, traditionally, its competitive advantage is that it offers more assistance to its listed companies in the areas of arranging investor conferences, meetings, and research programs.

All of its listing, disclosure, filing, and voting rights rules and requirements are similar to those of the NYSE—except that the minimum listing requirements are less demanding on the AMEX.

The minimum listing requirements for AMEX are:

- 900 shareholders, 600 of which must own at least 100 shares
- 300,000 publicly held shares
- Publicly held shares with a market value of $2.5 million
- Income before taxes of $750,000
- Net assets of $4 million

The Regional Exchanges

Regional stock exchanges serve distinct regions. They are involved with the trading of stocks nationally, but their emphasis is on stocks that have a particular regional interest. Stocks on regional exchanges can also be traded OTC. Now, with the advent of the International Trading System, stocks listed on the NYSE can be traded on any exchange.

Prior to the crash of '29, there were 15 to 20 regional exchanges. One of them, the Boston Curb Market, had the reputation of being a famous old playground for skip-shop promoters. These were unsavory promoters who offered phony stocks to the unsuspecting investor and then disappeared with the proceeds. That was a common occurrence among all the regionals during the Roaring Twenties. After the implementation of the securities acts of '33 and '34, along with the establishment of the SEC, regionals either went out of business or consolidated.

By the early 1960s, only eight regional exchanges were still in business. They were in San Francisco, Los Angeles, Chicago, Detroit, Philadelphia, Baltimore, Boston, and Washington. There was also the Cincinnati Stock Exchange, which is regional, but has gone into a computerized system called the Multiple Dealer Trading System. It matches orders and executes them immediately by computer. To improve their business, the other regional exchanges started accepting memberships. Pension funds, banks, and other institutional investors joined as a way of saving on commissions.

By the late 1960s, the need for regional exchanges had diminished greatly. However, there was a growing concern on the part of Wall Street and the SEC over the heavy influence of institutional trading through the regionals. New rules were passed in the 1975 Securities Acts Amendments that effectively prohibited the joint ownership and operation of institutional managers and brokerage firms. Additionally, the deregulation of commissions wiped out the effectiveness of these associations.

Today's regional markets are essentially option trading markets, the most notable being the Chicago Board. The remaining exchanges have consolidated further into the Pacific, Midwest, Philadelphia, and Boston. They list less than 100 companies in total as regional stocks, and they continue to trade dually listed securities from the NYSE and AMEX as well as OTC. The impact of the regionals is minimal, and most Wall Streeters predict a bleak future for them.

The Forth Market

The Forth Market is a recent development encouraged by the continually increasing large stock positions held by institutional investors. These investors consist primarily of pension funds, mutual funds, bank trusts, and insurance companies. Together they have formed a system whereby they execute buys and sells among themselves without the intermediary of a broker. These large block trades are reported to the exchanges, but both the NYSE and the AMEX are seriously concerned about the growing Forth Market. They are trying to devise ways to halt, limit, or supervise this seemingly runaway growth. The computerized and preprogrammed trading by these institutions has come under increasing scrutiny and investigation, especially since Black Monday 1987. The obvious benefit to these large institutions is that it saves them a lot of commission dollars.

The Over-the-Counter Market

The over-the-counter (OTC) market is subdivided into Pink Sheets, the National Association of Securities Dealers Automated Quotation Systems (NASDAQ), and the National Market System (NMS). Its daily trading function and mechanism differs from the exchanges in that its business is conducted via telecommunications through broker/dealers across the country as opposed to the procedures used by the NYSE and AMEX. The interconnect is via phones and computers, and each broker/dealer provides a bid and ask price for each of the individual stocks he or she chooses to make market in. There are no specialists along the lines of the NYSE, which creates a true negotiated marketplace. The broker/dealers buy and sell on an inventory basis.

Their governing body, the National Association of Securities Dealers (NASD), is composed of broker/dealers themselves. They have a paid administrative staff numbering in the hundreds, located around the country. NASD, as a nonprofit organization, establishes and enforces the regulations for the OTC market. Its chief concerns are:

- To protect the investors from illegal actions by the listed companies and the broker/dealers
- To establish and implement rules of fair practice for the broker/dealers
- To ensure that all broker/dealers comply with federal and state securities regulations
- To arbitrate grievances or disputes between broker/dealers and investors

Pink Sheets

The Pink Sheets are so named because they are printed on pink paper (over 300 pages measuring 6-by-14 inches). They are printed daily and are available by subscription from the National Quotations Bureau, a subsidiary of Commerce Clearing House. Each trading day's list, which is compiled the previous afternoon from all the market makers across the country, will show the bid and ask price quoted from the market makers.

Pink Sheets are considered to be the OTC trader's bible. By looking up a company by name, the stock, warrant, or bond and the firm that makes the market in each security can be identified. Each market maker's trading line phone number is listed. If the company is on the NASDAQ system, its symbol is also shown.

The first level of the OTC markets are the companies that trade in The Pinks. This includes most of the OTC-traded stocks—over 15,000. Approximately two-thirds of these companies have either chosen not to, or are unable to meet the requirements to, trade on the NASDAQ system.

There are actually no listing requirements for the Pink Sheets. If the company is publicly traded with two market makers, it is automatically listed. It is the responsibility of the company's management to secure the market makers and broker/dealers to trade its stock. A broker or trader that wants to trade the stock for an investor would look up the company in The Pinks, identify the market makers, call them on the phone, request quotes, and then execute the trade to the customer's best advantage. Confirming paperwork is processed through the broker/dealer clearing system.

The NASDAQ System

In 1971, the National Association of Securities Dealers (NASD) introduced the National Association of Securities Dealers Automated Quotation Systems (NASDAQ) service and drastically changed OTC trading. NASDAQ is a computer-based quotation/trading system with terminals in broker/dealers' offices all over the country. This system is able to display up-to-the-minute firm quotations.

Today the system is divided into various levels of service. It will show quotes of the best bid and the lowest offer, and the more complex terminals will show all the market makers in each stock, their quotes, last trades in price and amount, and continuous volume. The terminal systems are subscribed to by broker/dealers from NASDAQ.

Over 400 firms are listed market makers on NASDAQ, and the average company trading on its system has eight market makers versus *one* specialist on the exchanges. What's more, the services of the market makers are voluntary, whereas the specialists on the exchanges are assigned. This seems to suggest that the OTC may offer a company better stock trading advantages.

There are also over 4500 companies listed on NASDAQ. The listing requirements are brief and simple:

- A minimum of 300 shareholders
- A minimum of 100,000 publicly traded shares
- Total assets of $4 million

- Total net worth of $2 million
- Two or more market makers

As this book goes to press, the National Association of Securities Dealers (NASD) has put into motion a set of revised entry and maintenance standards for the listing of companies on NASDAQ. The new standards have been proposed to take effect January 1, 1991. A comparison chart between old and new standards is presented below:

Entry Standards

	Present	Proposed
Total assets	$2 million	$4 million
Capital & Surplus	$1 million	$2 million
Public Float	100,000 shares	same
Market Value of Public Float	none	$1 million
Market makers	2	same
Bid price	none	$3
Shareholders	300	same

Maintenance Standards

	Present	Proposed
Total Assets	$750,000	$2 million
Capital & Surplus	$375,000	$1 million
Public Float	1000 shares	100,000 shares
Market value of Public Float	none	$200,000
Market Makers	1	2
Bid Price	none	$1
Shareholders	300	same

A company's stock will be determined to be deficient in its maintenance standards if the issue fails to maintain any of the following individual stated requirements for 10 consecutive trading days: the market value of the public float, the number of market makers, and the bid price. Should any failure occur, the company will be notified promptly and will be given 90 calendar days in which to comply with the *entry*-level standard of the specified area failed.

The OTC Bulletin Board

Additionally, the SEC has instigated a one-year pilot program called the OTC Bulletin Board. This is an experiment to create an "electronic computerized" Pink Sheet trading report. Initial operations have been successful and enthusiastically received by both Pink Sheet companies and the brokers that trade them. All indications are that the OTC Bulletin Board will be implemented on a full-time, ongoing basis. This will be very helpful for the small companies that are unable to meet the higher listing requirements of NASDAQ.

During market trading hours, this computerized system displays the *firm* and *non-firm quotations,* and indications of interest in eligible OTC stocks that are not listed on the NASDAQ market.

All Pink Sheet stocks that were listed when the Bulletin Board went into effect are "grandfathered" as regards their initial eligibility. The decision for determining initial tradeability lies with the market makers and broker/dealers. New listing can be instagated, or reinstatement can be made by complying with the SEC Rule 15c2-11.

The Bulletin Board functions very much like the existing NASDAQ system. Each company has a designated symbol on the screen. Firm quotes (bid or ask) are shown, as are non-firm bids, wanted and unpriced entries. Each listing has the name and phone number of the market maker who is trading the stock being quoted.

The cost for listing is paid by the market makers and is free to the companies. Because of the complications and restrictions in the system, quotes will only be shown on the screens at trading desks as opposed to screens normally found in a brokerage office.

The NMS Market

The National Market System (NMS) came into being in 1975 when President Ford signed the Securities Acts Amendments. The purpose was to ensure a national trading structure that would result in a more efficient level of stock trading. It brought stock trading on the OTC to its highest level. It functions through the NASDAQ computer system. By 1982, through a series of improvements, it included the last trade of the day. Currently it shows trading activity similar to NYSE and AMEX, in that companies that are traded on the OTC NMS show their most recent stock trades, with continuous volume updates throughout the trading day.

The listing requirements for NMS are divided into two categories—developing and operating companies.

Developing companies are required to have a minimum of 800,000 publicly traded shares, $8 million in total capitalization, 4 years of operating history, and two market makers.

Operating companies are required to *maintain* a public shareholders' base of 300,000 shares, $1 million in operating capital, $300,000 in income, a minimum bid of $3, and two market makers.

In 1985, NMS stocks were granted automatic margin status, which acknowledged full equality with the exchange-listed stocks. This marginable status indicates increased liquidity and therefore attracts more institutional trading. The result has been that an increasing number of OTC stocks are now being found in institutional portfolios because of the high average growth rate of the OTC stocks compared to exchange-traded stocks.

Public Listings

The company should take advantage of the services of its financial public relations firm to arrange for listings in as many publications as possible. Shareholders should also be informed, on a continuing basis, as to the various publications in which they can find the company's stock quoted.

Most newspapers and financial publications today list the OTC. Its exposure is growing daily. *The National OTC Stock Journal* and *The Penny Stock News* are two major OTC papers that are published biweekly. They contain information on the OTC market, and news releases and feature articles about many companies and industries. *The OTC Review* is a nationally recognized monthly magazine that also emphasizes NASDAQ and NMS stocks, plus providing coverage of the market as a whole, including Pink Sheet stocks. As of now, over 100 daily newspapers carry the NMS and the NASDAQ National list. *The Wall Street Journal* carries the NASDAQ "Additional List" of over 1800 companies. Many regional daily newspapers also carry a supplemental list of companies that have a regional interest.

Standard & Poor's Index is a widely accepted index of market performance and trends. It includes the price activity of a broad base of 500 leading listed and OTC stocks, including industrial, transportation, financial, and public utility stocks.

Moody's is an investment rating service of corporate bond issues, preferred stocks, and selected common stocks.

As a point of information, all listed stocks and bonds must have identification numbers. They are provided by the Committee on Uniform Securities Identification Procedures (CUSIP), a NASD agency.

Broker/Dealers and Wholesale Market Makers

The difference between broker/dealers and market makers can be confusing to the layperson. There are many old sayings and cliches that could easily apply to the relationship between broker/dealers and market makers, such as, "It's a wise child who knows its own father," or "Never let your right hand know what your left hand is doing." The reason is, taking it to extremes, they could possibly do business with themselves.

Generally, a broker will execute a buy through a dealer for his or her client and sell a stock for a client through a dealer . . . who can also be a market maker (establishes the price). The broker operates on a commission basis, purchasing or selling stock/securities from a dealer. Dealers can also be the persons who make markets on various stocks. Their money is made from the spread, such as on the OTC market, between the bid and the ask price. Although most firms operate in the capacity of broker/dealers, they seldom make a market in all the more than 15,000 OTC-listed stocks.

There are also wholesalers, who are primarily dealers. They make a market (dictate the price of a stock from available information on the stock) and keep an inventory in a number of securities (selling shares of stock that they themselves have purchased for sale). They function in the capacity of dealers to other broker/dealers or to those who are just brokers. As a rule, they have few retail accounts (as brokers).

A market maker is essentially a securities firm that makes markets (designates the price) by always being ready to buy and sell certain securities. They could be brokers or dealers and operate retail or wholesale.

NASD market makers are bound by the rules enforced by NASD, which require them to trade at the prices quoted in the Pink Sheets or displayed on the NASDAQ system. Their quotes must be "reasonably related" (an SEC term) to the prevailing price of the security.

It is usually the responsibility of the company to make certain that there is a market maker for the company's stock. This often takes a certain amount of wining and dining on the company's part. Of course, the market maker prefers to handle a security that shows trading activity. The more trading activity, the more opportunity for the market-making firm to make money on the stock, and the less of a chance of keeping the firm's capital at risk. A good company public relations effort is also important to keep the stock in the public eye (see chapter 11). If the price of the stock goes down and the market maker has a lot of it in inventory, the market maker could lose. By the same token, if the market maker has sold a security without having inventory, it must now go out and buy some. In the meantime, if the price has gone up, the market maker stands to lose. Some market makers prefer to stay flat (hold no inventory) on some securities. The names of market makers can be found in the Pink Sheets.

Since market makers wear several hats, it's important for the company to throw in with the market makers whose hats can make the company look good.

Summary

The OTC market is fast becoming the market trading system of the future. Its daily trading function and mechanism differs from the NYSE and AMEX exchanges in that its business is conducted via telecommunications through broker/dealers across the country. The auction/specialists method of trading used by the NYSE, AMEX, and the regional exchanges is slowly losing ground to the OTC market. More and more, institutions are turning to the OTC system. Even England gave up its auction market in 1987 to adopt a system modeled on NASDAQ. Many other European countries are watching this transition closely and are already changing or considering changing their auction markets in the near future. The International Stock Exchange (ISE) is already established, with London being its biggest market. Its Stock Exchange Automated Quotation (SEAQ) system is the international equivalent to our NASDAQ.

With our world's continuing evolution toward an international economy, a computer/telecommunications trading system similar to the one adopted by the OTC market, which can be accessed any time of day, seems to be the only answer. It's no wonder that thousands of NASDAQ-traded stocks that qualify for trading on the exchanges choose to remain OTC.

The listing requirements for the OTC are also less severe than those of the NYSE and AMEX. There are no special listing requirements for the Pink Sheets. Also, where the exchanges use a specialist to conduct trading activities, the OTC uses market makers, which creates a true negotiated marketplace.

Although entrepreneurs first look to the OTC for their IPOs, it could easily remain their best BET.

PART V

COMPLETING THE PUBLIC OFFERING

31

Aftermarket Trading

Aftermarket trading begins after the new issue has been sold to the original purchasers, who bought the shares via the prospectus. The entrepreneur should be aware that the aftermarket trading of a small best effort IPO is pursued differently from that for a large firm commitment IPO. In the larger firm commitment issues, the underwriters have *their* dollars at initial risk as well as their reputations for pricing an issue (see chapter 15). For the smaller best efforts offering, the *public investors'* dollars are at risk. On a larger issue, the underwriters are geared to "stabilize" the stock price. That is, they will support the market price of a new issue in order to keep it from falling below the initial offering price when the trading of the stock goes into the aftermarket. When a new issue discounts (goes down) on first trading, for whatever reason, it reflects true supply and demand for the first time. That could result in it being negatively branded for months. Underwriters want to avoid that possibility. Discounting a new issue also adversely reflects on the judgment of the lead underwriter as well as the analysts in the selling group as regards the pricing strategy. So they turn to stabilization, a form of legal manipulation, which has the approval of the SEC.

When a stock starts trading, the underwriting group hopes for an even market—an equal number of buyers and sellers. The ideal is a gradual rise in the price of the stock. Stabilization is not put into effect unless there are too many sellers, which forces down the price of the stock. The market maker will then step in and buy the stock to stabilize the price. The market maker will hold the stock in inventory to keep the price from going down. For the smaller best efforts offerings, the new issue stands on its own. Stabilization is less frequent, if used at all.

Although the SEC allows stabilization, the underwriter must furnish detailed reports to the SEC if it is undertaken. Furthermore, the stock purchased for stabilization cannot be resold at a higher price. It must be resold at the purchase price or below. If losses occur as a result, they are shared pro rata by the total selling syndicate. Also, if the stock price continues to fall after stabilization has been put into effect, the underwriters may withdraw support at their own discretion without notice. In fact, the underwriter is not obligated to support the issue by stabilization.

Underwriters will make every attempt to place the stock in strong hands among the syndicate members to avoid the necessity for stabilization. If investors sell immediately after trading commences, it indicates that the syndicate member could not control its clients from selling out just because the stock price didn't go up. This could cause the syndicate member to be eliminated, or at minimum, be offered reduced participation on future offerings.

Over-Allotment

Just as investment banker/underwriters don't relish a steep discount or the falling price of an IPO, they find it hard to deal with a hot issue. Either extreme presents extenuating circumstances that call for legal manipulation. Where an offering that discounts from the initial offering price will require stabilization, a hot offering with a large initial demand or a drastic increase in the initial offering price will usually see the use of an *"over-allotment."*

The purpose of an over-allotment, like stabilization, is to ensure an orderly aftermarket. It allows the underwriter to sell up to 15 percent more of the stock than what was originally settled upon. For example, if the underwriter had a $5 million underwriting at $2.50 a share, it would be able to sell 300,000 more shares of stock. This is called a "green shoe" option. The name for this option comes from the first company to ever use it, which was the Green Shoe Company. It is often used if the syndicate members' initial indications are that interest in the stock could be higher than anticipated. It is put into effect if there is a big demand for the stock and it becomes a hot issue. The additional monies raised by the green shoe go to the company, less selling commissions. The purpose, as mentioned earlier, is that the extra shares reduce the upward pressure on the price of the stock and insure an orderly aftermarket.

When the underwriter anticipates either over-allotment or a possibility of engaging in stabilization activities, that fact must be disclosed on the front cover of the prospectus as follows:

IN CONNECTION WITH THIS OFFERING, THE UNDERWRITERS MAY OVER-ALLOT OR EFFECT TRANSACTIONS WHICH STABILIZE OR

MAINTAIN THE MARKET PRICE OF THE COMMON STOCK OF THE COMPANY AT A LEVEL ABOVE THAT WHICH MIGHT OTHERWISE PREVAIL IN THE OPEN MARKET. SUCH STABILIZING, IF COMMENCED, MAY BE DISCONTINUED AT ANY TIME.

Smaller Issues

It is not common for smaller best efforts IPOs to use a green shoe. They will use a minimum/maximum offering, which is the common over-allotment method for best efforts underwritings. For example, if the offering is for 2 million shares, the underwriter may get an indication from syndicate members that they can probably move between 1½ million to 2 million shares. In that case, the minimum/maximum would be 1½ to 2 million.

Stabilization, as a rule, is also *not* used on smaller offerings. If the stock discounts—it discounts. The best that can be hoped for is that the primary market makers will purchase the stock for their own inventory if it goes down. Most market makers are usually capable of holding the position long enough to stabilize the discount or downward trend.

If the market goes down, it is often because a weak syndicate member is cutting losses rather than an indication of the market reception to the new issue.

Trading activities are fairly predictable. A study has been made of 21 new issues of at least $5 million that had price/earning multiples of 10. The average P/E multiple on the Dow Jones at the time was 12. A 10 was considered a good quality issue. This study showed that during the first 3 days of trading, as much as 35 percent of the publicly held shares turned over, which is about the same average as smaller issues. Generally, the first month or so can see a high degree of volatility in the pricing and trading volume of a new issue. Unfortunately, the company is at a disadvantage in affecting this trading activity. The reason is that the issue is still in its quiet period—the 90-day period during which there can be no form of public announcements and no hyping of the stock without stickering the prospectus. This is the time when speculators are still coming in and going out. Therefore, the company can only depend on the support of the underwriters and the selling syndicate to maintain its stock at a reasonable price and trading levels.

During this quiet period it is important for the entrepreneur to establish a strong rapport with individual brokers involved in the issue during the selling period. If the company's stock discounts, it is helpful to be able to reassure the brokers that the company is as strong as when the offering came to them. It's important to point out that with money in the bank, the company is even stronger, and its goals and projections are more likely to be met.

Ideally, the stock has been priced by the underwriter at a 10 percent to 20 percent discount below what the company felt it was really worth. That gives enticement to the investor to buy the stock at the offering price. The inevitable speculators will usually get out during the first 30 days of trading. This allows the brokerage community time to find committed shareholders who will hold the stock for the long haul because the company shows promise and in hopes that the stock price will go up as anticipated. This is the ideal. Unfortunately, the ideal is not always attainable. But who's to say it can't happen?

Summary

Initial aftermarket trading of the large, firm commitment IPOs, versus the aftermarket trading of best efforts offerings of smaller issues, are quite different. In the larger issues, the underwriters have their dollars at initial risk. They also have certain SEC-approved methods they can use to stabilize a stock. For the smaller best efforts offerings, it is the public investors' dollars at risk, and stabilization is rarely used.

If the stock of a firm commitment underwriting climbs excessively high in the immediate aftermarket, the underwriter will exercise an over-allotment. The term used is *green shoe.* This allows the underwriter to sell up to 15 percent more of the stock than was originally planned in order to ensure an orderly aftermarket. On best efforts underwritings, instead of a green shoe, a minimum/maximum offering is the common over-allotment method used.

Since the company has to depend on the support of the underwriters and the selling syndicates to maintain its stock at a reasonable price and trading levels, it is important to establish a strong rapport with individual brokers during the selling period. It wouldn't hurt to be friendly with them afterward either.

32

Continuing Reporting

Continuing reporting is the one thing that public company officers complain about most. According to popular consensus, it's one of the disadvantages of going public. Once a company achieves public operating status, it is required to file, on a continuing basis, a stream of never-ending reports to the federal regulators (SEC) and to the shareholders. We will examine the various reports that are required by the government, and we will attempt to shed some light on how a public company can take advantage of these reports by making them reader friendly for distribution to the shareholders as well.

The reports fall into two general areas—legal and public. They must be filed on a timely basis, in formats that do not leave much room for self-expression. They are time consuming and expensive to produce. The legal side is burdensome. It deals with the requirements that must be complied with according to the rules and regulations of the SEC, the exchanges, and the markets.

The legally required reporting starts immediately after going public and continues at an unrelenting pace forever after.

The optional public reporting leaves room to lighten up and personalize the process. This is especially true as regards annual reports and shareholders' letters. Keeping the investment community interested in a company is no easy task, and it's also expensive.

It is not unusual for a typical small public company to spend as much as $100,000 annually for printing reports and for financial public relations. Continuing legal and accounting expenses could comprise half again this amount. The annual accounting audit is vitally important. It must be reviewed and kept current throughout the year.

Continuing legal advice should also be figured into the budget, as all required reports must definitely be reviewed by legal counsel. Projects such as acquisitions, mergers, and divestitures all call for legal expertise to meet SEC requirements. Even press and shareholder releases should go through legal counsel review.

The whole complex matter of shareholder relations, with the preparation of quarterly and annual reports, is best handled by professional financial public relations people. They are familiar with the proper distribution techniques. They have established financial press relationships. And they know who the PR reports should be sent to, such as market makers, individual stock brokers, prospective investors, newspapers, magazines, and broadcast sources. Successful public companies have recognized that continuing reporting is an opportunity to maintain and enhance the value of their stock.

It is management's decision, of course, whether to hire a PR firm on a retainer or strictly on a project basis to produce the quarterly reports to the shareholders, the annual report, shareholders' letters, and other specific PR information.

The quarterly and annual reports should be professionally prepared. The first year's expense for printing and mailing alone could easily run in excess of $10,000. Good financial public relations may seem expensive, but it is an important adjunct to continuing reporting (see chapter 11). Now, on to the reports.

Form SR: Application of Proceeds

The rules require disclosing information concerning the expenses of the offering and the use of the proceeds on a continuing basis. Once the company has received its IPO money from the underwriter (less the underwriter's commission), the company must report to the SEC how much money it received and what the money is going to be used for. Form SR is a required filing every 6 months, for as long as the company would be using the proceeds, as was stated in the prospectus. The designated period is usually 12 months, but it could extend for years.

On a small best efforts IPO, an initial filing of the Form SR must be made to the SEC within 10 days after the first 3-month period following the effective date of the registration statement. If the offering was a firm commitment, and the application of proceeds was immediate, Form SR must be filed within 10 days after the proceeds were applied, and every 6 months thereafter.

Form SR is the SEC's way of making sure that the company is using the proceeds in the time period prescribed and for the purposes it said they would be used. For example, a company may have stated in the prospectus that it intended to spend $.5 million for marketing, $.5 million for equipment, and $.5 million for operating capital. If, instead, the company spent $.5 million on an office building, without declaring that in the prospectus, the SEC would consider it to be a fraudulent use of the proceeds.

It should be noted that the form can be confusing and tricky. It may require some creative financial accounting and help from legal counsel and auditing accountants. There is no consideration in the form for any type of interest from money on deposit until spent, for income derived by the company, or for profits earned. The SEC doesn't allow for that in the form. Hence, 6 months down the road when the next Form SR is filed, the company will have to sort out information that will show that the application of proceeds was as stated in the prospectus—with no accounting for the income realized.

The entrepreneur should be pleased to learn, however, that the Form SR is not a public disclosure form. It is only filed with the SEC and is not sent to the media or shareholders.

Form 8–K: Current Reports

Form 8–K is a report that a company must file when a significant event occurs that could materially affect decisions on buying, selling, or holding stock in a company. The event could be internal or external. The report must be filed no later than 15 days after the event occurred. Timely disclosure rules may also require companies to issue a press release prior to disclosing the particulars that are reported on Form 8–K. Legal counsel plays an important role when reporting on Form 8–K, especially on the interpretation of "other materially important events." Events that are considered significant are:

1. *Changes in control of the company.* This principally refers to changes among persons who control or own big blocks of the stock. For example, a principal of a company could leave the company and his or her stocks would change hands. Or the controller of a large block of stock dies. The public must be advised that there is a change in a big block of stock and management in the company. The requirements are very specific regarding the financial aspects. (See discussion of forms 3 and 4 and Schedule 13–D later in this chapter; forms 3 and 4 concern officers and directors of corporations holding 10 percent or more of the stock; Schedule 13–D refers to anyone who acquires 5 percent or more of a company.)

2. *Acquisition or disposition of assets.* This applies to majority-owned subsidiaries, if the asset value is greater than 10 percent of the company's assets.

3. *Bankruptcy.* This is considered a very significant event. In such cases, instructions are specific that Form 8–K is to be filed immediately after receivership is appointed. All the pertinent facts must be noted, including the court involved, the date of the event, name of the receiver, and date of the appointment of the receiver. An amendment is also required confirming the plans for reorganization or arrangements for liquidation.

4. *Change of auditing accounting firm.* This requirement is aimed at determining whether the change is taking place because of a policy dispute between the auditing accountants and the company management. For example, management may want the auditing accountant to take a depreciation on a piece of equipment that would not be an ethical procedure. The accountant informs management that it would not be proper. Management fires the accounting firm. The departing audit accountant files a letter of comment, noting that the departure was not amicable.

   This section could also contain an accounting or format change made by a new audit accounting firm.

5. *Directors.* Resignations or the election of a new director are not required to be included in 8–K report. However, if a director resigns and specifically requests the company to disclose the resignation along with the reasons for it, the company is obligated to do so on Form 8–K. A copy of the resignation letter should be attached as an exhibit, and management can include a statement regarding the resignation if desired.

6. *Optional.* This is a catch-all for other materially important events. If management and the board want to report a situation of material importance, they must file by the tenth of the month following the occurrence of the event.

   The company can report the event or distribute 8–K reports detailing the event to its shareholders. Actually, it seems to be better just to inform the shareholders by a friendly letter or by issuing a press release rather than mailing out copies of the 8–K.

Form 10–K: Annual Report

This is the annual report that must be filed with the SEC by corporations with more than 500 stockholders and assets over $2 million. It provides an overview of the company's business. It must be completed and filed with the SEC within 90 days after the end of the company's fiscal year.

The 10–K is comprehensive in its reporting requirements. Divided into four parts with 13 subheadings, it calls for audited financial statements with associated footnotes and thorough coverage of the company's operations during the past year. For instance, if the company leased a building, an explanation must be given for leasing the building and a complete description of the building must be included. Also, management must explain what happened, historically, during the year such as, the company introduced two new product lines, started a new subsidiary, signed a licensing agreement in Europe, sold a plant in Chicago, increased the truck fleet, sold off a product line—anything and everything having to do with the company's operations, including sales and marketing.

This report requires the signatures of all the officers and members of the board of directors, so they should all have ample time to add their input and to review it carefully. The SEC attaches a great deal of importance to the 10–K report.

The SEC also encourages inclusion of business projections, which could present a problem. The 10–K may be included in the annual report that goes to stockholders. If a projection is not met, it could result in a complaint from an irate stockholder, who may even threaten to sue the company. Therefore, the SEC provides the company a "safe harbor," which allows that projections do not always have to be fulfilled. The company can make them, but is protected as long as it states that these are just projections and may never reach fruition. Many companies refuse to use projections because of the problems they can cause. If projections are to be used, all aspects should first be thoroughly discussed with legal counsel and audit accountants.

Since the 10–K becomes the basis of the annual report, it should be considered a very important document and handled as an important piece of investment communication.

Form 10–Q: Quarterly Report

The 10–Q is a quarterly report required by the SEC. It contains information similar to that which is in Form 10–K. The report must be filed for each of the first 3 fiscal quarters and is due within 45 days of the close of the quarter. The main purpose of the quarterlies is to reduce the number of surprises during a company's fiscal year reporting.

Like the 10–K, the quarterly report has specific guidelines. It would be in the company's best interest to secure help from legal counsel and audit accountants in its preparation. Although audited financial statements are not required, there are substantial financial disclosures that must be made.

Part I of the 10–Q requires disclosure of the following information:

- Income statement, balance sheet, and statement of sources and application of funds
- A text analysis by management of the quarterly income statement (particularly in reference to material changes)
- Information about capitalization (and changes)
- Information about shareholders' equity (and changes)

The following information, as applicable, must be disclosed in Part II:

- Legal proceedings involving the company.
- Changes in securities. For example, another company may step into the picture to purchase part of the company. It could be issued preferred stock, which would change the basic securities structure. Issuance of warrants would also constitute a change.
- Changes in security for registered securities. For example, the company may have received a large contract and decided to buy back some of the stock. It must declare in this form that it has made an offer to repurchase some stock.
- Default on senior securities.
- Increase or decrease in the amount of outstanding securities or indebtedness.
- Submission of matters to a vote of shareholders.
- Other materially important events.
- Particulars and summary of 8–Ks filed during the reporting quarter. As stated earlier, an 8–K is a current report that provides information on certain specified material events that could affect a decision to buy, sell, or hold stock in the company. It must be filed within 15 days of the event.

The second part of the 10–Q report is not required to be presented to the public shareholders.

The company should think of the 10–Q quarterly report as a natural opportunity to communicate with the investing public and shareholders. The fact that it contains financial statements should make the recipients inclined to read the quarterly report more carefully than if it was just a shareholders' letter. It would also be worth taking a salutary approach to the report by making it reader friendly, rather than simply presenting the cold, hard facts. And since the data is all gathered for the report, management should consider including it in a warm, personal shareholders' letter.

The Annual Report

After the company becomes public, *the annual report is the single most important document the company produces.*

Since there are so many publications that deal with the annual report in detail (check local libraries), we will only touch on points that we think are worth remembering.

The annual report is standard reading in areas that are not considered strictly financial, such as customer relations and supplier relations. It is widely recognized as the voice of management reporting on the health and promise of the company. Naturally, it is a vital communication link between management and the shareholders. Therefore, before starting, management should thoroughly discuss the report with legal counsel, the auditing accountants, and the PR firm.

There are two distinct parts to the annual report. The first part is the corporate message—information about the goals of the company and management, which can take up to half the total pages. The second part usually deals with the financial picture.

Preliminary planning should include an evaluation of other annual reports in the industry. Management should have an idea of what they like to see, and what they don't like. The input from other sources, such as underwriters, brokers, and analysts should be solicited. A brainstorming session with the PR firm, designers, and printers can be most helpful in determining the overall theme, the style of type, the pictures, the illustrations, and the number of pages that will be needed. Management should be open to suggestions and ideas from these people. (Remember, they have a lot of experience in this area.) A budget and timetable should be determined and adhered to. A decision should be made on the information that will accompany charts and illustrations. A distribution list needs to be compiled.

As to the contents—the company, the people, the products, the programs, and the prospects should be well defined. The chief executive's opinions on important issues, such as strength, growth, profitability, and the promise of the company should be thoughtfully placed and highlighted.

The final product should also fit the company's image. Generally, small companies tend to go all out in publishing annuals, especially their first one. A full-blown, four-color major production may not be the answer—just as simply sending out photocopies of the company's 10–K is not the answer. The underlying purpose of the annual report is to favorably influence the financial marketplace. Everything in the report requires careful planning—and easy reading.

Corporate Message

The president's report usually leads off the corporate message portion, which is probably the most widely read section of the annual, as readers particularly like to hear it from the horse's mouth. It's the *one* opportunity for top management to communicate directly with all the owners (shareholders) of the company. It should be composed in a personal, reflective, and intimate style. Here is the president discussing the company's current and future operations.

Here are some key ideas to include:

- History: the company's story, implying in a positive way that the future will be significant and monetarily rewarding.
- Strategy: describe how the company is being run today in accordance with long-term strategies.
- Markets: indicate how the company is competing better.
- Governance: explain how the company is being run by the board of directors to assure survival, profits, and ethicality.
- Future: specify corporate goals for the next 5 years.

A photograph or a portrait-style picture of the president would be most appropriate.

Design

If a picture is really worth a thousand words, good layout and design for an annual report are essential and should be eye-catching. A good design visually holds readers and leads them further into the contents. Consider color, art, photos, illustrations, charts, maps, size, and typography; select a good paper stock and cover stock. Headlines and captions are the first things read. In case the reader reads no further, these should capsulize the whole story management has to tell.

The art director, working with the financial PR firm's creative team, can usually be depended upon to come up with good ideas on the art and photographs—whether they should be stock photos or shot on location; whether to use black-and-white, color, or shaded halftones. Before proceeding, there should be a combined decision on the charts and graphs that best depict the company's operations. The SEC requires specific type sizes and type styles for some parts of the financials. Other than that, allow the creative people an opportunity to suggest underlines, boldfaces, and line spacing. Obviously, there is always a concern for cost with paper. But good quality paper for an annual report must have top priority. Remember, management always has final approval.

As a general rule, companies print three to four times as many copies as they have shareholders. This policy makes sure there are enough reports to cover the fringe areas—brokers, analysts, requests, and media. To further assure that these additional copies get into the appropriate hands, it's important that the mailing list be kept up to date.

A saleable annual report requires a great deal of effort and attention to detail by all concerned, including top management. It is important to start planning early—as much as 3 to 4 months ahead. But the results can be far reaching and well worth the effort.

Proxies

Webster defines proxy as "authority to act for another." In the case of a public company management, proxies are a request for shareholders to allow management to vote their shares.

Under state corporate laws and stock exchange rules, most matters that materially affect stockholder rights must be submitted to stockholders for approval. This is done through a special shareholders' meeting. The proxy statement is used to inform stockholders about the nature of the meeting and to identify the management soliciting the proxies.

Typically, proxies account for a large majority of the votes cast at a shareholders' meeting. Stockholders may withdraw or revoke their proxy at any time prior to a final tabulation of the vote. The proxy, then, is a power of attorney granted by a shareholder for the special purpose of authorizing another individual to vote his or her stock. In most cases, this solicitation concerns the company's annual meeting, which includes the election of the board of directors. For these situations, the proxy package must contain the company's annual report, including the audited financial statements, the names of the directors to be elected, information about them and the management team, and a disclosure of management remuneration.

However, at various times, the company will need to inform its shareholders of other important matters pertaining to the operations of the company. This could be in reference to events such as a major acquisition, divestitures, or stock splits. These are usually information notices and nonvoting situations. In either case, the information contained in the notice must be a description of the matter to be considered or voted on and any pertinent information relating to the matter.

According to SEC proxy rules, derived from Section 14(a) of the '34 act, all proposed proxy material must be submitted to the SEC 10 days prior to being sent to shareholders. That allows time for the SEC to review the submitted materials for misstatements and omissions. If the SEC has no comments within the 10 days, the proxy materials can be distributed to the shareholders. Proxy materials should not be mailed until this clearance is obtained.

Mailing

Getting the proxy material to the actual shareholder is no easy matter. Since the late 1970s, there has been an increase in the complexity of the mailing process. First, there has been a large increase in the number of shares held in "street name" (in the name of the brokerage firm on behalf of the owner). In 1975, this included just a small percentage—today, it is estimated at over 45 percent of stock purchasers. Secondly, there is an increasing layer of stock ownership by brokerage firms holding certificates in street name through a Depository Trust Company (DTC; a computerized go-between for securities transfers that charges and credits each member's account). Thirdly, over this period, there has been a general decline in the U.S. mail service, which, coupled with the fact that the traditional proxy time coincides with the mailing of tax returns and refunds, usually results in the system being overburdened.

Fortunately, most companies have found a way to relieve themselves of this headache. Today, the actual process of mailing, receiving, and tabulating proxies is most frequently handled by the company's transfer agent. Its personnel also attend the annual meeting and, with the help of the secretary of the company, supervise the counting and tabulating of the votes on the issues.

FCPA: The Foreign Corrupt Practices Act

The Foreign Corrupt Practices Act (FCPA) is a major post-Watergate piece of legislation. It is also deceptively named, especially as pertaining to IPOs. However, the IPO management team should not ignore this act just because it appears, on the surface, to only deal with foreign operations. In reality, it relates to record keeping and applies to all public companies. Failure to comply with its provisions could lead to serious problems.

The FCPA has nothing to do with foreign activities or corrupt practices. It was originally passed by Congress in 1977 because investigations revealed that a certain amount of questionable payments, often illegal, were made by large U.S. corporations to foreign governments, suppliers, agents, and customers. Examples cited were improper political contributions, improper overseas payments, and the establishment and use of off-balance-sheet slush funds.

The FCPA was passed specifically to deal with companies in this country. Part of it prohibits payments of bribes by U.S. companies, their officers, directors, shareholders, or agents. Another part deals with two areas that affect a public company's internal controls and record keeping. First, the company must "make and keep books, records, and accounts" that detail transactions and dispositions of its assets. This is a statutory accounting requirement in addition to SEC accounting controls. The company must keep detailed records that accurately show and fairly depict any financial transaction involving the company's assets. Second, the company must "devise and maintain a system of internal accounting controls." An accounting control system must be implemented that assures an accurate tracking of all assets and their disposition.

It is important for the company's audit accountants to review the present system and recommend changes, if necessary, to make sure that the company is complying with the act.

Form 3

Form 3 is a relatively simple report that is filed with the SEC prior to a company's public offering becoming effective. It requires any officer, or director, holding 10 percent or more of the company's stock to file a statement of ownership with the commission. The same holds true for any other holder of 10 percent or more.

Briefly, the report lists the numbers and types of securities held, the dates purchased, and the method of payment, such as cash or exchange of services, stock, or assets. It describes all stock owned by the individual of record, beneficially (by family members of the immediate household), or otherwise.

It is also necessary, in the event of the election of new directors or appointment of new officers, that a Form 3 be prepared and filed with the SEC with respect to their stock ownership within 10 days of the event.

Form 4

Form 4 is the continuing equivalent of Form 3. Any officer, director, or holder of 10 percent or more of the company's stock must file with the SEC if any change occurs in the securities owned. Any purchase or sale of the company's stock must be reported on Form 4, including the number of shares, the price, the resulting total ownership, and any other significant related transactions. It applies to all classifications of stock—common, preferred, convertible holdings, rights, options, or warrants and the conditions under which they were received or purchased.

As with Form 3, the report must be filed within 10 days after the end of the month in which the change occurred.

Insider Reporting and Trading Restrictions

An insider is anyone with inside information. Using that information specifically to buy or sell securities is considered a form of collusion or fraud by the SEC. Under Rule 10b–5, insiders are those who come into possession of undisclosed material information in the course of their business activities and those who are "tippees" (persons or groups who receive such information from an insider or a third party). These include employees, consultants, retained counsel, accountants, underwriters, broker/dealers, analysts, investment advisors, and those who are informed directly or indirectly by any of these people. Within the purview of Rule 10b–5 they are all insiders.

The Insider Trading Sanction Act of 1984 granted the SEC authority to obtain civil penalties up to three times the amount of profits gained *or* losses avoided. Liability extends to reporting persons, insiders, and tippees who trade on material nonpublic information.

Naturally, the whole area of insider trading is looked upon with great concern by the SEC. And because it is a complicated and constantly changing issue, it is imperative that management seek legal counsel any time any management team member, director, advisor, or employee wishes to buy or sell stock in the company.

> Don't take chances. The SEC has made it very clear that it considers the elements necessary to establish liability for insider trading to be that the information in question be (1) material and non-public; (2) that the tippee who receives the information directly or indirectly, knows or has reason to know that it was non-public and has been obtained improperly by selective revelation or otherwise; and (3) that the information be a factor in his/her decision to effect the transaction (in the security of the company involved).

Under Rule 10b–5, liability could be found even in cases where someone innocently comes into possession of, and uses, information that he or she has reason to believe is intended to be confidential. Such persons can be held liable if, based on such information, they effect a transaction in the securities involved.

Short Selling

In addition to Rule 10b–5, the reader should be aware of Section 16, which deals with "short swing" profits. This provision applies to any "quick" profits on the company's securities that are realized during any 6-month period, whether it's as a result of buying long or selling short. Insiders who profit on those transactions are required to turn over those profits to the company without any offset of losses should they occur. The company can sue the insider, as can any shareholder, on behalf of the company, to recover the profits for the company.

The '34 act also prohibits reporting persons (those filing forms 3 and 4) as well as insiders from selling shares of stock they *do not* own—otherwise known as "short selling." "Sales against the box," which is selling "owned" shares but not delivering them within 20 days after the sale, are also prohibited under the '34 act.

It is very important for the CEO of an OTC-traded public company to establish strong controls to protect the confidentiality of inside information. One help would be to coordinate all press information having to do with news releases and contacts with brokers, analysts, and shareholders through one single source. Furthermore, all persons privy to inside information must be made aware of the need for confidentiality and the serious consequences that can come from trading on or tipping that information.

Schedules

Because of the nature of the Schedule 13s, the reports must be filed with the SEC and with the stock exchanges on which the company's stock is traded or, in the case of OTC-traded companies, NASD/NASDAQ. The company must also keep complete files on these reports.

Schedule 13–G

This schedule discloses the names of each person or group who owns 5 percent or more of the company's stock. Within 45 days of the end of each calendar year they must file a Schedule 13–G with the SEC. This is a relatively simple form, requiring information concerning share ownership with no intention on the part of the owner of changing or influencing the control of the issuer.

Schedule 13–D

This is considered the takeover alert filing. Any shareholder or group of shareholders who are acting individually or together with the intention of making a tender offer, friendly or unfriendly, must file a Schedule 13–D.

The schedule requires information on the following:

- Identity of the buyer or buyers
- Number of shares owned or controlled
- Dates of purchase
- Source and amounts of funds used to acquire shares
- The reason for the purchase

The alert number is 5 percent or more. As an illustration, if an individual or a group has established a position of 4 percent ownership of the stock in a company, and if that position is increased to 5 percent or more, the SEC regulations stipulate that the holder must file an amended Schedule 13–D. That usually is a clear signal that a takeover will be attempted. There are people in Washington, D.C., whose sole job for their company is to read all the Schedule 13–Ds that are filed to find out if the takeovers will be friendly or unfriendly.

Other 13s that are noteworthy are:

Schedule 13–E–3

This filing schedule is used by a company if management intends to take the company private or if it intends to reduce the number of shareholders to such a point that the company is no longer required to file the periodic reports with the SEC.

Schedule 13–E–4

This filing schedule (called an Issuer Tender Offer Statement) is used by companies with securities registered under Section 12 of the '34 act if they are making a tender offer for their own securities.

Other Forms and Schedules

The following forms and schedules are listed here simply because they will be required from time to time, and management should be aware of them:

Form 8–A

This form is used to register securities under the '34 act. It must be filed immediately upon completion of a public offering, usually in conjunction with S–18s that call for registration of securities not to exceed an aggregate offering price of $7.5 million. The form is occasionally used as an optional version of Form 10 under an S–1 filing (which is the basic registration form that can be used to register securities for which no other form is authorized or prescribed). Form 8–A is fast becoming obsolete, but it is noted here because the government has not yet eliminated it.

Form 10

This form is used to register securities with the SEC after a public offering is in effect. Upon filing it, the company becomes fully reporting. All the information needed to complete it can be found in the offering prospectus. It calls for the following items as disclosures:

- Description of the business
- Financial information
- Description of properties
- Securities ownership of officers and directors
- Names of officers and directors
- Executive compensation
- Certain relationships and related transactions
- Legal proceedings
- Dividend information
- Recent sales of unregistered securities
- Description of securities to be registered
- Existing indemnification of officers and directors
- Financial statements and supplemental data
- Difference of opinion with accountants

Form 10–C

This form is only used by companies whose securities are quoted on NASDAQ. It is used for reporting changes in the number of shares outstanding when the change exceeds 5 percent. It is also used to report a name change of the issuer.

Schedule 14–B

This form is used in the event that there is a proxy contest with respect to the election or removal of a company director. Any person who instigates or is a participant in this type of contest is required to file a Schedule 14–B.

Schedule 14–D–1

This form is commonly used in takeover attempts. It is used by any person, other than the issuer, who is making a tender offer to purchase securities that would amount to over 5 percent ownership in the company. It must be filed at the time of the offer.

Form 15

This form is used to officially notify the SEC of the suspension of the responsibility to make periodic filing reports, or it is filed by the company as notice of termination of a registration statement.

Form 20–F

This form is used only when there is foreign company involvement.

There will, no doubt, soon be more forms to file—as soon as the SEC can think of a reason for them.

Summary

Continuing reporting makes it necessary for the company to have a thorough knowledge of all the various areas that require reporting.

There are so many forms, schedules, reports, proxies, and restrictions that need to be filed by a public company—it's enough to make an entrepreneur wonder if it is really worth the trouble. Obviously it is. Witness all the IPOs that are being undertaken.

There's no getting around it, it takes the full cooperation of the company's SEC counsel and audit accountants to make certain that the SEC receives the reports on time and that they are properly presented. These professional people must prepare checklists of the trigger dates and events to make sure that all the requirements by the SEC are complied with.

The reports should also be well conceived and well written, as a majority of them can easily be used as PR reports for the company, in the form of news releases, press notices, annual reports, and shareholders' reports.

The company must just get used to the fact that the reporting is continuous. It never stops—just like the money that keeps rolling in . . . we hope.

33

Rule 144

Rule 144 sets forth the criteria for sale of restricted stock without registration.

When a registration statement is filed for an initial public offering, the stocks that are sent out to new shareholders are newly issued shares of the company. There are also existing stocks that are held by the officers, directors, and other inside shareholders, which were probably purchased in a private offering prior to the registration statement. They are called "restricted," or "lettered," stock. These are stocks that have not been registered with the SEC and cannot be sold or freely traded in the new public market for a *designated* period of time. However, there are some provisions under Rule 144 under the Securities Act of 1933 that allow "leakage" (selling) of these securities. Rule 144 was enacted in 1975 to clarify the restricted stock situation for affected investors and, incidentally, to further protect the public shareholders from the possible harmful effects of unchecked insider sales.

Two-year Period

Generally speaking, the designated holding period on restricted securities is 2 years from the date they were purchased. At that time, the stockholders who purchased the stock can proceed with the filing of Form 144, which allows them to sell (in any 3-month period) formerly restricted securities. However, they may not sell more than 1 percent of the total amount of shares outstanding of that particular class of stock during that 3-month period. Or, if they choose, they may sell up to 1 percent of the reported weekly trading volume on an exchange or NASDAQ during the 4 calendar weeks preceding their filing of Form 144. The most widely used approach is the 144 sales form based on the 3-month period observed by the OTC as opposed to the weekly trading volume on NASDAQ. The reason is it's too difficult and complicated to track the weekly volume, because brokers don't have that information readily available. If the securities filed for sale under Rule 144 are not sold within the 3-month period, an extension can be filed for an additional 30 days.

The restricted stock usually carries a legend, customarily stamped on the front or back of the certificates, noting that they are restricted securities:

> The shares represented by this certificate have not been registered under the Securities Act of 1933 ("the Act") and are "restricted securities" as that term is defined in rule 144 under the Act. The shares may not be offered for sale, sold or otherwise transferred except pursuant to an effective registration statement under the Act, or pursuant to an exemption from registration under the Act, the availability of which is to be established to the satisfaction of the company.

In addition to the legend noted on the stock, the company's transfer agent, who keeps track of all stock certificates and sales of that particular stock, is automatically issued a "stop" on all restricted securities and will not initiate a transfer without first receiving notification that the transfer has been cleared by the company.

Three-year Period

After a 3-year holding period, a noncontrolling, or nonaffiliated share-holder, who probably bought the stock in a private placement, becomes free of almost all the restrictions of sale. The paperwork amounts to just one simple letter (144–K), which prevents the company from blocking the sale.

144 Letter

This letter is in reference to the "stop." It is actually a notification that comes in the form of a letter from the company's legal counsel. It tells the transfer agent that the company has assumed the responsibility and that the intended transfer conforms with SEC Rule 144 regulations.

The reason for the letter is that the SEC allows the sale of restricted stock only if adequate current information on the company is available to the public (mainly that the company is current in its filing of all 10–Qs, 10–Ks, and 8–Ks). This must be attested to by both the company and the restricted selling stockholders.

Affiliates

Broadly interpreted, an affiliate is a person who directly or indirectly, through one or more intermediaries, controls a block of the company's stock. For example, Mr. Smith, who is not part of the company in any way, but who knows a director of the company, made a private purchase of a block of the company's stock before the company entertained the idea of going public. Now that the company's stock is publicly traded, Mr. Smith is still deemed an affiliate because he owns a block of the stock, even though he has nothing to do with the company's operations. Should he purchase additional shares in the open market, the certificates will not be imprinted with the standard restrictive legend. Technically though, Mr. Smith is considered an affiliate, which makes him a "control" person. So he can't freely trade his stock. Therefore he must file special forms (forms 3 and 4) in order to comply with Rule 144 if he wishes to sell his stock.

An affiliate can also be (1) any relative (child, cousin, aunt, uncle, and so forth) or spouse of such person, or any relative of such spouse (in-laws), or a person who lives in the same home of any of the above; (2) any trust in which the person owns 10 percent or more of the stock or serves as a trustee, executor, or in a similar capacity; and (3) any corporation or organization where such person is the beneficial owner of 10 percent or more.

Other Considerations

Form 144 restricted stock can only be sold via a "broker transaction"—through a broker/dealer. The seller (who owns the stock) is prohibited from arranging for a buyer for his or her stock, or from making any kind of arrangements between the potential buyer of the stock and the broker. The broker must do that independently. What's more, no payments are allowed except the normal broker commissions; there are exemptions regarding estates and nonaffiliates.

Although the selling shareholder is responsible for informing the broker, at the first contact, that the transaction is a 144 affiliate or nonaffiliate stock sale, the brokers and their firms are still somewhat at risk in 144 transactions. They must justify their actions by keeping complete files and copies of all the documentation that goes with the Rule 144 transaction.

Many entrepreneurs have resigned themselves to looking upon their 144-restricted sales as a necessary break in the action before proceeding again. That's because a certain amount of caution is required on the part of the sellers. Insiders, especially officers and directors, must consider the impact of timing in the sale of their 144 stock. Any insider buys or sells must be reported to the SEC, from which there seems to be a direct line to the financial press. The street (Wall Street brokers) doesn't like to see management bailing out, as they affectionately call it, even if the management team has spent 4 to 5 years building a successful and profitable company and justifiably believes it has a right to cash in on hard-earned gains.

It's legal to sell. The rules are there. Management knows it can't sell more than 1 percent of the market. Unfortunately, 144 sales are usually regarded suspiciously. Before insiders make their move, they must be cognizant of the trading volume. They don't want to sell in a down market, as that could further depress the stock prices. Since, generally, the number of shares held by the public (public float) is thin (small in numbers compared to the total outstanding) on OTC stocks and the moves of management are public knowledge, management must be aware of the public mood at the time and take care that its trades don't jar the market or the prices. An influx of management 144 sales could seriously impact on the bid or selling price of the company's stock. To keep or not to keep, that is the dilemma.

Summary

SEC Rule 144 was enacted to clarify the restricted stock situation for those investors who smartly bought or obtained their stock privately and were having a trying time selling it publicly.

Since the stock is not registered, they must receive an exemption from registration, which was helped by Rule 144. But getting through all the restrictions is as difficult as going through a maze. A 2-year waiting period must elapse before the stock can be traded, a letter must be sent to the SEC by the company indicating that the transfer of the stock conformed with the SEC rules, and, of course, forms must be filed.

Affiliates—friends, relatives, others, even management—who own restricted stock are only allowed to sell a percentage of their stock within a given period of time and under specified conditions. Insiders such as officers and directors must exercise great care when selling their stock, even though their company is successful, in order not to cause a negative impact on the trading and price of the stock. Other than that, the owners of restricted stock stand to make a killing—if they can just make it through the legalities and frustration of the process.

34

Alternatives to Going Public

Growing companies are constantly on the search for new capital, either through debt or equity, though it's not always easy to come by. But for the entrepreneur, raising money is a way of life. Going public is one way to secure needed capital. It can relieve the pressure, and it can also turn out to be the pot of gold at the end of the rainbow or the "Open sesame" to Ali Baba's door. The problem is—it takes money to make money. The process of going public often requires a lot of money up front to cover the cost of services and fees, and fees, and fees. But look at it this way: If it was all easy to come by there would be nothing special about entrepreneurs.

Some entrepreneurs consider going public no different from other alternatives to raising money. What's more, they have proven it time after time. But the process does require time—and it costs money. The first thing to be done is to put together a business plan to use as a fundraising tool. Second is the actual raising of the financing. Each alternative to raising money requires a different approach to the business plan. It happens fast in the movies and on television, but generally speaking, it is never quick, it is never simple. In fact, it is usually quite painful and exasperating. Entrepreneurs often find themselves chasing down blind alleys.

What all entrepreneurs soon discover they must reckon with in pursuit of the elusive dollar are high interest costs, dilution of equity ownership, potential restrictions on daily operating flexibility, and even constraints on future growth.

274

Going Private

For some entrepreneurs, the best way to accomplish private equity financing has been through the use of Regulation D, which is a limited offer and sale of securities without registration under the Securities Act of 1933. (A major portion of this book is devoted to that subject.) The most common form for raising private capital, however, is to borrow it, for either the short or long term. Short-term debt is traditionally used for working capital and some equipment purchases. But most often new businesses require long-term debt or permanent equity capital to support major expansion and anticipated rapid growth. The advantages of borrowing are that it is a relatively simple process to arrange. It does not take a great deal of time and does not dilute equity ownership. The disadvantages are that it is a high-risk strategy as far as the company's growth is concerned, in that incurring debt subjects the company to a firm obligation. A downturn in business or an increase in interest rates could result in the inability to service the debt payments.

If borrowing is the answer, the question is, from whom? The following pages will address the various types of financing, and other potential borrowing sources, as well as identifying other possible capital sources.

Debt Financing

Pure debt (loan/borrowing) financing can take several forms. It is available from various sources such as banks, finance companies, or leasing companies. It is considered increased risk for the company since borrowed funds require repayment. However, loans do increase the borrower's return on equity (leverage). Costs to be considered in using debt financing are not only interest, which can be high, but also indirect costs that can be associated with some forms of debt, such as *compensating checking account balances,* where the borrower is required by the lender (bank) to maintain a stated minimum balance in a non-interest-bearing checking account. This means, if the borrower received a $100,000 loan from the bank, the bank would insist that the borrower keep a minimum of $10,000 in the checking account, with the stipulation that the account cannot go below the $10,000. The borrower would be required to pay interest on that $10,000, even though it can't be touched. This is a very common business practice. Additionally, the lender may impose strict loan covenants in the form of performance ratios that must be maintained. That means, in effect, that the company's net worth versus assets cannot fall below a certain level, the company's inventory must remain at a certain level, receivables cannot go over a certain level, and payables cannot exceed a certain level. If any of these situations occur while the loan is in effect, the loan or portions of it can be called due.

Since the late 1970s, the cost of borrowing money by new companies has seen wide fluctuations. Interest costs on unsecured loans has gone as high as or higher than 25 percent. What's more, long-term loans often carried "equity kickers" in the form of stock warrants or rights to purchase stock. (This has become common practice with venture leasing companies and many sources that make private side offerings.) An *equity kicker* is a deal made with the company by the lenders. The gist of it is that because the company is new and considered high-risk, the lenders are betting that the company will become successful. If that happens and the company goes public, the lenders want the company to give them a warrant that allows them to buy x number of shares of the company's stock at today's prices as compensation for loaning the company money.

It may smell like usury, but savvy entrepreneurs know that those are often the costs of borrowing money to start up a business. Unfortunately, prime rates of 15 percent plus—the cost for short-term borrowing from finance companies—can spell death for a small enterprise. The only hope is to try to obtain longer-term debt which could serve as a junior or secondary to a bank loan.

Subordinated Debt

An alternative to bank borrowing is the placement of subordinated convertible debt debentures with private lenders who are venture capital firms, also referred to as Small Business Investment Companies (SBICs; discussed later in this chapter). Most subordinated debt is unsecured and, consequently, junior (secondary) to bank loans. For example, Company A has a $500,000 bank loan that is secured by inventory and receivables. Company A wants to borrow another $500,000 to put in a new production line and buy more equipment. The equipment will ordinarily be enough to secure the new loan. However, if Company A goes bankrupt, the bank has first claim against the assets, and the venture capital firm must take a secondary position against the assets. It is second in line for payment after the bank. That's what makes the venture capital firm subordinated. But assuming that the loan helped Company A reach its goals, the convertibility clause allows the venture capital firm to convert the subordinated debt debentures to stock at an agreed-upon date at prices to be determined at the time of the loan or on the date of conversion. In essence, the loan is subordinated, but it is also convertible to stock.

Putting together subordinated debt placements takes experienced legal and accounting advice. Additionally, careful consideration must be given to the long-term effects of equity dilution, as it is possible that subordinated convertible debt holders could team up with other minority shareholders and, by their conversion rights, gain effective control of the company (this is not very likely).

Sources of Debt Financing

Commercial Banks

Banks are traditional lenders for secured short- or medium-term loans. These loans are usually revolving lines of credit to finance inventory buildup and are quite often seasonal or loaned against a particular contract. Banks will also make mortgage loans on a longer-term basis against buildings, real property, and equipment. They do not ordinarily provide loans that are unsecured or lend to start-up companies. Their modus operandi is consistent with other banks.

	Commercial Banks
Costs	Floating rates to 5 points above prime
Maturity	30–90 day notes; credit lines to 3 years; long-term mortgages to 7 years
Proceeds	Working capital; inventory; receivables; machinery
Collateral	Unsecured; secured against specific assets; personal guarantees
Advantages	Usually lower costs than other lending organizations; many branches
Disadvantages	Prefer established business; require personal guarantees and/or collateral

Commercial Finance Companies

Finance companies provide asset-based lending, most commonly against receivables and occasionally against inventory. Their rates are usually higher than those of banks, and they usually require a regular monthly reconciliation of their collateral (receivables/inventory).

	Finance Companies
Cost	Floating rates to 7 points above prime
Maturity	Depends on loan size; usually 1 to 8 years
Proceeds	Working capital; acquisitions; machinery; equipment; real estate
Collateral	First liens on assets; personal guarantees

Leasing Companies

Leasing companies tend to offer the entrepreneur more flexibility than banks. The company may lease an asset (equipment), or buy it, sell it to the leasing company, and then lease it back (lease-back). Leases can often be made for longer time periods and set up with varying payment plans. Payments can be scheduled monthly, quarterly, semiannually, and in some cases, annually. Depending on tax advantages, the lease contract may also contain balloon payments.

	Leasing Companies
Costs	Prime plus 6 to 8 points
Maturity	Negotiable: operating leases as short as 6 months; financing leases for useful life of the asset
Proceeds	Machinery; equipment; real estate; acquisitions
Advantages	Easy deals; 100 percent financing; lessor carries risk
Disadvantages	High cost; no ownership benefits

Savings and Loan Associations

Savings and loans have been experiencing upheavals, changes of ownership, and financial setbacks. But they are still operating. The entrepreneur should not overlook the fact that even with all their problems, the distinction between S&Ls and banks is lessening, except S&Ls are still more inclined to finance against real property.

	Savings and Loans
Cost	Competitive with banks; fixed or variable rate tied to prime rate
Maturity	Long term to 15 years; occasionally lines of credit
Proceeds	Real estate; some working capital; equipment

Collateral	Always secured; personal guarantees
Advantages	Attractive rates; experienced real estate lenders
Disadvantages	High minimum loan amounts; restrictive covenants

Small Business Administration

The SBA is a lender of last resort. A company must be turned down by other lenders to qualify for an SBA loan. In most cases, SBA will provide guarantees securing loans up to $500,000. It has a number of different loan programs with various qualifiers. Rates are reasonable, but programs are subject to government funding availability. They have a lot of restrictive covenants and require a lot of paper processing.

	Small Business Administration
Cost	Floating and fixed rates; tied to prime
Maturity	7 to 25 years
Proceeds	Working capital; machinery; equipment; real estate (only when other financing is denied)
Collateral	Secured by liens; personal guarantees
Advantages	Last-resort lender; low cost considering risk; does not finance some types of assets
Disadvantages	Liens; personal guarantees

Industrial Revenue Bonds

Industrial revenue bonds are not for start-up or early stage companies, with the exception of those companies that have substantial equity financing. They are mostly issued to finance large real estate projects or companies with large equipment requirements. Also, in most cases, the issuing agency holds title to the property and leases it back to the company.

	Industrial Revenue Bonds
Cost	Floating or fixed rates at 70 to 85 percent of prime at tax-exempt status
Maturity	Usually 5 to 15 or more years
Proceeds	Real estate; equipment; machinery; acquisitions
Collateral	Secured by the fixed assets
Advantages	Low rates; good maturities
Disadvantages	Depends on market availability; strict government rules; high closing costs, especially legal

Life Insurance Companies and Pension Funds

This type of financing is specifically for established companies with substantial equity financing. Additionally, it is obtainable for large investment projects that frequently run into the millions.

	Life Insurance and Pension Funds
Cost	Fixed rates tied to long-term markets
Maturity	5 to 25 or 30 years
Proceeds	Real estate; machinery; equipment
Collateral	Secured assets; debentures
Advantages	Interest rates; long-term maturity
Disadvantages	High minimum amounts; restrictive loan agreements

Leveraged Buy-out (LBO)

Leveraged buy-outs (LBOs) are a form of financing that has been around for decades, but it became glamorized in the '80s. It simply amounts to borrowing against the assets of a company and then using the cash flow realized from that loan to pay off the debt. Buyers frequently sell off some of the assets to reduce the debt and, as part of their operating procedure, drastically cut operating costs to increase the cash flow. Sources of financing for LBOs are commercial banks, asset-based lenders, industrial bonds, and private investment pools. LBOs usually get their initial funding from investment banks.

We have just presented a number of ways to go for debt financing. But the entrepreneur should know that there are also alternate avenues that can be pursued for equity financing besides public offerings and semiprivate offerings. There are many professionally managed firms out there, composed of sophisticated investors, whose sole business is venture capital funding. However, it takes a capable, well-informed management team to access this kind of money. The following are some areas worth considering:

Professional Venture Capital

These are professional management companies who manage high-risk funding. Their capital is supplied by institutions such as insurance companies, pension funds, and some limited partnerships.

Professional Venture Capital

Amount Avail.	Usually $500,000 and up; occasionally for start-ups
Structure	Convertible preferred stock
Cost	Generally a minimum 30 percent per annum compounded return
Proceeds	For very high growth to sales of $50 million
Advantages	Large amount of capital available
Disadvantages	Must have high growth potential

R&D Partnerships

Prior to the tax code changes of 1986, R&D partnerships were a major funding source for small companies. Some forms of these partnerships are still available. For instance, real estate partnerships are still being done. Some astute entrepreneurs are also involved with real estate partnerships tied in with historic building renovation. They form an R&D partnership to buy the building, which would be used to house their business. Since the financing for the building came from outside the company, it further leverages the money raised in going public. Entrepreneurs who find this method applicable for their purposes should discuss this funding source with their CPA.

Small Business Investment Companies

The SBA licenses and provides leveraged financing to SBICs, which in turn provide various forms of venture capital to entrepreneurial enterprises, usually in the form of convertible/subordinated debt. As proof that it really works, during the '87/'88 fiscal year, 445 SBICs extended $550 million in loans and equity to small companies.

Small Business Investment Companies

Amount Avail.	$100,000 to $1 million
Structure	Convertible debt; debt with warrants
Cost	Reasonable interest; dividends; equity
Proceeds	Working capital; acquisitions; LBOs
Advantages	Subordinated capital; 5-year debt; fixed interest
Disadvantages	Equity dilution; must prove fast growth

Minority Enterprise Small Business Investment Companies

MESBICs are identical to SBICs except for the fact that they are designed for, and only available to, minority-owned businesses. There are presently about 130 MESBICs across the country.

Small Business Innovation Research Grants (SBIR Grants)

Several grant programs are funded and administered by various federal agencies. The grants (first stage up to $50,000, second stage to $500,000) are primarily available for new product development. The product, if successfully developed, belongs to the company. But the stipulations are that the government has an option to purchase the technology. These grants are also offered to individuals as well as companies.

Small Business Innovation Research Grants

Amount Avail.	First stage to $50,000; second stage to $500,000
Structure	Grant by federal agency
Cost	Documented proposal must be submitted
Proceeds	Seed capital for research/development of product
Advantages	Low cost; no equity to give away
Disadvantages	Limited capital commitment

A point of information: Numerous grants are available from the federal government, foundations, and private sources, and not exclusively for research and development. It is estimated that the total grants from all sources amount to $100 billion annually. A directory listing most of the grants that are available in the United States is published by the Office of Management and Budget. Someone —we don't recall who—once said that there is a grant for every purpose that was ever thought of.

Finally, there is one more means of finding capital that is frequently overlooked by entrepreneurs, and that is a *combination of funding*. Considering all the possible sources that are available, using a combination of multiple sources of capital may be just the answer to building a business that is successful and profitable. All it takes is a little re*source*fulness.

Summary

Entrepreneurs often become short-sighted in their search for capital. They make the common mistake of not considering all the resources available to them. There are innumerable sources available for private equity financing. Many have been mentioned in this chapter, including borrowing, debt financing, subordinated debt, commercial banks, commercial finance companies, leasing companies, savings and loan associations, the Small Business Administration, industrial revenue bonds, life insurance companies and pension funds, leveraged buy-outs, professional venture capital, R&D partnerships, small business investment companies, minority enterprise small business investment companies, small business innovation research grants, and of course, Regulation D. Resourceful entrepreneurs should surely find something in this bag of goodies to fit their specific needs.

35

The Financial Press

Every day, every week, every month of the year, financial publications across the country pour out stories about the goings on in the financial world. Millions of facts, figures, and interesting bits of information about companies, mergers, tender offers, stock prices, even local, national, and international news items with a financial slant, are funneled through these publications.

Those stories don't just appear out of the blue, somebody produces them. That *somebody* is usually a company's financial public relations person or firm.

To fully understand the relationship between financial public relations and the press, one must understand that it is literally impossible for today's financial press to accumulate all those pages of information by itself. The human factor as well as the cost to go around and dig up those stories would be prohibitive. The fact is that much of the financial news that appears in financial publications is fed news—fed by financial public relations firms and by the companies who make the news.

Astute editors of financial publications welcome and rely on fed information to fill their pages. It is the most direct way they have of obtaining reports on items of interest to their readers. Of course, they have their own staffs of reporters, and they do check on the authenticity of a release, but they would be much less effective without the input from financial PR firms. This does not mean that financial publications will accept articles of no particular significance. Any story or release should be newsworthy and of interest to the publication's reader profile, and it should be simply stated. Editors recognize a printable item when they see one. Professional PR people know it is an insult to editors' professional intelligence to send tout pieces or trivial releases.

Financial public relations, especially in the area of press relations, is an intangible commodity. It is often difficult to measure its effect, success, or failure. Because of this, many public company executives are tempted to handle their own public relations. That's a mistake! It takes a professional to do a professional job. Entrepreneurs should ask themselves, Am I a qualified expert in financial public relations? Do I really know the procedures? How well connected am I with the financial press?

When hiring a financial public relations firm, it is most important to choose one that has an intimate knowledge of and a good working relationship with the financial press. Financial publications are forever faced with tight deadlines. Their reporters, writers, and editors appreciate those who respect and have an understanding of how they work and the standards they must meet.

Financial PR people must also be prepared to verify their sources to the press—to confirm the facts, figures, and content that create the news stories they are responsible for and to provide backup to the stories.

Another significant area of financial PR that companies should seriously consider is buying advertising space in the sections of the press generally titled "Corporate Reports." Almost all the OTC financial publications provide such sections. Two of the better known ones are *The National OTC Stock Journal* and *The OTC Review.* They are also found in publications such as *Inc., Barron's, The Wall Street Journal, The OTC MarketPlace, Fortune,* and others. These are sections where the company can place an ad to advertise itself. The ad could be in the form of a specific favorable report taken from their annual report. Or the company can use the space for a press release, a shareholders' report, or a particular important corporate event, such as obtaining major financing or a valuable contract.

Having a good relationship with the financial press can pay off with big dividends. Here are some guidelines on dealing with business and financial editors:

- Be impartial—give the news to everyone at the same time.
- Don't pass an old story off as new.
- Don't ask to see a story before it is run.
- Don't expect to be notified if your story is used.
- Don't expect your story to be run as submitted. That's why editors were born.
- Don't be too commercial; if possible, mention your company name only once.
- Don't make exaggerated claims.
- Don't call it news if you ran it as an ad.

- Don't call a news conference if mail will do.
- Don't sit on a story, news is perishable.
- Write for the reader.

When dealing with the financial press, deal directly, honestly, and openly, and you will usually find that you will be treated fairly during good times as well as bad times. Finally, it's worth mentioning again, that every publication has a closing date. If, for whatever reason, the company doesn't get the release or ad in to the publication on time, it's sayonara.

Summary

Entrepreneurs with dreams of one day being featured in one of those prime financial publications after taking their company public don't have to wait until some distant tomorrow. If their story is worth telling, it's worth printing whenever they're ready to tell it.

A company going public should make every effort to align itself with a creative and knowledgeable public relations firm that has a good working relationship with the financial press.

There are many fine financial publications across the country today, and they all depend on financial PR firms and companies to fill their pages. They are all accessible and willing to work with anyone who has information for the financial world that would be of interest to their readers. Entrepreneurs should not be embarrassed to wave their company's flag. If nobody sees the flag, nobody will know about the company.

36

Market Makers

Market makers are securities firms that make markets. They stand continuously ready to buy certain securities for their own inventory or to sell securities from their own inventory.

To be more explicit: market makers are broker/dealers. They put their money at risk by buying or selling a stock with their own money, as opposed to brokers who, without putting up their own money, will buy the stock from one source (the market maker) and sell it to another source (a client). They won't buy a stock unless they have a selling transaction lined up. Market makers actually buy the stock and hold on to it until they find a buyer. Many brokerage firms are also market makers, such as Merrill Lynch. They may own stocks from hundreds of companies. Other firms only make market in a few stocks. They are always prepared to buy or sell those stocks at the quoted price on the exchange.

NASDAQ market makers are bound by the rules enforced by the NASD, which require them to trade at the price displayed on the NASDAQ system or the quotes in the Pink Sheets. Additionally, they are forbidden to jump in and out of securities during the day. They must always be ready (at risk) to buy or sell the stock and hold it in inventory. This rule also applies to market makers on the NYSE and all stock exchanges. NASDAQ also requires that the quotations the market makers give or display must be reasonably related to the prevailing market in the security.

Market makers can be either wholesale or retail. Wholesale market makers may have just a few individuals that they make trades for, and consequently, almost all their business is in trading between retail brokers, which is called wholesaling. Ideally, one would expect them to carry large amounts of the company's stock in inventory. On a practical basis, they maintain relatively flat inventories, playing the spreads when the stocks move up or down. Nobody likes getting caught with his or her stocks down.

A retail market maker is the trading department of a retail brokerage firm. Most often it carries inventory to accommodate the brokers in the firm, usually concentrating its positions in securities that were underwritten by the firm. Generally, a wholesaler will make a market in hundreds of stocks, while a retailer will only make market in a couple of dozen.

A market maker actually does more than just hold on to inventory of a stock. Good market makers form a working partnership with the company whose stock they trade to provide the best possible market for the existing stockholders and prospective stockholders. The market-making firm will do this in a number of ways: (1) by assigning an able trader to the company's stock (one who has faith in the company); (2) by furnishing adequate capital to support the market in the company's stock (having enough money available to buy more stock if necessary and also to be able to hold the stock until buyers present themselves); (3) by taking risk positions in the stock and being long or short as appropriate (the market maker tries to equalize the market; if more stockholders are trying to sell, for example, the market maker will take a long position and hold the stock in inventory until the buyers come along; on short sales, the market maker must be able to transact a sell order and buy back later, even if it means losing money on the transaction—what is called covering the short); (4) by providing liquidity for a strong and effective market in the stock (having money ready and at risk); and (5) by acting as a salesperson for the company when talking to securities firms throughout the country (when a retail brokerage firm solicits information about the company for a client, the market maker will provide the information and sell the stock to the brokerage firm). Incidentally, a company can have many market makers.

Why Firms Make Markets

The obvious reason for market making is that customers of a firm are interested in certain securities. Often, the decision to make a market will be sparked by a retail broker who has contact with the company that is attempting to create interest. Since the business is customer driven, the best reason for trading a stock is to sell it. If a stock is in demand, market makers want to trade it. Additionally, firms make a market in a stock if they have participated in the selling syndicates that distributed the company's shares in an IPO.

Firms also make markets in stocks that are recommended by their analysts who think well of the stock's potential for price appreciation. However, the stock must also be able to generate interest by the firm's customers. That's one reason why, as a rule, the analyst's recommendation has to be seconded by the firm's sales department—the brokers who work for the firm.

Let us not overlook one of the big reasons why many firms make markets: It is primarily for the trading profits that might be realized. Their trading department could easily be their key profit center, as they will always try to sell the stock to the buying broker for more than they paid for it. Some firms, however, believe the trading department should fulfill a service function, based not on making trading profits, but on the retail sales activity that the trading department generates. They will sell the stock to the brokers for their cost plus reasonable expenses. They may be selling for less than other firms, but they do it to get the business. And some market makers will trade stocks for their arbitrage possibilities. They will simultaneously sell the same security in different markets. The arbitrage is a way of profiting from the differences in price on the two exchanges.

Before the entrepreneur gets involved with a prospective market maker, he or she should have answers ready that will satisfy the market maker's concerns, such as:

- Are the company's prospects promising; if not yet, when are they expected to become promising?

- Is the company's stock an attractive product now or likely to turn into one soon?

- Does the company have a good overall investor relations program that can assist the market maker's efforts to promote it?

- Is management willing to keep the market makers informed and to keep an open line to the traders, the corporate people, and research departments?

Depending on what is required by the market makers, management must be ready with a complete package of basic information. It should include complete financial statements, business plans, details of the present stock ownership, and a favorable annual report (the company's most important sales tool).

After the deal is set, management needs to establish a communication line with the market maker's *very* key people. Every shareholder letter or mailing should be forwarded to the market maker and followed by personal contact. The market maker should be invited, in writing and by phone, to all corporate social functions, annual meetings, open houses, and product display presentations. They should also be sent all 10–Q, 10–K, and 8–K mailings.

Maintaining a good relationship with market makers should be a number 1 priority for company management. A determination must also be made to continue to bring new market makers into the fold. Remember, they are the bread-and-butter people. (Of course, margarine may be substituted for butter for health reasons.)

Summary

Market makers are indispensable in the trading of a company's stock. They are the ones who, more or less, set the buy and sell prices of certain stocks. Actually, NASDAQ market makers are bound by the rules enforced by the NASD, which require them to trade at the prices displayed on the NASDAQ system or the quotes in the Pink Sheets. They are also bound by rules set by the NYSE and other exchanges.

Each market maker will buy and sell certain securities for and from its own inventory. A wholesale market maker will do almost all of its business in trading between retail brokers. Retail market makers will usually carry inventory to accommodate the brokers in their firm.

Entrepreneurs should make every effort to maintain good relationships with their company's market makers. They must keep the market makers fully informed about the company's operations, including its business plans, financial statements, and the special things that make the company look attractive to the investor. They should also try to interest as many market makers as possible in representing the company.

Good market makers are hard to come by. Finding the right ones may necessitate the entrepreneur's catering to their idiosyncrasies and eating a little humble pie from time to time. But the higher the stock goes—the better the pie tastes.

37

Analysts

Analysts are opinion leaders in the brokerage community. They are usually employed by brokerage firms, banks, and institutional investors such as universities, pension funds, insurance companies, and an increasing number of financial planners. In large Big Board firms, analysts may specialize in just a few stocks or in a specific industry.

Analysts generally issue reports to the brokers in their firms, who then use them as a guide in advising their individual customers. Most analysts also write or contribute to market letters, which often have a great influence on customers.

On New York's Wall Street

> securities analysts have been called Wall Street's "idea men," "financial detectives," and "wizards of odds." They are billed as impartial judges of companies, but their employers increasingly judge them on the trading volume they generate from their recommendations to buy "favored" stocks.

About 15,400 analysts regularly chronicle the daily dramas of America's public companies. Nearly 4,000 work for brokerage houses, spewing out reams of research reports.

Analysts seem to feel compelled to lend their expertise to something that studies suggest they have never been good at—picking stocks that will enjoy immediate glory. They rarely use the word *sell* in a report, though they may utter it privately. They have a tendency to couch bad news in dazzling, creative phrases. For example, a stock does not collapse in price, it "underperforms the market." Part of their wizardry image stems from the fact that they are often put in a position of making value judgments to determine whether a stock is underpriced or overvalued in its present market price and its near- to long-term investment prospects. It is because

291

of this intuitive aspect of their work that most analysts consider their business to be both a science and an art.

Regardless of what the rest of the world may think, analysts are looked upon as a friend by companies. Management must go out of its way to cultivate relationships with them, to let them know who the company is, what the company is about, and all the great things that are happening in the company. What's more, it should be done on a continuing basis. Out of sight, out of mind.

The Haves and Have Nots

The problem is that analysts in the low-priced OTC market are a rare commodity. In the small brokerage firms (fewer than 10 brokers), there will most likely not be a designated analyst. Medium-size firms (10 to 50 brokers) will possibly have someone who functions in the capacity of a combination analyst/syndicate manager. The larger firms (more than 50 brokers) can be counted on to have a full-time analyst.

Unfortunately, analysts in the larger firms tend to concentrate only on the firm's own underwritings. They usually are not interested in small companies. Medium-size firms, who as a rule do not have a preponderance of underwritings, are often open to working on outside stocks, while small brokerage firms can't afford to do much.

What Analysts Look For

Here are a few items for management to consider, and a few suggestions that analysts, brokers, and individual investors should look for in an IPO. The company must present convincing evidence that it meets or will meet the following criteria:

- High and sustainable levels of earnings growth
- High levels of profitability
- Low levels of debt as a percentage of capital
- Solid and improving balance sheets
- Positive cash flow dynamics
- Reasonable market valuations and price to book value relationships
- Dominant positions in small but rapidly growing markets; unique products; aggressive strategies in large, highly fragmented markets

- Management teams that are competent, understandable, and predictable

Another part of the study asks for an evaluation of the management team:

- Who are the members of management, and what are their professional histories and track records?
- Are the business plans and the corporate strategy simple to manage, understand, and evaluate?
- How well does management articulate the business plan and strategy?
- To what extent does management show its confidence in the company by owning stock in it?
- What incentives for good management performance (and penalties for poor performance) does the company provide?
- Does management really accept its responsibility as a public company and treat shareholders as partners?
- Does management scrupulously avoid any conflicts of interest?

Do's and Don'ts

The report also included a few wise Do's and Don'ts for dealing with analysts:

- Use direct mail.
- Participate in local, regional, and national securities industry conferences.
- Make presentations to analysts' societies.
- Keep the investment community continuously informed.
- Keep management accessible.
- Don't be overly aggressive in corporate strategy.
- Don't overemphasize minor events.
- Don't be overly optimistic in communications.

Group Presentations

There are not a great many analysts involved with low-priced OTC stocks. Consequently, the OTC entrepreneur should make every effort to cultivate the few that are available.

Occasionally, management is presented with an opportunity to address analysts' societies or social gatherings. These can prove invaluable ways to get the company story to the right ears. Financial PR firms are usually aware of such meetings and can assist in securing an invitation.

If invited, management must decide whether the CEO/president should make the company presentation alone or whether to involve other top executives who possess special expertise. Audiovisual presentations should be considered, or a slide presentation of not more than 15 minutes. Another acceptable form of presentation would be for the CEO to simply extemporize for the time allotted. After all, who knows the company better? It can also be a more intimate presentation.

A common mistake made at analysts' meetings is rehashing volumes of information that is commonly known or easily obtainable by reading existing materials. It can be far more profitable to spend the time telling analysts about future strategies and projections, both short and long term, and give them a feel for the philosophy of the company.

Just for the prestige, analysts prefer to meet the CEO or CFO of a company. Successful OTC companies that have participated in similar meetings know that. They consider it to be part of the strategy in building and maintaining a friendly relationship with analysts.

These meetings should also be followed up by a mailing that includes a financial public relations packet on the company. If the contact seems worthwhile, the mailings should continue. In some quarters, the feeling is that analysts can't do much for the little guys. Well, a lot of the little guys are now big guys because they didn't follow that advice.

Summary

Stock analysts are people who are considered specialists in analyzing the pros and cons of certain securities by those in the financial community as well as the general public. Their "impartial" opinions are often what make stocks go up and down.

Many of them work exclusively for large broker/dealer firms and dispense their eagerly awaited information to the firm's customers.

Getting a stock analyst to devote time to a small OTC IPO is not an easy task. Small brokerage firms simply don't have analysts in their employ, and analysts in larger brokerage firms tend to concentrate on the firm's own underwritings. Entrepreneurs of small IPOs do, however, manage to get analysts to do their company. They make the contacts through their broker/dealers or by participating in meetings or conferences attended by analysts. If the company has something going for it, analysts are receptive. It never hurts to try.

38

Shells and Pools

The best general definition for a *public shell* is that it is an "inactive public company." The best general definition for a *blind pool* is that it is an "artificial shell." Both are backdoor ways of going public, as the entities are, for all intents and purposes, nonoperating public companies. They also come with an existing shareholder base ranging from a few dozen to thousands of individuals.

Shells and blind pools are two other alternatives entrepreneurs can consider in their quest for a public company. They can very well save the taking of lots of aspirins to ward off the headaches encountered in going through an IPO. They can also end up giving more headaches than one would receive from going through the regular process. We will examine them one at a time.

Public Shells

A public shell is a corporation that has marketable and tradeable shares of its stock registered with the SEC and held by the general public. More than likely, it is not currently engaged in any active business operations, and its stock may or may not be currently trading. Additionally, it may or may not be current in the required filings with the regulatory agencies, especially the SEC.

Shells are appealing for many reasons. One is the time and money saved from going through the tedious and costly process of taking a company public. There are also companies that are not glamorous enough to generate public acceptance if they went public. But the owners, for whatever reasons, believe it would be to their advantage to become a public company. The easiest way is to acquire a shell company—a company that was once a public company and is no longer active. By merging their private company into the shell, they automatically become a public company.

There is an essential difference between going public via an IPO and going public with a shell. Characteristically in an IPO, the public pays a premium for participating in ownership, diluting its investment and increasing the net worth per share of controlling shareholders. In the case of a shell with little or no assets, the original shareholders receive an increase in per share net worth since the shares of the shell have little or no value.

On the liability side, if there are assets, there may be offsetting liabilities, such as a mortgage against an office building. Or there may be debts that have accrued against the shell, maybe from lawyers or accountants, maybe rents that have not been paid, or equipment rentals or loans. Very likely, there will be liabilities and no or minimal assets. These are the things that must be looked into when purchasing a public shell. The reason these things are possible is that public shells used to be operating, publicly traded companies. Many were probably started during some hot market period by well-intended entrepreneurs who had high hopes of heading a successful company.

During the late 1970s and early 1980s, many of today's shells were oil and gas or other energy-related operations conceived to help solve the country's energy crisis. They were IPOs that raised hundreds of thousands, if not millions of dollars. The companies got caught in the downturn of the energy market, and they floundered. In some cases, management disbanded operations, salvaging what it could by selling off properties for cash. In other cases, the companies kept operating until there was no cash left, and management left. They also incurred debt that may still remain on the books.

The most desirable shells are those with few or no assets, minimal or no liabilities, and little or no negative net worth, with the controlling shareholder base held by only a few people. These people may have been the original founders who have gone on to other endeavors, hoping that one day someone will come along and offer them, if not a profitable buy-out for their control stock, at least a face-saving solution for all investors.

Unfortunately, shells do not end like movies. More often than not, a shell is formed when a publicly traded company fails and the executives who operated it do not dissolve it. In any case, the major problem with all shells is past liabilities. Although those liabilities may still be on the record, in most cases they can be settled. The big question mark comes from the ghosts in the closet, if any. These could be disgruntled shareholders who lie low until new management comes along with cash in the bank and then file suit against the new management for the old management's sins. It is extremely difficult to protect against this kind of action. The best hope is that the investor can be convinced that the new company has great potential to make back the money invested plus more and leave well enough alone.

History

Shells have been around as long as the public market has existed. They have weathered good and bad reputations. In the late fifties, the SEC prosecuted two notorious shell hustlers named Alexander Guterman and Lowell Burrell. According to reports, these two gentlemen used shells to fleece investors and loot numerous companies. They manipulated stocks by spreading phony rumors to create grossly overvalued market prices and then unloaded their unregistered stock into the U.S. and foreign marketplace.

The same kind of operators are still around, but the SEC continues a careful surveillance, and the abuses are fewer. Today, going public via a shell is recognized as a very legitimate approach. In fact, many shareholders of public companies have no idea that their company was once a shell. There are many honest and dependable shell brokers who have been very helpful in bringing buyer and seller together. Even so, caution is advised.

A study by Alfred D. Morgan* of Southern Connecticut State University attests to the legitimacy and acceptance of going public through a shell. The study points out that an analysis of ads that ran in *The Wall Street Journal* from 1976 to 1986 showed that the shell market increased fivefold over the 10-year period. The same study also concluded that the supply exceeded the demand by at least three to one.

Clean Shells

Some shells start out as clean shells. They are brand new. Many of the new ones were first set up in the state of Utah, which has been a continuing source of supply, the work mainly of attorneys, accountants, and other business people. They form a small interstate public company with a few thousand dollars invested in an interest-bearing account. The shell only has a handful of shareholders, who hold on to their stock to "mature" it. The company does not have any operations, it just exists as a public company, or shell. The owners hold it for at least 2 years to comply with SEC Rule 144, which stipulates that restricted securities cannot be sold before 2 years from the date they were purchased. At the end of the 2 years, the owners simply sell control to the new managers, who put their operating company into the shell. The original shareholders profit by selling the stock. They sell enough of it to the new management so that it can

---

*Alfred D. Morgan, *Journal of Business Venturing*, "The Public Shell: Vehicle for Venture Financing," New York Elfevier Science Publishing Co., Volume 3, No. 1 (Winter) 1988.

have control, but they hold the rest of the stock to sell into the market when the stock starts trading with new investor interest. If the company is successful, they stand to reap a harvest. The advantage of this type of shell is that since it does not have any operations, the liability risk is negligible. The disadvantage is that the company lacks full registration, does not have any market makers, and has a very small shareholder base.

Advantages and Disadvantages

Every shell has its advantages and disadvantages. There really is not a perfect shell. If it is workable, it fits. The entrepreneur should look into the shell carefully and ask a lot of questions. For example, how financially clean is the shell? What are its assets? If there is cash in the shell, it may become more attractive. The company may need the money to cover the cost of completing the final reports to get the company operating. The company, then, will "buy" the money, but will probably have to pay a steep price for it—instead of getting 90 percent control of the company, the entrepreneur may have to settle for 70 percent control. Depending on the potential price of the stock, that could be an expensive exchange. Also, if there are tangible net assets, do they justify the increased cost of obtaining the shell? On the question of liabilities, the entrepreneur would want to know if the creditors would be willing to discount the debt or settle for stock. Net liabilities or technical bankruptcy do not make a shell unusable.

A shell that is in favor is one that has been around for long enough that the statutes of limitations have run, thus limiting past liabilities. However, these types of shells can present other problems. Most dormant companies became delinquent in filing reports before they actually ceased doing business. Consequently, all missing reports, quarterly and annual, will have to be updated prior to relisting for trading. The reconstruction of these reports can be expensive and time consuming, and in some cases make the shell completely unacceptable.

There are also some shells that are not fully reporting. They filed under Reg A or an intrastate filing, which meant that they did not have to file quarterly reports, only annual reports. A fully reporting company must file quarterly reports as well as the annual report. If the shell was not fully reporting, purchasing it may not be such a good move, as the refiling process could be almost as extensive and costly as doing an IPO.

Control

The control of the shell must also be weighed carefully. Rather than buy the shell, a company may arrange to merge with the shell. The question is—how to work out the post-merger percentage of control. Here's where the public float (shares held by the public) comes into play. Let us say that 60 percent of the company was restricted stock held by the original owners of the shell. The public float amounts to 30 percent as a result of the IPO. Private financing owns the 10 percent balance and the original owners can't decide whether to sell the new company 90 percent of their 60 percent or just 30 or 40 percent of it. They decide instead, to issue more shares, which dilute the percentage of the public float, and give them and the new company the lion's share of the outstanding stock. Now the public stock may be down to 5 to 10 percent of the total outstanding shares, which is too small a public float as far as brokerage firms are concerned. It means that the inside shareholders have too much control. Should they decide to trade 2 years hence, when they can sell their 144 stock, it could drive down the stock price. The actual control percentage is the obvious number that the new management is concerned about. They will ultimately want majority control of the outstanding shares. Many shells are acquired in multiple stages. A second acquisition could be conducted shortly after the first, with additional shares issued to the principals, thereby giving them control. There are many ways to obtain and then retain control, including the issuance of different classes of common or preferred stock. These should be discussed with the SEC counsel and accountants to be sure that all areas are covered concerning the total shares publicly or privately held and the new management's holdings. Many of these problems can be avoided by simply starting out in full control of the shell.

More Questions to Ask

- What was the company's product or service? Could use of the product result in liability lawsuits?
- What was the trading history? Did the stock have wild price fluctuations that may have caused disgruntled shareholders?
- What is the status of the founding second-round shareholders? Are they willing to sell out their original shares at a reasonable price or, at minimum, will they be cooperative in the timing of selling their shares back into the market?
- Were there any second- or third-round original investors that need attention now to prevent future problems?
- Did the original company do any desperation, late-round financings that could carry forward added liabilities? (Late-round financings can take the form of preferred stock or subordinated debt.)

- Are there any outstanding options, rights offerings, or warrants? Are there any underwriter's warrants outstanding? (These usually extend for 4 or 5 years after the original effective date of an underwriting.)

An ideal shell could also be a company that is currently operating whose management wants to take it private. This is usually a no-asset, no-liability, currently reporting, very clean situation. If the shell in question is currently trading, questions to ask are:

- Who are the market makers, and how many are there?
- What is the current stock price, and what was the last year's or last active trading period's history?
- Is there a current list of the brokers that maintain positions in the stock?
- What is the current status of all required SEC reports, including 10–Ks, 10–Qs, and 8–Ks?
- What is the status of state and local reports?

Note that there are no questions here about tax-loss carryforward. The government canceled that in 1986. It used to be a big perk for entrepreneurs obtaining shells. For example, Ms. Entrepreneur buys a shell that shows $1 million in losses. She would put her company into the shell and she wouldn't have to pay taxes on the first million dollars she made, because she had a tax-loss carryforward. Under the 1986 Tax Reform Act, tax loss is virtually useless for mergers or shells. At best, only a small fraction is retainable.

Shareholders

There is a definite advantage in having a large number of shareholders on the books of a shell as opposed to just a few, as there are in new shells. Popular consensus is that 300 to 1000 is an ideal number, showing that there is a large enough base of stock out there to get the market makers interested in trading it. Fewer than 300 may not show enough public float. But more than 1000 can create excessive shareholder contact expense for a new company. All those shareholders must be communicated with when the trading is reactivated. That comes to a lot of letters and reports that must be sent out.

Compiling all the shareholder names can also be a problem. A lot of stock today is held in street name through brokerage firms, which makes it difficult to get a firm handle on the number of shareholders. It requires direct contact with the brokerage firms to determine the actual figure. Also, dormant companies usually have outdated lists, which makes it even more difficult to reestablish contact. But it is important to get to these shareholders.

Most reactivated shells have a base of shareholders who purchased the stock at substantially higher prices than the reactivated trading price. Consequently, they rarely sell out immediately. Instead, they wait until the stock has, at minimum, regained its purchase price. This is a great opportunity for management not only to hold these existing shareholders, but to encourage them to make additional purchases and become faithful to their born-again company. The fact that the existing shareholders now own stock at higher prices can create new buying that can move a stock price up dramatically.

Finding a Shell

The OTC market and the National Securities Dealers Pink Sheets are good places to start the hunt. Hunters look for stocks quoted at pennies, often with no bid, and only one or two market makers. But these factors can also be misleading. It's possible that the company in question is just marginally profitable, with thin market trading, and management has more interest in perpetuating salaries than producing shareholder returns.

A more fruitful method may be to watch ads in the financial press, contact broker/dealers, or make a direct contact with a shell broker. Most broker/dealers do not get involved in the purchase of shells directly, but they will refer inquiries to finders.

Finders, or shell brokers, make it their business to seek out shells or distressed companies that most likely will become shells. Their fees are negotiated, and often include retention of stock. They can give a prospective purchaser a feel for current market pricing. Many shells are controlled by individuals who may or may not have a realistic value established as to the worth of their holdings. Then the purchase price becomes a major bargaining point.

Cost of Shells

There is no set off-the-shelf price list for shells. Prices can range from $20,000 to $100,000 and up. Many variables come into play including: the amount of control, how clean the shell is, net assets, board control, number of shareholders, and reporting status.

Acquiring a Shell

There's more to acquiring a shell than meets the eye. A number of steps must be taken. Here is an example:

1. The new management team purchases control of the shell by buying stock from the existing controlling shareholders.

2. They then set up a new, wholly-owned subsidiary of the parent company, whose only asset is the parent company's stock.

3. The subsidiary acquires the private company in exchange for the parent company stock, thus increasing control by the new management group.

4. Since the parent company owns 100 percent of the subsidiary, it then votes an upstream merger with the subsidiary (takeover).

The result is that the parent company has merged with the private company without going to the shareholders for approval. At this point, an information statement should be sent to shareholders and ratification of the action is usually put on the agenda at the next shareholders' meeting.

Basically, this has been a simplified approach to shell acquisitions. The purpose is to leave the reader with a fundamental understanding of how shells work. Even with this understanding, it is not wise to acquire a shell without the help of qualified legal counsel. One reason why Rule 144 came into existence was the abuses that occurred in shell combinations. Be aware that the SEC continues to tighten its requirements for proxies and other filings concerned with shells.

One more thing of interest about shells. They seem to run in cycles. When the number of IPOs go down, interest picks up in shells.

Spin-off Shells

Until the mid 1960s some existing public companies created subsidiaries for newly formed operations and spun off a portion of the subsidiary's stock to their shareholders as stock dividends. The result was that a new public company was formed without the need for registration. Subsequently, if the subsidiary did not perform well, the parent company enjoyed a residual value by selling the subsidiary's controlling shares. A deliberate abuse of this loophole caused many spin-off shells to be created. The SEC stepped in and started challenging these spin-offs when, in its opinion, there was no justification for their existence.

In the mid 1980s, the spin-off syndrome started again. Today, many states' merit review process restricts the percentage of "promotional stock" issued—that is, stock issued at no cost to the shareholder. Consequently, registered distribution of stock and warrants by way of spin-offs is again receiving the careful attention of the SEC and regulatory bodies across the country.

Blind Pools

Blind pools are similar to shells . . . only different. They have, at times, been considered the first phase of a shell. They are offerings in which participation money is raised, but the investment or company is not identified. The investor depends on the expertise and integrity of the blind pool founders to make the investment pay off.

Blind pools were first conceived in the oil and gas industry. As the story goes, a group of successful oil men wanted to prospect for oil. They realized it would take more money than their finances would allow. So they approached investors to invest in them blindly, without their even knowing themselves where they would drill or how they would spend the money. It was called a blind pool. Blind pools have also been referred to as blank check companies and artificial shells. Many have been used as a means of bringing needed financing into an existing operating company. These companies often turn to blind pools because underwriters didn't feel the companies presented a glamorous enough image and therefore didn't show interest in an underwriting. In essence, they are publicly traded, often not fully registered shells, with cash. Their corporate charters are written in broad language to allow the companies to engage in all lawful activities. Investors put their money into these companies, often without knowing who runs them or what they are going to do with the money.

Blind pools were further encouraged by the 1980 Business Development Company Act. This federal legislation eased the Investment Holding Company rules designed to promote small business. They came into modern-day prominence in the mid 1980s in the Rocky Mountain region, primarily in underwritings by the small OTC firms in Utah and Colorado. From 1984 to 1988 the percentage of blind pool underwritings rose from 5 percent to 65 percent of the total underwritings.

Abuses

In the early eighties, a lot of fast-buck operators abused the system. By mid 1986 the SEC had charged 32 blind pools with violating securities laws. Charges included:

- The use of undisclosed principals, major shareholders, and investors
- Having prearranged mergers set up
- Insufficient disclosure of conflicts of interest

- Issuance of cheap stock to promoters
- Unjustified salaries to founders
- Bonuses to finders
- Misuse of proceeds

Additionally, the SEC stepped up surveillance of broker/dealers with attention on market manipulation, churning of customer accounts, investor suitability, trading spreads, and financial disclosure.

Recently, the states of Utah and Colorado revised their securities regulations to effectively stop new blind pools in their states. This was accomplished by requiring all blind pools to escrow a large percentage of their proceeds until an acquisition was identified, and then all shareholders were allowed to vote on the proposed acquisition.

Unit Offerings

As promoters became more sophisticated in the assembling of blind pools, they recognized that they had to raise the ante. They began to offer acquired companies more than the standard $50,000 to $500,000 they had been offering. This resulted in the *unit offering.* The new stock was now sold in units of common stock and warrants.

A unit was priced at 10 cents and consisted of one share of common stock and two warrants—an "A" warrant exercisable at 15 cents and a "B" warrant exercisable at 20 cents. Some of the warrants had qualifications. The "A" warrant was good for 1 year, and the "B" warrant was good for 2 years. The time may be extended over and over again by the Board of Directors. However, the price can only be reduced and not increased.

The concept behind the unit offerings was that if the company was successful, the price of its stock would increase and consequently the investors would exercise their warrants with the company.

As an example, the initial offering would yield gross proceeds of $500,-000, assuming the offering was for 5 million shares (units) at 10 cents. A year later, if the company had been successful and its stock was trading at 18 cents to 20 cents per share, the shareholders would exercise their warrants, which would bring $750,000 into the company (5 million "A" warrants at 15 cents each). The second year the process would be repeated with the "B" warrants, bringing in $1 million (5 million "B" warrants at 20 cents). Thus one blind pool underwriting could easily total $2.25 million in proceeds to the company over the 2 years.

Many variations to this approach have been put together, with some unit offerings having as many as four or five warrants.

Warrants' Exercise

In theory, the concept of warrants being attached to a blind pool is a good idea. In practice, it has presented many problems. For instance, the original units are often issued in one of two ways. One is as an attached unit, where the warrant stays attached to the common stock. The other offers a detachable warrant, where the warrant is separated from the stock and trades by itself. The bookkeeping, or tracking of the detached warrant holders, can be a transfer agent's nightmare.

In either instance, attached or detached, the responsibility to get the warrant exercised is the company's. Some companies prefer to contact the warrant holders directly to remind them it's time to exercise their warrants. Others prefer the lead underwriter to handle the chore. Either way takes a lot of effort and precise tracking to obtain successful results.

What makes the task seem so thankless is that most investors in blind pool units view the investment strictly as a gamble. Consequently, the dollar amount of their investment is usually small, maybe $500 to $2,000. Their hope is that the stock price will quickly increase 50 percent to 100 percent, and they can "turn out" for a quick profit. The bottom line is that the original investor is usually not interested in any further investment in the warrants.

There are also rules that apply to warrants:

- A purchase warrant simply offers the holder a right to purchase a specific amount of stock at a specific price, exercisable at a specific time.

- The exercise price can be reduced but cannot be increased.

- The shares underlying the warrant must be registered, which requires the company to file a post-effective amendment. (This filing is equivalent to a full S–18.) The reason behind the SEC requirement for such an extensive update filing is because the whole nature of the company changes when a merger with a blind pool occurs. In effect, the company loses its privacy.

Costs

The cost of acquiring a blind pool is comparable to the cost of a shell. It can vary from $20,000 to $100,000 and up. The process usually requires the company to purchase control positions from the founding control shareholders. The deal often includes sizeable options for additional shares for the founders.

Some blind pools are set up with differing classes of stock in order to assure that management will control the voting rights. They would sell common stock with no voting rights to shareholders and preferred stock with voting rights to management to give it control. The original founders use these inside stock positions as bargaining points.

Hidden Costs

A major deterrent to becoming involved with a blind pool is the eventual total cost to complete the whole deal. Audited financial statements are a specific requirement. First, audited financial statements are required from the private company shortly after combining with the blind pool. Then audited financial statements will also be required of the combined companies. There are also legal fees and filing fees to be paid for the immediate and continuing reports.

The entrepreneur must realize up front that purchasing a blind pool does not relieve the company from the reporting requirements of a publicly traded company. A lot of blind pools will only have met minimal reporting requirements, so getting the new blind pool company up to full reporting status may require just as much time and dollar expenditure as it takes to accomplish a new IPO. Which, of course, takes us all back to the beginning of this book.

Summary

For the entrepreneur, going public through a shell or a blind pool is a legitimate way to achieve public company status. By definition, a shell is an inactive public company. In many cases, by buying a shell, the entrepreneur can save a lot of the time and money it would take to go through an IPO. In other cases, it may take more time and money than starting an IPO from scratch just to bring the shell up to fully reporting status.

Some shells have assets that can be absorbed. Some have liabilities, and often these liabilities are not obvious. They can crop up later by way of suits by disgruntled owners of the former company's stock or through debts that have been accumulated. It requires sophisticated advisors who are familiar with the legal, accounting, and regulatory pitfalls of shell acquisitions to make the right choice. But a good shell can be a shell of a bargain.

A blind pool has been referred to as an artificial shell. It is a publicly traded, often not fully registered shell—with cash. Unlike a shell, which at one time may have been an operating public company, a blind pool is not. Many investors consider a blind pool a gamble. It can also cost more to bring it up to a fully reporting public company than does an IPO.

Stock ownership of shells and pools have the same high leverage potential that is sought in any public company. And like a shell, a blind pool is an expedient way of going public, if not gone into blindly, of course.

39

The Next Step

The next step may be the most difficult, most nerve-wracking, most anxi-ety-ridden, most agonizing step an entrepreneur could take . . . which is *going public.*

It's alright to dream about it, but to be honest, the door to the dream won't swing open simply by your saying "Open sesame." It takes more than just a few magic words or rubbing lamps. Actually, rubbing *is* in-volved—rubbing hands, rubbing heads, and burning a lot of midnight oil. But it's not an impossible dream. Stories abound about entrepreneurs turned multimillionaires because of taking their companies public. Going public can reap the same kind of harvest that Ali Baba experienced when he proclaimed his first "Open sesame."

As we have repeated throughout this book, our focus has been on the small OTC IPO. We believe, as complicated a process as it is, the rewards are well worth taking a company public.

We have also presented alternative ways to going public that work as well. To be sure, there are pitfalls, but a far-seeing entrepreneur will find that the benefits easily outweigh the negatives. There's no trick or special secret to the process. Going public is a process in which a business owned by one or several individuals opens its doors to public participation by offering the public an opportunity to invest in the company. Everything that must be done to go public is spelled out in detail by the government for anyone who is interested.

However, to protect the innocent investor, the government has estab-lished rules and regulations. A lot of them. We discussed most of them in this book. We touched on some things, and we went into depth on others, among them—the importance of timing; the need for advisors and consul-tants; the way to find the right legal and accounting people; the advantages

308

of private financing; finding and dealing with underwriters, market makers, and brokers/dealers; and the necessity for good PR. We presented alternative methods for going public and deluged you with a lot of rules and regulations.

Through this book we traveled a significant distance together. We agonized over the decision of going public, we dissected the team, we struggled through the preoffering period, we sympathized with the entrepreneur through the registration process, and we successfully completed the offering. If you stuck with us through it all, you're awarded an MBA in IPOs.

Of course, one reading alone will not allow you to retain the thousands of essential points that have been covered. However, your base familiarity with the book's contents will allow you to use it as a continuing reference source. It can serve you as a manual of techniques, systems, and guide points to give you assurance and assist you in meeting your goals.

Going public is a heavy experience. We hope that after you accomplish it, you will share your experience and expertise with others. Teach them, mentor them, use your organizational skills and leadership gifts to help them and to encourage them. Pass your tenacity on to those who can benefit from it.

This book hasn't given you the experience. However, when you do it yourself, you'll find it has furnished you with the knowledge you'll need. You've learned that timing is important in the world of IPOs, that you need to be prepared to take advantage of the windows. You've learned that there's a lot yet to learn. As John Case, the senior editor of *Inc.* magazine said, "When the investment bankers aren't tripping all over themselves to take companies public, is precisely the time to study up on the subject."

You understand that selecting the best professionals to assist you is important. You have learned that it is possible to effectively work within the guidelines of regulators. You have also studied the world of underwriters. You know the registration process.

Building a company is a dynamic process. It takes a continuing, unrelenting, and committed attempt to create value. You must strive to achieve new insights, encourage innovation, pursue excellence—excellence in your product or service, excellence in your management team, and excellence in customer results.

The rewards are achievable. They're significant. They can feel good—both in your pocket and your heart.

Our entrepreneur's wish to you is that this book has helped you gain the confidence you need to go after it—to be able to sing out Ali Baba's "Open sesame" and capture the dream.

Index

311